CW01306419

Backpacking With A Bunion

A Journey of Discovery and Adventure in South East Asia

Terry Grigg

"I travel not to go anywhere, but to go. I travel for travel's sake. The great affair is to move."
Robert Louis Stevenson (1850 - 1894)

authorHOUSE®

AuthorHouse™ UK Ltd.
500 Avebury Boulevard
Central Milton Keynes, MK9 2BE
www.authorhouse.co.uk
Phone: 08001974150

© *2008 Terry Grigg. All rights reserved.*

No part of this book may be reproduced, stored in a retrieval system, or transmitted by any means without the written permission of the author.

First published by AuthorHouse 3/25/2008

ISBN: 978-1-4259-9918-6 (sc)
ISBN: 978-1-4259-9919-3 (hc)

Printed in the United States of America
Bloomington, Indiana

This book is printed on acid-free paper.

Front Cover Image:
Author with Long Neck Karen,
Mae Hong Son, Thailand Dec 2001

*In memory of my mother Edith, who sadly
passed away shortly before publication*

Contents

		Page
	AN INTRODUCTION	1
1.	WELCOME TO THE LAND OF SMILES	5
2.	BANGLUMPOO OR BUST	12
3.	BANGKOK AND BEYOND	18
4.	HELLFIRE AND BRIMSTONE	25
5.	PAI IN THE SKY	39
6.	POWER TO THE PEOPLE	48
7.	KHMER TODAY, GONE TOMORROW	63
8.	KAMPUCHEA, OUR MOTHERLAND	78
9.	GOOD MORNING VIETNAM	84
10.	SAME, SAME, BUT DIFFERENT	104
11.	HALONG HAS THIS BEEN GOING ON	111
12.	HEY JOE	119
13.	BAHALA NA	127
14.	THE GOLDEN WONDER	137
15.	A BALANCING ACT	145
16.	THE ROAD TO MANDALAY	150
17.	BRICKS IN BAGAN	161
18.	CANOES, CATS, CAVES, CHURCHES AND CHEROOTS	166
19.	A NE WIN SITUATION	174

		PAGE
20.	FROM SAMET TO SAMUI	178
21.	PIERCED IN PHUKET	186
22.	CLIFFS AND CAVES IN KRABI	193
23.	PENANG, PEARL OF THE ORIENT	207
24.	A CAMERON HIGHLANDER	217
25.	OM AMRITESWARIYAI NAMAH (SALUTATIONS TO THE IMMORTAL GODDESS)	221
26.	MERDEKA MELAKA	227
27.	SINGAPORE SLING	236
28.	THE OLD MAN OF BORNEO	245
29.	A SARAWAKY DUDE	253
30.	KITSCH IN KUCHING	262
31.	THE OLDEST RAINFOREST	270
32.	SEARCHING IN SUMATERA	277
33.	JALAN, JALAN, JAVA MAN	290
34.	BALI HAI	297
35.	ENTER (AND EXIT) THE DRAGONS	306
36.	IN CONCLUSION	316
	QUOTATIONS	318

Illustrations

	Page
GRAND PALACE, BANGKOK, THAILAND, MAY 2003	95
ON THE DEATH RAILWAY, KANCHANABURI, THAILAND, MAY 2003	96
WAT THAWET LEARNING GARDEN, SUKHOTHAI, THAILAND, JUNE 2003	97
VILLAGE LIFE, LUANGNAMTHA, LAOS, DECEMBER 2001	98
CHILDREN AT ANGKOR WAT, CAMBODIA, JANUARY 2002	98
THE ABODE OF THE GODS, TA PROHM, CAMBODIA, JANUARY 2002	99
GUARDIAN DRAGON LION, SHWEDAGON PAYA, YANGON, MYANMAR, NOVEMBER 2003	100
CHAUKHTATGYI BUDDHA, YANGON, MYANMAR, NOVEMBER 2003	101
BALANCING BOULDER STUPA, KYAIKTIYO, MYANMAR, NOVEMBER 2003	102
ORANGE SELLER, KYAIKTIYO, MYANMAR, NOVEMBER 2003	103
STREET VENDOR, KYAIKTIYO, MYANMAR, NOVEMBER 2003	200
COOKING IN KALAW, MYANMAR, NOVEMBER 2003	200
MUSLIM FISHING VILLAGE, PHANG-NGA, THAILAND, AUGUST 2003	201

	PAGE
DHAMMIKARAMA BURMESE BUDDHIST TEMPLE, GEORGETOWN, PENANG, MALAYSIA, AUGUST 2003	202
SNAKE TEMPLE, PENANG, MALAYSIA, AUGUST 2003	203
UNCLE TAN'S JUNGLE CAMP, KINABATANGAN, SABAH, MALAYSIA, APRIL 2002	203
SARAWAK LADIES, KUCHING, MALAYSIA, MAY 2002	204
MINANGKABAU WEDDING, BUKITTINGGI, SUMATRA, INDONESIA, AUGUST 2003	205
CHILDREN, TUK TUK, SAMOSIR, DANAU TOBA, SUMATRA, INDONESIA, JULY 2003	206
BOROBUDUR, JAVA, INDONESIA, JULY 2002	206

An Introduction

To say that for me a mid-life crisis began at 40, is I believe a bit of an understatement. For it was then that the yearnings of youth finally caught up with me and the travel bug bit good and proper. It's NEVER too late to travel.

When I was in my twenties, world travel was mainly confined to the wealthy (though compared to me nearly everyone was wealthy). There was of course the 'Hippy Trail' to Kathmandu, and a few guys managed the States for a couple of months. Europe by InterRail was the usual 'fix', but slowly and surely new exotic destinations were being opened up for the adventurous traveller.

The nineties saw a huge explosion in such travels - overlanding across Africa, backpacking through South-East Asia and working one's way across Australia and New Zealand. In 1999 I chose Africa as the place to go - five months travelling through ten countries from Nairobi to Cape Town.

Most - no all - of my travelling companions were much younger than I, and in backpacking circles this was always going to be the case. Hence the 'bunion' bit (which I really do possess - one of life's little irritants), just to put a more mature perspective on things. Only joking. Would I fit in, would I look stupid, could they relate to me (I was old enough to be nearly everyone's father, perish the thought), could I relate to them - the girls were pretty attractive, and so on. Who cares? I did it and was proud I did it. There is a saying, "You're only as old as you feel", or as Groucho Marx would say, "You're only as old as the woman you feel."

Just before I set off on my big trip to the Orient, I had a vivid dream - something to do with the salty sea and waves, seals on a rocky coastline and a train entering a tunnel. This can be interpreted as pleasant and happy travels, a lonely life, lack of judgment, troubles and strife with close associates, extravagant tastes and finally, the prediction of illness. This didn't seem to be a good omen, and while I was writing this book came news of the tsunami, which affected some of the areas I had visited.

South-East Asia is an amazingly diverse area in terms of geography, scenery, climate, history and culture. It stretches from the Himalayas in Burma in the north to Irian Jaya across the Equator in the south-east. The vast majority of the land lies within the tropics, with a wet and dry monsoon climate. It contains the largest archipelago in the world, and most of the countries, apart from Laos which is landlocked, have extensive coastlines.

The region is one of the great centres and crossroads of world trade, and has seen widespread colonisation by the Western powers. Most of the economies are based on agriculture and, to a growing extent, tourism. Manufacturing is becoming prominent in the more wealthy countries of Thailand and Malaysia. The City States of Singapore, a major shipping and transport hub, and oil-rich Brunei stand alone. The principal religions are Buddhism and Islam, though Christianity has made some inroads, especially in the Philippines where ninety per cent are Christian, and there are Hindus in Malaysia and Bali. Animism and spirit worship is common in some rural areas. Travelling in this relatively small area can be almost as diverse as the scenery. From bemos, cyclos, túk túks, motor-bikes, minivans, pick-up trucks, taxis, horses and carts to bicycles, buses, bangkas, canoes, rafts, outriggers, ferries, trains and planes.

What are the highlights? Well for me, the temples in Angkor, Bangkok, Bagan and Yangon; the hill-tribes of Thailand and Laos; the amazing cultures of the Batak and Minangkabau in Sumatra; the colourful and vibrant festivals of the Philippines; the volcanoes of Java, Bali and Flores; the limestone crags of Krabi and Halong Bay; the jungles of Malaysia; the soaring heights of Kinabalu; the orang-utans and proboscis monkeys of Borneo; the Komodo dragon; the bustling high life of Singapore and Kuala Lumpur; the Chinese shop houses of Penang and Melaka; the floating markets of Thailand and Vietnam; the beaches; the coral reefs; the forests; the mountains; the wildlife; the food; the people; but most of all, the fact that I was travelling. And not stuck in cold, wet, miserable Britain. One hears of all these so-called 'mature gappers' who get homesick after a couple of weeks. What wimps! Why bother in the first place? I still wasn't homesick after two years. Never once did I think I'd be better off back home - whatever home meant.

But back home I eventually came to write it all up. And I have my memories. The sweet smell of jasmine rice, the exotic colours and shapes of tropical fruit, saffron-robed monks, sunrises over mountains and sunsets over temples, crowing roosters at dawn, lying in a hammock by the beach or the misty Mekong, noisy festivals with firecrackers, climbing up hills, trekking through jungles, fording across rivers and swimming in the warm tropical ocean. South-East Asia has all this and more.

However, I have never regarded myself as a particularly adventurous person. I haven't sailed round the world, crossed the Sahara, scaled the heights of Mount Everest, or trekked to the South Pole (though I know someone who has). And I hate camping in the cold and wet. But I have a *sense* of adventure and with that perspective in mind I set off on my travels. And my first port of call was going to be Bangkok, the City of Angels in the Land of Smiles.

CHAPTER 1
WELCOME TO THE LAND OF SMILES

Many countries like to have bold and colourful slogans to describe their culture and disposition. South Africa - The World in One Country; India - Land of Dreams and Fantasies; Malaysia - Truly Asia. With Thailand it's the 'Land of Smiles' and it's true. As soon as you go through Immigration at the new Suvarnabhumi International Airport you are met with a smile. Such a refreshing change from coming into Heathrow. I think this is mainly to do with Buddhist teachings, a genuine desire to help and serve and 'sanuk', meaning fun. A tradition of friendliness and hospitality, which is best exemplified in the 'wai', a Thai greeting where the hands are placed together in a prayer-like posture, accompanied by a bowing of the head. It is still widely used, and denotes a combination of age, status, wealth and power. Thais are generally a fun-loving people with a philosophy of 'mai pen rai' (It doesn't matter).

However, the two areas of life where it does matter are religion and the monarchy. The King is held in great respect and it is a grave insult to the Thais to make criticisms, or not to stand when the national anthem is played. Something I was reminded of when I was sitting on a park bench and the anthem came blaring through some speakers. So beware: you don't want to end up like Oliver Jufer, the Swiss guy found guilty of spray-painting pictures of the King, and then sentenced to ten years for the crime of lèse majesté. Though thankfully now he has received the King's pardon. Buddhism is regarded in a similar vein, so don't point your feet at, or climb on, a statue of the Buddha. No touching the head, being the highest part of the body, and remember in temples cover your legs and go barefoot. And keep the spray paint at home.

Thailand is also known as *Prathet Thai*, the Land of the Free. For unlike its neighbours, it has never been colonised or suffered civil war or racial conflicts. It is a fiercely independent and proud nation, proud of its culture, proud of its religion and proud of its King. But it is also a very welcoming country, pleased to greet and accommodate foreign ways and tastes, and ready to adapt and change - but at its own pace.

Sure, there are some problems. Thousands have been killed over recent years in a drugs crackdown; prostitution and the treatment of women could certainly be looked at with a very critical eye; and there is still a great deal of inequality and poverty. Environmental and animal welfare issues (despite the Buddhist outlook) are also a major concern.

Out of a total population of sixty-two million, eighty per cent are ethnic Thai, plus Chinese, a small number of Malays in the south of the country, Cambodians, Burmese, Vietnamese and hill-tribes in the north. Ninety-five per cent are Theravada Buddhist. There are some 32,000 monasteries and 200,000 monks. This form of Buddhism came from India via Sri Lanka and means 'Teaching of the Elders'. I am not a religious person myself, but the idea of karma or 'Dhamma' - Buddha's teachings, the path to freedom, that fate or destiny is nothing but the collective force of one's own actions performed in past lives - rather appeals. The wheel of cause and effect forever turns.

Thailand is roughly the size of France, with a shape like an elephant's head, the trunk forming part of the Malay Peninsula. The distance from north to south is about 1860 kilometres, giving quite a diverse monsoon climate. There is also a great range of scenery, from mountains in the north (the southernmost part of the Himalayas) to the limestone islands and tropical beaches of the south. Just fifty years ago, seventy per cent of Thailand was covered with natural forest. Logging and agriculture have taken their toll, and this has now been reduced to an estimated twenty per cent. With loss of habitat, wildlife has suffered greatly, with some species becoming extinct. A large number of protected parks have been created since the 1970s to counterbalance this loss, and the government hopes to increase forest cover to forty per cent within fifty years. The illegal trade in wildlife doesn't help. The marine environment is also threatened with pollution and over-fishing.

But it's not all a gloomy picture. Environmental awareness is increasing, not just with the creation of parks, but also with protests against dam-building, the elimination of coral dynamiting, and the removal of some damaging developments. Eco-tourism also helps: education is the key for tourists and locals alike to act in a responsible and sustainable way. We can all do our bit to help care for the planet.

Something which has been in the news recently is the sorry plight of orang-utans, those beautiful and intelligent creatures whose homes have been decimated by deforestation in Malaysia and Indonesia. They have been smuggled into Thailand illegally and then used in kick-boxing bouts at the infamous Safari World Wildlife Park. This park has long been the target of animal rights campaigners and the bouts are now suspended.

But if you prefer to see humans behind bars instead of animals, then make for Bang Kwang prison, made famous in the films *Bangkok Hilton* and *Brokedown Palace*, and more recently a TV documentary. It is now a tourist attraction in its own right, and inmates welcome gifts of food and books. There are now over 7000 of them - mostly drug offenders - and hundreds have been sentenced to death, mercifully now by lethal injection instead of firing squad.

I've been reading a couple of books on the experiences of two women prisoners in the Bangkok Hilton recently. The first is *Free! - True Release in Christ in a Bangkok Jail* by Rita Nightingale. There's an interesting quote on the cover from Solzhenitsyn, the famous Russian author imprisoned in the gulags, about the meaning of life: it's not the prospering that counts, but the development of the soul; materialism won't bring you happiness. Secondly *Forget You Had A Daughter* by Sandra Gregory. *"Amid the degradation she found redemption, and the strength to rebuild the life she had thrown away."* (Mail on Sunday).[1] Or, for a real horror story, read *Welcome to Hell, One Man's Fight for Life inside the Bangkok Hilton* by Colin Martin. Bribes and brutality - Thailand corrupt to the core: the other side to 'The Land of Smiles'.

Some forty thousand Brits travel to Bangkok every month, the vast majority heading to Pattaya, Phuket or Ko Samui. A TV series called *Bangkok Bound* showed what goes on. A man who made his living photographing naked women, a mother visiting her son in prison, sentenced to fifty years for smuggling heroin. A Thai transsexual who had just had the chop - "I am so happy now I am lady. One hundred per cent." (Thailand is the place to go if you want to go on a gender bender.) A married man from Devon who was having a gay fling (apparently he was bisexual). Tragically his lover was murdered. And finally a lady who went to visit her father's grave in Kanchanaburi.

He died building the Thai/Burma Railway in 1942, aged just 25. All human life is out there.

Thailand of course has a reputation for its sexual proclivities, whether it be in the sois of Patpong, the clubs and bars of Pattaya and Patong, or the village girls in Chiang Mai. One interesting point: only ten per cent of the customers are Westerners - the vast majority are Thai, with a significant sprinkling of Chinese. But the stereotype prevails of the sixty-year-old fat pot-bellied German businessman with his petite teenage Thai girlfriend. And I can testify to that. On a visit to Bumrungrad Hospital in Sukhumvit to have my eyes examined, there was the said German businessman with a Thai wife, not only a third his age, but a third his size. It is an excellent world-class hospital by the way, more like a hotel: clean, efficient, and I would recommend it to anyone. Puts the British NHS to shame.

And then there's the headline *'Fleeced by a Thai Gold-Digger'*. The story goes something like this. Lonely divorced man heads to Bangkok looking for love. Pays an inordinate amount of money to a dating agency. Looks through photos and videos, finds a girl/woman, takes her out for an expensive meal and later they make love. Man becomes infatuated, showering upon her jewellery, clothing and other gifts. They get married and more money is spent. On arrival in the UK there's the visa application, he buys her a car, but she sleeps in the spare room. No more sex, and certainly no love. Then she flies back to Bangkok saying that her father's ill - no more contact. And at the same time she's had about ten other guys on the go. This little tale came from the Daily Mail, Wednesday March 12, 2003 with the inscription *'He was a lonely divorcé, she was a stunning young Thai girl. Yet when SHE proposed a week after they met, he still didn't smell a rat. Now his naïvety has cost him £40,000.'*[2] Male folly and female manipulation - not a good combination and neither party come out with much credit. I have heard of one or two other incidents in this ilk, which I will recount later. But I'm sure most Thai/Western relationships work out OK - you just have to be cautious. Although it is reckoned seventy per cent of marriages end in divorce - that's about the rate in the UK now, isn't it?

Thailand is justly famous for its music, theatre and dance. The classical Thai orchestra is called the pìi-phâat and has from five to twenty players. It is not unlike the Indonesian 'gamelan' from Java and Bali, consisting of tuned gongs, drums, flutes, a xylophone-like instrument and the pìi. This woodwind instrument is heard at Thai boxing contests and reminded me of the sounds of a Middle Eastern bazaar, or maybe a snake charmer. The entire ensemble is used to accompany dance dramas like the Ramakien and shadow theatre, and in concerts. If you want to experience Thai dancing then pop along to the Vimanmek Teak Mansion or the Rose Garden Country Resort, 32 km west of Bangkok, where you can see such delights as the fingernail, bamboo, kala (coconut) and yoey (flirtation) dances. There are also sword-fights, a wedding ceremony (you might even want to try the real thing) and mock Muay Thai (Thai boxing). Really tacky I know, but quite fun and relaxing.

I am a vegetarian, for health, ethical and environmental reasons, which has led to many heated debates with fellow travellers, but I always stand my ground. This can lead to problems in some countries, as there can be limited choice - there have been times I've survived on bananas, noodles and biscuits. But not in Thailand. From street vendors selling Pad Thai, cafés, curry-houses, Western bars and guest-houses, to Thai and Chinese restaurants, I nearly always get what I want. Certainly in Bangkok, Chiang Mai and major tourist resorts, there is a wide selection of vegetarian food. There are indeed a string of Thai vegetarian restaurants across the country run by the Asoke Foundation, a Theravada Buddhist sect. And then we have the great argument on whether all Buddhists should be vegetarian. More on that later.

I like to start my day with a huge fruit salad of banana, pineapple, mango, papaya and dragon fruit for example, together with a cappuccino, and all for just over a pound. Lunch then consists of a cheese salad baguette and a fruit smoothie. And dinner is nearly always rice or noodles, a red, yellow or green curry, and a Big Chang to wash it down - that'll knock your head off. Traditional Thai food is hot, pungent and spicy, courtesy of the 'mouse-shit' peppers. Other essential ingredients include lemon-grass, coriander, basil, ground peanuts, lime juice and of course coconut milk for the curries. The finest quality rice is jasmine-scented rice, but there are many different types. The 'sticky' rice of the north is rolled into balls and is so full of gluten to me - almost indigestible.

We are going to start our journey in - of course - Bangkok, or Krung Thep, City of Angels. It is by far the country's largest city - a concrete mêlée of traffic-clogged fly overs, bustling streets and open-air markets, huge shopping malls, high-rise hotels and office-blocks, neon-throbbing night life, Buddhist monks in saffron robes, schoolgirls in white blouses and black skirts, smoke-belching buses and the ubiquitous túk-túks. But away from the busy main streets you will find maybe a peaceful wat (Buddhist temple) where you can relax and contemplate in a green oasis. And if you're backpacking you'll certainly head for Banglumpoo, the backpacker's haven.

CHAPTER 2

BANGLUMPOO OR BUST

I lay hot and sweaty in the bare whitewashed room, bathed in the glare of blue neon. Above me the incessant whirring of the ceiling fan did little to pierce the hot sultry air. As I wiped my brow, a cockroach scuttled in a dark corner and a friendly gecko awaited its next mosquito meal. Outside in the street I could hear the roar of túk túks and next door the squeaking of bed-springs and laughter. Memories of Alex Garland's *The Beach* immediately sprang to mind. I had well and truly arrived in Banglumpoo and the Khao San Road.

People often used to denigrate Banglumpoo as a backpacker's ghetto, but I think it's a great location. Just five minutes to the river for the ferry to other sights and access to the Skytrain. A great innovation in such a crowded city, where you can see most of the sights in air-conditioned elevated comfort. Much better than bus, taxi or túk túk (a three-wheeled and very noisy motorised vehicle). The Grand Palace and Museum are only a stone's throw away, and Chinatown not much further. Loads of guest-houses, restaurants and cheap eats. What it doesn't have is high-rise tourist hotels and all the multinationals, although I noted sadly that McDonald's has crept in. And Ronnie McDonald performing a 'wai' - what an insult to Thai culture. I suppose there will be a meditating or reclining Ronnie next. Fortunately the offending statue has now been removed.

The Khao San Road is very much a young person's place with all the paraphernalia of street vendors selling everything from noodles, 'Big Chang' beer, colourful cocktails with names like Goodnight Bangkok and Ladyboy, henna tattoos, hair braiding, pirated CDs, T-shirts (OBL and GWB still seem to be the favourites - 'Weapons Of Ass Destruction'), to fake documents, masks, hammocks, balloons, puppets, tacky toys, huge jars of honey that would last months and cigarette lighters with enough fuel to launch a rocket into space. But it's also the best place to get cheap flights, and organise tours and visas, and it certainly has a great buzz about it. And you can satisfy all your medical and cosmetic needs at the local branch of Boots.

New Year's Eve on the Khao San - what mayhem. Makes Trafalgar Square revelries look like a meeting of the Women's Institute. The road is only 300 metres in length but the number of people crammed into it was astonishing. It is busy at the best of times, but tonight was frightening. Every conceivable type of music blaring out from all directions - trance, hip-hop, rock, reggae, Thai pop, the Thai National Anthem and a blind guy singing karaoke. The road was covered with tables and chairs, but cars and bikes still trying to get through. Finally got through the crowds to my hotel - lots of screaming, swearing, firecrackers and fireworks. Well that's the end of another year.

A lot has changed over recent years though. The more seedy guest-houses and bars are being swept away to make way for modern, well-appointed and comfortable, but not pretentious, establishments. I don't think Bangkok will ever be regarded as a pretentious place. The general infrastructure has been tidied up and new pavements laid; though I'm not sure if making one's progress in amongst the túk túks, motor-bikes and street vendors will be any less calamitous. It was hilarious trying to negotiate the cement lorries arriving at a new building site. Though not much fun for the drivers, and up in the skeleton of the new structure welders were hard at work. All amongst the commotion of the Khao San Road.

The Banglumpoo district covers a relatively small area on the east side of the Chao Phraya River just to the north of the National Museum and Grand Palace. It's a great place to walk around and it doesn't take much effort to find the 'real' Bangkok, where the influence of the West (and Westerners) just falls away. I was sitting in a restaurant maybe a hundred metres from Khao San and didn't see any for a couple of hours.

Of course it is at night time that Bangkok really comes to life. Urban Thais are very much night-owls, and Bangkok is truly a city that never sleeps. I've arrived in Banglumpoo at all hours of the night and there's always something going on. You can get a beer, a bottle of water, Pad Thai (noodles) or a full restaurant meal if you like at four in the morning. VW camper vans are set up as mobile cocktail bars in the forecourts of gas stations: out come the tables and chairs, and a couple of bamboo parasols, and hey presto - you have it. Wacky or what! Wires everywhere - Bangkok must be an electrician's nightmare - but somehow it all works. I've never yet experienced a power failure. More than can be said of the UK.

In a bar in Banglumpoo - all (stereotypical) human life was there. Western films being shown on the big screen. Two Western alcoholics (well that's obligatory in any bar in the world), two Western guys with their very pissed off 'Thai brides'. Another Western guy who apparently spoke fluent Thai and wanted the world to know about it. A group of Asian Americans showing off, demanding the best, looking down on their hosts. One guy was really into red snapper - I could have put one down his pants. And finally a group of genuine Thais, who were very reserved and polite. So there you have it - a night in Banglumpoo - plus the girl selling flowers, the blind karaoke singer, various amputee beggars and Akha hill-tribe women flogging jewellery.

Then there are the ladies of the night or more likely ladyboys. There I was, minding my own business in a ladyboy bar, sipping my Ladyboy cocktail, served by a ladyboy, when two more ladyboys come in and started pole-dancing. But then they stripped off until completely naked. With just a casual observation I noticed they'd had the chop (cut them off I say). Fully-developed breasts and no bodily hair completed the transformation. Complete gender reassignment. They were a bit tall (for Thais anyway) and the body language exaggerated, but I suspect many men, especially if drunk, have been fooled. And there was an article in the Bangkok Post not so long ago about a piece in the UK press. *"Your chance to come love me long time baby." Win a free holiday with a ladyboy.* You dirty Katoey. A complaint was made that it denigrated Thai culture and advocated sex tourism. The complaint was upheld by the Advertising Standards Authority. More to the point, in Buddhism, Thailand being a Buddhist country, women are not supposed to touch monks, and articles must be passed to them indirectly. But are ladyboys allowed to touch monks, whether or not they've had the operation? This must be the most intriguing dilemma in Buddhism today.

When it's very hot and sticky and I'm sweating buckets - April and May are pretty horrendous - I like to chill out at my favourite spot by the Chao Phraya River at Phra Sumen Fort, shaded by Golden Showers, Thailand's national tree. Or is it the Lumpoo tree? I love the conflicting semantics here. You can see the usual jugglers and other entertainers, chat with a monk or schoolchildren wishing to improve their English, or just watch the world go by. Unfortunately Bangkok doesn't have many green spaces, so it's all the more pleasant for that. The area is known as Little Kensington after its London namesake, for the proliferation of bars, restaurants and coffee-shops - in historic Chinese shop-houses - filled mainly with well-to-do young Thais. You can really chill out here, in the luxury of air-conditioning. I've spent many happy hours in Ricky's, sipping my cappuccino and reading the Bangkok Post, or in the Saffron Bakery indulging in apple pie and cream. How decadent and Western is that?

Later in the year - October to be precise - I watched from this very spot the Royal Barge Procession, a dress rehearsal for the APEC Summit. The river frontage was closed off by police on the actual occasion. I didn't know there were so many barges - like gilded Roman galleys shimmering across the river. The largest is nearly fifty metres long with a rowing crew of fifty men plus seven umbrella-bearers. The King's personal barge has a huge swan head, the Suphannahongsa, the mythical steed of the Hindu god Brahma. Made from teak, it is the largest dugout in the world. Others were in the shapes of birds (garuda) and serpents (naga). As these magnificent vessels drifted past in the night, men dressed in red, white and black tunics started chanting. With their voices and the boats fading into the distance, the crowds dispersed and the ceremony was over. Traditionally the ceremony is held to mark the end of the Buddhist Rains Retreat, when the King presents robes to monks.

And when the likes of Bush, Putin, Howard and co did arrive for the APEC Summit; their cavalcade rolling down Ratchadamnoen Klang Avenue - the stars and stripes flying on a bullet-proof limo, they were met with a surging, angry throng of anti-globalisation protestors throwing bricks and fire-bombs. The police responded with rubber bullets and tear gas. Then a direct hit on the McDonald's by the Democracy Monument (what totally opposed concepts), with the flames lighting up the sky like it was the 4th of July. Actually it all went off very peacefully, the whole operation tightly controlled and security cordons everywhere. There was a massive clampdown on beggars, vagrants, street vendors, prostitutes, stray dogs; even litter bins were hidden. Protests and demonstrations were banned - something of an irony, considering it was the 30th anniversary of the student-led Democracy Uprisings. Around 20,000 personnel were involved. Was it all worth it?

But the Thai Prime Minister, Thaksin Shinawatra was eventually to be on the receiving end himself, with the military coup of September 2006. Although popular amongst the rural poor, he was not so well-liked in Bangkok, especially with his financial dealings. So Thailand continues on the military/democracy merry-go-round. At least it was a bloodless coup and everyone hopes for a slightly more stable democratic future.

CHAPTER 3

BANGKOK AND BEYOND

So what is there to see outside the Backpacker enclave of Banglumpoo? Well, a visit to Bangkok would not be complete without going to see the Grand Palace and Wat Pho. It is the Taj Mahal, the Versailles, the Coliseum, of Thailand. From Khao San it is about a twenty minute walk or a two stop ride on the Chao Phraya ferry. The Grand Palace dates back to 1782, and was originally the residence of the Royal Family. It is surrounded by high white walls and covers an area of roughly one square mile. There are more than one hundred buildings in the complex, with gleaming gold stupas, mosaic-covered pillars, orange and green roof tiles and rock guardians. The largest of the Palace buildings is the Great Hall of Chakri built in Italian Renaissance style and topped by *mondops,* Thai ornamented spires. But most spectacular of all, Wat Phra Kaew - the Temple of the Emerald Buddha. The image itself is tiny in comparison, not much more than 60cm in height, and it was originally covered in plaster and gold leaf. It is actually made from jade and seated on a throne of gilded wood.

One of the most venerated sites in Thailand, there are always plenty of pilgrims seated in the mermaid posture and paying homage. You might get chatting to a monk or a group of giggling schoolgirls if you're lucky - with clipboards ready they wanted to know all about my home country and what I thought of Thailand.

Next to the Grand Palace is Wat Pho, home of the legendary reclining Buddha, the largest in Thailand. And with a distinct smile on his face. It is 46 metres long and 15 metres high and illustrates the passing of Buddha into Nirvana. Made from plaster with a brick core, it is covered in gold leaf. The feet are three metres high and five metres long. The soles are adorned with mother-of-pearl inlay, displaying the 108 auspicious *laksanas* or characteristics of a Buddha. You will often see scaffolding erected - the maintenance must be like painting the Forth Road Bridge.

Apart from the huge Buddha there are also such marvels as Chinese rock guardians, made from cement, some wearing top hats, with weapons in hands. And panels depicting episodes from the Ramakien (Thai version of Indian Ramayana) with lions, horses, elephants and cows. Wat Pho is famous for the teaching and practice of Thai medicine and massage. *Teaching Thai Tradition Massage from the fundamental of the stone inscription massage texts and Yoga models, which have been collected and inscribed by King Rama III decree at Wat Pho.* It is said that all the massage techniques throughout the country have derived from this site. And you can also have your palms read.

Nearby is the City Pillar, made from a teak tree, almost half buried in the ground, which was used to inspire the Thais over the Burmese in their many conflicts. Classical Thai dancing takes place daily, as well as offerings of severed pigs' heads with sticks of incense sprouting from their foreheads. Well, I think I'll give that one a miss. If you enjoy wandering around markets, spend a while at adjoining Tha Tien and

Pak Klong Talard, with their profusion of fruit, vegetables and flowers. The confusion and chaos of Chinatown isn't very far away - but it's a bit too much on a hot and humid day.

Across the river is Wat Arun, Temple of the Dawn, named after the Indian God Aruna. The 82-metre Khmer-style tower or prang is covered in a mosaic of broken multicoloured porcelain. Evening is a good time for a visit, as it glistens in the rays of the setting sun over the Chao Phraya. You can climb up some steep stairs to a great lookout point over Thonburi and the river.

Just to the east of the Grand Palace and south of the Democracy Monument is Wat Suthat, with two large meditating Buddhas and a quadrangle of smaller Buddhas. Like a smaller version of the Grand Palace but without the crowds. However the murals did need a lot of renovation. A couple of guys were repainting some Buddhas, in shorts, I hasten to add. Not setting a very good example to Westerners in dress etiquette. Then there were statues of people praying, all light-skinned apart from one. And it was here that I saw my first dark-skinned aboriginal Thai woman (with the flat nose, bulbous lips and angular jaw), with an even darker daughter. Just supporting my deliberations that the original inhabitants of the country were more Negroid in appearance: most Thais now are descended from Chinese, Tibetan and other central Asian races.

Next door were some Hindu shrines, one for Shiva/Ganesh, the other for Vishnu. Across the road is the famous 'Sao Ching-Cha' or Giant Swing; two towering red pillars with a crossbar between them. Contestants used to swing from this in honour of the Hindu God Shiva to reach a bag of gold suspended from a bamboo pole, but so many died, the practice was banned. Round about is a plethora of Buddha warehouses - thousands of Buddhas in all shapes and sizes to satisfy even the most ardent follower.

A bit further to the east is the Golden Mount, built on top of a much larger monument which collapsed, making an artificial mound. Steps wind up through gnarled trees to the summit. It is a great vantage point with an excellent 360-degree view of Bangkok, showing the various wats, the Royal Palace and the river. A description of the view is given by Frank Vincent, an American writer who wrote *The Land of the White Elephant* in 1871: *"The general appearance of Bangkok is that of a large, primitive village, situated in and mostly concealed by a virgin forest of almost impenetrable density."* A lot has changed in 130-odd years. To the north is Wat Indravihara, which is renowned for the gigantic 32-metre high Buddha, standing on a lotus-petal base, alms-bowl in hands and nine-tiered umbrella above the head.

In Dusit Park to the north-east, stands Vimanmek Teak Mansion, the largest golden teak building in the world, with displays of Thai art such as ceramics, crystal and silverware. This is a great place to watch traditional Thai Dancing. If you're into photography, there's King Bhumibol's Photographic Museum nearby, with pictures of the family, various royal ceremonies, Ramakien scenes, village life, natural wonders and building developments.

Another 'must see' is the house of Jim Thompson, the American silk entrepreneur who went missing in the Cameron Highlands in Malaysia in 1967. He collected parts of derelict Thai houses and then reassembled them as a whole in 1959. Contained within is a great Asian art collection and his personal effects, including the Chinese Mouse House, where children watch their pet mice running between the separate rooms, but never finding the exit. The house is not far from the Skytrain terminal at the National Stadium alongside the Klong (Canal) Saen Saep.

A good way to find out about the culture, art and history of Thailand would be to visit the National Museum - and it's probably the closest place of interest to Banglumpoo. Bucketloads of Buddhas, Hindu sculptures, religious artefacts, ceramics, wood-carvings, weaponry (with a life-size model of an elephant in full battle array), textiles and Thai musical instruments. Of particular note are the Royal Funeral Chariots, the diorama depicting the Burmese invasion, and the Buddha mural painting at Buddhaisawan Chapel.

In complete contrast, there are the sois of Patpong with their tacky neon-lit market-stalls, sleazy girlie bars, overpriced drinks, bikini-clad dancers, massage parlours and erotic cabarets. Not forgetting screw boys a go-go, street touts and sex shows with such lurid delights as vaginal ping-pong and bottle-opening. It gained its notoriety with American GIs coming over for some R & R from the Vietnam War. Since then it has gone from strength to strength, and the rent from the area alone makes the Patpongpanich family in excess of £150,000 per month. There is a book called *Patpong Sisters: An American Woman's View of the Bangkok Sex World* by Cleo Odzer, which readers might find interesting.

From the heights of human achievement and expression to the oldest profession, Bangkok has it all. If you've got weeks to spare you could try countless more wats, temples, shrines, mosques, exhibitions, galleries, museums, houses, markets, monuments and parks. And Thai dancing, music and art, Thai boxing (Muay Thai), nightclubs, cabarets, sex shows or whatever takes your fancy. Yes, Bangkok is frenetic, but it's great fun. It's polluted, dirty, hot, smelly, sweaty, but the smiles make up for it. Above all it has a great buzz - there's always something to do twenty-four hours a day. Or you can just chill out in a park, on the river, in a street bar or café, or on the street itself.

Around Bangkok there's a lot to see within an hour's drive or so. The easiest thing to do is organise a tour from an agent on the Khao San - for a few pounds you can have a great day's entertainment. Let's start with Ayuthaya, which means 'unassailable' in Sanskrit. It is 86 kilometres north of Bangkok, and was the Siamese capital, the great centre of Thai culture, before Bangkok took over in 1767. I call it 'Cock City' on account of the number of rooster statues on display. You can even buy some to be shipped back home if it takes your fancy. Ayuthaya Historical Park is a UNESCO World Heritage Site, and depending on time available and/or enthusiasm you can get around by boat, bicycle or on foot. It contains the usual surfeit of wats and Buddhas, some unfortunately disintegrating. There is Wat Phra Si Sanphet, the one time Royal Palace and home of a gold Buddha melted down by the Burmese. There is Wat Phra Mahathat with the Buddha's head in a Bodhi tree, and Wat Phanan Choeng with a 19-metre high sitting Buddha image, named after a Chinese explorer. Or Wat Yai Chai Mongkhon, with a large reclining Buddha and a community of monks and nuns.

Just to the south of Ayuthaya is Bang Pa-In Palace. You can go on a day cruise from Bangkok or use the minibus. There is a pretty little pavilion in the centre of a lake, the Chinese style Wehat Chamrun Palace, and the Withun Thatsana building, like a lighthouse with balconies. A topiary garden where the bushes have been shaped into elephants is also worth a visit. But my favourite is Wat Niwet Thama Prawat, which is like a Gothic Christian church. You swing across the river to get to it, in a small trolley-like cable-car operated by the monks. When I was there it was pretty stifling. A small black dog lay curled up peacefully under the seat and was transported back and forth like this for most of the day, no doubt freshened by the breeze. I got chatting to a monk who kept laughing and making jokes. There are those smiles again.

And a rather interesting observation. One of the don'ts - do not stand behind a headless Buddha for a photo - that's the sort of thing the Japanese were doing. Actually it looked quite funny. But isn't it a little ironic how two very similar cultures, the same race almost, same colour and same religion (Theravada Buddhism) came to destroy the very thing presumably they both stood for. I'm talking about the Thai and the Burmese who have been fighting for centuries and destroying each other's temples and Buddhas in consequence.

I expect many of you remember the James Bond film *The Man with the Golden Gun*, when Roger Moore throws a boy into the canal and speeds off in a supercharged long-tail boat. Well, I'm not sure where exactly it was filmed - maybe Thonburi, but it could have been at the Damnoen Saduak Floating Market. The perceived image of the place is I expect of wooden canoes loaded with brightly-coloured fruits and vegetables, being paddled by women in indigo jackets and wearing wide-brimmed straw hats to keep out the glaring sun. Well to a certain extent that is still the case, but these days they will be overwhelmed by the hordes of day-trippers from Bangkok, me included. I'm not really into markets of any kind, but it was a relaxing way to spend a couple of hours. What amused me was not only some fat Americans spending their money on overpriced souvenirs, but boatloads of giggling camera-snapping Japanese wearing identical hats all bumping into one another.

CHAPTER 4

HELLFIRE AND BRIMSTONE

Kanchanaburi lies about 130 km to the west of Bangkok amidst hills and sugar plantations, and can be reached by car or bus in about two hours. Many visitors just come from Bangkok for the day to see the famous Bridge on the River Kwai, but I think it is worth a much longer visit. It makes such a refreshing change from Bangkok, being at a higher elevation with lush forests, several of Thailand's largest waterfalls and most extensive wildlife sanctuaries. And the nearer the Burmese border you get, the more remote and wild it gets.

The first thing you will come across on arrival is the Allied War Cemetery, with its neatly tended green lawns and flower-beds. It is the last resting place for nearly 7000 POWs, and the gravestones carry the names, military insignia and epitaphs of those involved. At the JEATH (Japan, England, Australia, Thailand and Holland) War Museum is a reconstruction of a POW camp with bamboo-atap shacks that housed the prisoners. It is tended by a monk from the local wat and was established in 1977.

The huts contain a collection of photographs from the war, news cuttings, weapons, helmets and a large bomb. Let's hope it doesn't go off. Some of the pictures by a Leo Rawlings reminded me of the paintings in the S21 killing rooms just outside Phnom Penh in Cambodia. For apart from the camp scenes, bridge construction, operations, diseases (scabies, malaria, beriberi, sores and boils), there were also scenes of torture. Holding up rocks for hours on end, being filled with water and hung up by the thumbs. And pictures of tropical ulcers that had gone gangrenous - so bad in fact that feet and legs had to be amputated. I have had these ulcers on more than one occasion, and if you don't get the appropriate antibiotics they don't heal up and they go septic. It is particularly bad in the rainy season and just a slight scratch or insect bite will do it.

So on to the Thailand-Burma Railway Centre. This museum shows the planning and construction of the railway, a scale model with an electronic map, photographs, POW artwork, relics and artefacts, and interpretive panels. Visitor's comments have been very complimentary. Of 60,000 Allied POWs, 12,399 died; but between 70,000 to 90,000 of the quarter million Asian labourers perished in constructing the line. Just puts the whole thing in perspective; what I found the most poignant was a couple of quotations - *"Never have I dreamt that I would see the day when human life would be held so cheaply"* from Major A.E Saggers, Malay Hamlet, June 1943, and *"It was like the Tower Of Babel - Tamils, Chinese, Malays, English and Australians and the Japanese herding us about, shouting the local pidgin, and underlining phrases with bamboo rods"* from Ray Parkin, HMAS Perth.

And yet another museum is the World War II Museum, which is decorated like a garish Chinese Buddhist Temple - the fat smiling Buddha with a beer belly; the physical and facial characteristics of the Buddha vary from country to country. There are some very elaborate wall murals showing Thai-Burmese battle scenes using elephants in siege warfare. One guy had his head, shoulder and arm cut off - he didn't look too happy about it. On the highest floor are pictures of the Chinese family who built the museum, positioned above the portraits of Thai kings. Well, that isn't showing much respect to the monarchy is it! Outside a smaller building are statues of leading war figures e.g. Hitler, Stalin, Churchill and Hirohito. It contains various relics such as photos and sketches, and a diorama of the bombing of the River Kwai Bridge on 28th November, 1944. Some life-sized papier-mâché POWs dressed in loincloths completed the scene. "The bridge got broken into pieces in a twinkle of an eye - the bodies of POWs lay higgledy-piggledy beneath" says the inscription.

But of course the centrepiece of it all is the Death Railway Bridge itself. It was constructed in 1943 but was bombed several times by Allied forces in 1945. Rebuilt after the war, the central section of rectangular girders is the only original part remaining. And you can walk over it if you like - just avoid the trains and the huge groups of Japanese making a return visit. Some old locomotives are parked in a display area nearby.

The bridge was just one of 688, and over 415 km of track were built between Thailand and Burma. Further up the line, the journey to the Hellfire Pass Memorial in Konyu Cutting - sponsored by the Australian government and completed in 1998 - is well worth the effort. The pass gained its name as it was lit up by torches at night during rail construction. A most apt description. Over seventy per cent of the POWs died in constructing the one thousand metre series of mountain cuttings, using little more than hammers, picks, shovels and some dynamite. A plaque is set in stone commemorating the deaths.

I took the train back to Kanchanaburi: great scenery, and certainly beats Connex and its successor - more efficient as well, despite the wooden bridge supports, but don't look down if you suffer from vertigo. Krasae Cave with its attendant Buddha made an interesting diversion.

If you want a break from all this turbulent history, Erawan National Park with its famous waterfalls makes for a fun day out, walking the trails - and it's great for swimming. There are seven levels of waterfalls with numerous pools and footbridges across. The uppermost fall is said to resemble the Hindu three-headed elephant Airvata (*Erawan* in Thai). The day I went, there was some kind of endurance trial with the competitors running through ravines and climbing up the waterfalls using nets. I contented myself with some relaxing swimming and was most intrigued to be 'bitten' by some passing fish. Actually all they do is eat your dead skin - quite a useful cleansing service, and very therapeutic.

I very much liked Kanchanaburi - lots to see and do, and had some very interesting conversations. In particular, the local tourist police were very helpful and informative. One guy I spoke to ran a restaurant and had studied English in Bournemouth back in the 1970s. He was about my age and there was a picture of him at Stonehenge in 1972 with shoulder-length hair. Just like me. He was very proud of that picture. He was into the Beatles, Phil Collins, the Stones and Dire Straits. We had a great time chatting about world affairs and the merits of Western and Eastern cultures. And he was against the war in Iraq too. Great guy.

But unfortunately some restaurant-owners are not so friendly, as reported in October 2004 with the headline 'Thai cop confesses to killing Britons.' The suspect, Sgt Somchai Visetsingha, owned a restaurant in Kanchanaburi, and it was here that a row broke out with the two Britons Adam Lloyd and Vanessa Arscott. Lloyd allegedly spat in Somchai's face, with the cop chasing after them when they left the restaurant. Lloyd was shot, and then Somchai mowed down Arscott with his car, dragging her down the road for 200 metres. Then she too was shot in the head and body. Just as well I didn't go to that restaurant. Another near miss. Somchai has been jailed for life, but has appealed against his sentence.

So it's time to say goodbye to Kanchanaburi and head north to Sukhothai, Thailand's first capital, now in ruins, another UNESCO World Heritage Site. I went by bus from Bangkok's Northern Bus Terminal near the Chatuchak Market. And very comfortable it was too - plenty of legroom, a great upstairs seat and free drink and cakes. Somehow I can't see that happening on National Express. Some of the best bus rides I've had have been in Thailand. Sukhothai is famous for its Historical Park with yet more wats. The grounds are well managed and I took a leisurely cycle round the area for about six hours. It was June and the beginning of the rainy season, so I got a little wet, but not as bad as in October. There are 21 individual sites altogether and four large ponds, but I'm not going to bore you with all the details. My favourite has to be the huge 15-metre seated blue-grey Buddha at Wat Si Chum. This is probably the most impressive, and certainly the most photographed.

However, what I had come to Sukhothai for was the Wat Thawet Learning Garden. To this end, I elicited the assistance of a German guy called Jurgens who had lived in Thailand for several years, including a year spent as a monk. He was a wealth of information on Thai culture and history. So off we went on his motor-bike, something which I have to confess gives me the shits, considering the state of the roads and of innumerable accidents. I'd already seen several people with exhaust pipe burns, broken arms and legs. One young man had a terrible red and purple scar all the way down his left arm where the skin had been ripped away. Horrendous.

The Garden was set up in 1975 by Monk Phra Sumroeng (1928-1995) and taken over by Phra Banthoeng. There are 100 life-sized concrete statues vividly depicting eternal punishments awaiting those who have sinned on earth. Those who killed animals have the heads of their victims: elephant, buffalo, duck or chicken. Those who have abused alcohol have boiling liquids poured down their throats. Those who have kicked or injured others have huge hands and feet. Those who have lied or used bad language have tiny mouths. The souls in torment are surrounded by tableaux depicting scenes from the life of the Buddha. And next to the garden there is a large temple with intricate relief figures of Buddhist deities nearing completion. A great example of karmic retribution. And something I learnt that day - Hell isn't just for Christians.

But my day tour wasn't over yet. There was also a visit to a rice mill which consisted of a large shed with huge flywheels and belts. And mountains of rice rose up from the floor to the roof beams. It had been working the same way for more than fifty years - to me it looked like something out of Dickens; a snapshot of Victorian factory life. As luck would have it, a monk was about to be ordained at a local monastery. So off we went to witness the event, but it was certainly not a solemn occasion. Family and friends were out in force with tables bedecked with a huge quantity of food and drink. And a young girl belting out Thai pop songs celebrated the event with much gusto. All Thai males are expected to become monks, if only for a few weeks between leaving school and starting work. I wasn't too sure how long this one was going to last. The occasion went off with great merriment - that's one of the things I love about travelling - spontaneity, not always knowing what's going to happen next.

At this stage my visa was running out - in Thailand they only last a month from the date of entry, unless you obtain one in advance.

And the nearest exit point for renewal was Mae Sot on the border with Myanmar, formerly Burma. On the bus journey there were frequent police checkpoints to flush out any illegal immigrants, which was a real problem considering the political situation in that country. It is very much a frontier town with very few Westerners - and they were all crowded into a couple of bars.

Most of the trade seems to be on the black market - drugs, gems and people mainly. Border skirmishes are frequent - not that I saw any - and the town is full of Karen and Kayah refugees living in the nearby camps, some wearing their distinctive 'longyis' (wrap-around skirts or sarongs). There were quite a few hill-tribe people as well. Actually, I thought the town was quite a relaxing place, apart from the dogs, by far the most aggressive in Thailand - and not just with barking. One Rottweiler wanted to take a chunk out of my leg, but fortunately without success, as it's not just the threat of injury, but also rabies that worries me. Then there was this Thai TV programme about dogs being killed for food. I've seen caged dogs in several places in Thailand - Pekinese and Poodles seem to be the greatest delicacies; the skinned carcasses displayed on hooks like something out of the Texas Chainsaw Massacre. Definitely a 'bad dog' day.

Heading over the Thai-Myanmar Friendship Bridge (make friends, not war I say) and into Myawadi, I had to surrender my passport and for 10 dollars could wander around the town for a few hours. There was only one other Westerner - a South African with his Thai bride – and even he had to renew his visa every three months. Very few people spoke English, or even Thai, apart from a couple of 'guides' who latched onto me.

The difference between quite wealthy Thailand and poverty stricken Myanmar was immediately obvious. Shacks replaced concrete buildings, dirt roads replaced tarmac and bicycle rickshaws replaced motorised taxis. I wandered around Shwe Muay Wan, a bell-shaped stupa gilded with gold and topped with over 1600 precious and semi-precious gems. My most vivid recollection was of almost slipping over on the wet shiny tiles - it was raining quite hard and of course I was walking barefoot. Unlike in Thailand, where barefoot walking is usually confined to the insides of temples, in Myanmar it's almost everywhere. I later caught up with my two friends and we shared a meal of noodles together - I had no-one else to talk to. He had quite a lucrative travel business in Bangkok. Then it was back to Mae Sot and my onward journey to Chiang Mai. My first trip to Myanmar had been interesting to say the least, and I was determined to make an in-depth return journey some day.

The first time I arrived in Chiang Mai I was not impressed. The old city consists of a neat square about a kilometre across bounded by a moat and crumbling walls. But what I didn't like was the interminable roar of motor-bikes turning it into little more than a racetrack. However the city does tend to grow on you and you learn to live with its bad points - it's a lot better than some South-East Asian cities I've been to. On subsequent visits I've explored several of it's over 300 temples - almost as many as Bangkok; half-hidden bars down cobblestone lanes, the Night Bazaar; enjoyed Thai as well as international cuisine, a kick-boxing contest, and a trip up the hill to Doi Suthep, one of Thailand's greatest wats.

Chiang Mai is Thailand's second city, more than 700 km north-west of Bangkok, surrounded by forested mountains, home to the many hill-tribes for which the area is famous. The climate is somewhat cooler than Bangkok's, and in winter the temperatures can go down to near freezing in the hills. It is very much a commercial and market centre, with cultural influences from neighbouring countries, including China to the north, a legacy of the old Chinese-Muslim caravan trading routes.

Called 'The Rose of the North' it is renowned for Thai massage, cooking, yoga and vipassana (insight meditation). I can really recommend the massage: a young Thai girl jumping up and down on you, giving a full body and foot massage for one and a half hours for just over £3 - can't be bad. But it's more complicated than you think. There is stroking and kneading the muscles, chiropractics and acupressure, all performed in a ritualised set pattern with attention to such things as circulation, tempo and energy lines. It is quite mind-boggling. I tried it during a meditation retreat in Pai, but without much success.

After your massage you could head for a meal at one of over 25 Thai/Chinese vegetarian restaurants, the best selection outside Bangkok - and most within walking distance of each other. Why not try the 'VegeThairians' in the Night Market? In recognition of its status, the World Vegetarian Congress convened in Chiang Mai in 1999. Curries, bean curd, noodles, stir-fries, spicy papaya salad and all the condiments - garlic, chillies, lemon-grass, ginger etc. etc. - just try and avoid the shrimp paste. And talking of curries, here's a little joke I found quite amusing.

A gay man has to decide on how to dispose of his deceased partner's remains. The funeral director informs him there are two main options. Burial or cremation. However the man has another idea. "What I would like to do," he says thoughtfully, "is cut my friend up into small chunks, cook the meat in a really hot Green Curry and eat it at a farewell feast." "That's very gruesome," replied the funeral director with some unease. "Why would you want to do that?" "Well," uttered the gay man with a wry smile, "I would like to feel him dribbling out of my arse one last time."

And I can tell you from experience that some Thai curries will not only make your eyes water, but will set fire to the other end of your digestive tract. After hearing that, you might want a change of cuisine. I can say that the Indian and Italian food is excellent, not forgetting the falafel and hummus at the Jerusalem restaurant. Or maybe you're not hungry at all.

Time for some Thai boxing (Muay Thai) at the Thapae Stadium. 'All are the Superstar Boxers in the Match Day' says the promotional blurb. Ten fights in all - the best were the last two. Almost anything goes in this martial sport - the whole body is considered a target. And fighters can use fists, elbows and knees as well as feet to despatch their opponent. The match starts with a boxing dance, the contestants paying homage to their gurus and the guardian spirit of Thai boxing. This ceremony is accompanied by the Thai oboe (pìi) and percussion. After much bobbing and weaving, they take off their sacred headbands and the fight begins. One bout had a ladyboy boxer with lipstick on and his hair in bows. I thought he was winning, but then both contestants fell out of the ring and he had to throw in the towel. Unlike the victorious kathoey in Lumphini Stadium in Bangkok. The last fight was really vicious. I don't know how they managed so many kicks and punches. It reminded me of the internet movie clip that was doing the rounds a while ago, where one guy broke his foot, leaving it dangling lifeless. Then he fell over. Agonising.

Right, it's off to the Night Market to purchase a dazzling array of handicrafts, fabrics, clothing, jewellery, pottery, wood-carvings (I love masks), basketry and Buddhas in just about every material imaginable. Plus western fake designer goods galore - plenty of retail therapy, although personally I'd rather chill out in the bar. And what better than an English bar called the Red Lion, and a German bar with a Thai guy dressed in lederhosen with a feather in his cap. Yes it really is that sort of place. A cultural nightmare or what. Costa del Chiang. And the local Chang (Elephant) Beer, at 7% alcohol is enough to blow your head off. Actually it was all quite amusing, although I do hope such developments don't spread too much and swamp Thai culture. Thais are a pretty accommodating bunch, but there is a limit.

Which reminds me of a night bus journey I took back to Bangkok. It was a miserable wet evening which set the tone, when a load of loud, leery English yobboes climbed aboard. How I detest large groups of any particular nationality travelling. It's as though they haven't got the gumption to go on their own or at least in pairs. Seemingly transplanted from San Antonio or Ayia Napa. One guy who had been drinking quite a bit of whisky thought he could get away with smoking in the toilet (it was a 'No Smoking' bus), until one Thai lady remonstrated with him. I think at one point she was going to thump him on the nose. That's why I like the Thais - they're very tolerant towards foreigners unless you take the piss - then beware. I think he should have been deported back to Essex.

On a slightly more spiritual level, to find out about Thai Buddhism and culture, you might wish to take part in culture and meditation training. Well now it's easy. In a new programme from Mahachulalongkorn (I never tried pronouncing it) Buddhist University, there are free courses every Sunday and Monday with an introduction to Buddhism, chanting, meditation, alms offering and Thai cooking to finish the programme off. Or if you prefer, just turn up for the Monk Chat. Learn about the life of the monks, discuss religion and topical issues and help them with their English.

Buddhism is not about God-worship; there is no divine message. The idea is to eradicate evil thoughts, words and actions and to purify the mind. Such purity of mind is called enlightenment. That just about sums it up. And to finish:

Though one should conquer
a million men in battle.
Yet he, is indeed, the noblest
victor who has conquered himself.

There is no fire like lust,
No crime like hate.
There is no ill like the body,
No bliss higher than peace (Nibbana)

But Buddhism isn't everything. At the Thapae gate I got an 'Answer the Call with the Camp Family Relation', an evangelical band singing Hallelujah. There was lots of flag, banner and arm-waving, with women in white dresses and men in orange T-shirts proclaiming 'The Time of Praise.' A Western guy comes up to me with some Christian literature. I don't know - being converted to Christianity in a Buddhist country - whatever next? Probably the evangelical preacher on the Khao San Road - Hellfire and Brimstone.

Doi Suthep is situated on a 1676-metre peak north-west of Chiang Mai, and commands spectacular views of the city, even when it's cloudy and overcast. Near its summit is Wat Phra That Doi Suthep, first established over six hundred years ago. Entrance to the Wat is gained via a naga (serpent) staircase of three hundred steps. Hordes of schoolchildren were there, puffing and panting, then hitting gongs and ringing the bells. At the top is a Lanna-style (Northern Thai, 13th to 15th centuries, influenced by Shan/Burmese and Lao traditions) copper-plated chedi (pagoda) surmounted by a five-tiered gold umbrella.

According to legend, some holy relics contained within were carried by a white elephant, which promptly died from the exhausting journey. The White Elephant Monument commemorates the event. It was most interesting watching young Thai girls praying and being sprinkled with holy water by the monks. One of the best wats I've ever seen - in excellent condition. A short distance away is the Bhubing Palace, the royal winter residence with some beautiful temperate gardens - roses, fuchsias, hydrangeas, ferns and huge bamboos. And forget the songthaew (a small pick-up truck with two rows of bench seats facing each other) on the return journey - I got a lift from a very nice Thai couple all the way to my guest-house. They wanted to improve their English.

Doi Suthep, a secret peak
Thai speaks of customs old
Where nature's beauty doth unfold
O'er the golden name of "Nakorn Ping."

Highest of all is the peak of Doi Inthanon, which rises to 2596m with three dramatic waterfalls cascading down its sides. Nam Tok Mae Klang is the largest and easiest to get to. It can get pretty chilly at the top, especially in the winter months. If you have plenty of time there is always the National Park to explore, with its mist-shrouded forested slopes home to innumerable bird species, the Asiatic black bear, macaques, gibbons, civets, deer and the giant flying squirrel.

The area is also inhabited by Hmong and Karen tribes-people, and most auspicious among these are the Padaung Long-Neck women. Many of them are refugees escaping from persecution in neighbouring Myanmar. The legends go that the brass neck rings protected them from tigers, snakes or men from other tribes, or that they were descended from dragons.

At five years old the first ring is fitted, then gradually added to over the next few years to mark important occasions such as marriage. The rings are actually soldered together to make a continual coil, which forces up the jaw bone and compresses down on the rib cage creating the impression of a 'long neck'. It has been said that if the ring was removed for any length of time, the woman would die of suffocation or atrophy. But the rings are often removed for cleaning purposes, without ill effect, and they in no way impede the woman's mobility or her ability to work.

The villagers make their living from selling handicrafts and having their photographs taken. Usually it's of young girls, but the lady on the cover picture was a little older. I have a classic post-card showing the happy smiling faces of the girls in question washing in the river. The Long-Neck communities are generally administered by Karenni ethnic groups fighting for an independent state in eastern Myanmar. No doubt there is some exploitation; still it must be better than the life many of them had back in their homeland.

CHAPTER 5

PAI IN THE SKY

Pai is one of my favourite places in Thailand. It is very laid-back, enjoys a beautiful location amongst wooded hills, and the people are friendly and welcoming. There are lots of great eateries and activities galore - trekking, white-water rafting, mountain biking, visits to the hill-tribes or meditating in a peaceful retreat. It's a small town of some 3,000 people, about halfway between Chiang Mai and Mae Hong Son. A local bus takes just over four hours from Chiang Mai up steep and winding roads - and it's usually packed.

The population are mainly Shan and Thai, with a sprinkling of Muslim Chinese. It is also the haunt of backpackers and hippy dudes come to chill out for a few days, or weeks, or months. You know the scene - Bob Marley, Jimi Hendrix, dreadlocks, sarongs, banana pancakes, happy pizzas, wacky shakes (bang lassies), water pipes, juggling, massage, reiki meditation and om mani padme hum mantras.

On my typical chill-out day, having woken from the slumbers of my A-frame bungalow in a tropical garden, I would enjoy a leisurely breakfast, maybe read a book over a coffee and go for a swim in the local pool. Amazingly there is a swimming-pool in Pai. Then a wander around town - to the market maybe, a lunch of sweet and sour vegetables and a delicious coconut shake. More reading, catch up on my e-mails, more coffee, more shakes. No, no, no - that's a little too chilled. I'd be on a mountain bike past the elephant camp and up to the hot springs - had them all to myself, and in one place you could boil an egg in them. Then it was to a waterfall just beyond the Pai Mountain Lodge, only to be intercepted by some guys selling opium. It is after all the Golden Triangle. On the way back stopping off at Johnny's (that wasn't his real name) Bar Guest House in the middle of nowhere, meeting a guy from Edinburgh, who incidentally was born in Malawi. So we sat in a hot-tub and chatted about Africa, travelling, and the world, anything really, over a few beers.

Back in town I got chatting to a nice Thai lady who ran a restaurant - all you can eat for 60 baht, or something like that. She said she didn't like farang (Western) food, to which I replied, "Do you use chillies in your cooking?" Well that was the end of that topic of conversation - they were introduced by the Portuguese in the 16th century. Just goes to show that food tastes and culture are constantly in flux. There is now what is called 'Fusion Cuisine'. Like pizzas with a Thai curry topping - and I'm not joking. We went on to discuss the effects of mass tourism on the Thai way of life, especially in rural areas. She said quite simply that without the restaurant, she would have to leave her home-town and family behind, and work in either Chiang Mai or Bangkok. The world is governed by economics. End of story. Her one complaint however was about her Finnish boyfriend who was cold and emotionless. She said - and I quote - "He only come to me for the fucking." The brides are getting restless. West meets East in more ways than one.

At night time, the usual place to hang out in Pai is the Bebop Bar, which used to be located in a mock Shan-Yunnanese shop-house, decorated with Asian hippy gear. But now it's in a new larger, air-conditioned establishment and unfortunately has lost some of its old charm. Everything changes. But the bands still play Rock, Rhythm and Blues and you can still get drunk on San Som (Thai Rum) as I did, completely wrecked on one occasion. How I ever got back to my A-frame I'll never know. So much for chill-out days.

A short distance from the centre of town is the Temple on the Hill (Wat Phra That Mae Yen) - there is a climb of 353 steps to the top for some spectacular views. Bougainvilleas and poinsettias are everywhere, with huge butterflies flitting from plant to plant. It was very quiet and peaceful until a mangy dog came past - I think it was frothing at the mouth. Then there was a weird dude with a hillbilly smile staring vacantly into space - just like the banjo player in *Deliverance*. But then Pai is full of such characters, and how often does that movie come up in my travels. Inside the wat were some more scenes from Hell. People being sawn in half, tongues pulled out with pincers, mass hangings, boiling liquid poured down the throat, internal organs removed and eaten by crows, being burnt alive and forced to climb a tree embedded with spikes. There was a fasting skeletal Buddha, very feminine in character, and murals depicting his life. The reclining Buddha had the beginnings of a hornet's nest growing on his helmet - nasty. Well, there is a picture of the Buddha sitting under the Bodhi tree with a wasp nest just above him.

Now for something completely different. It just so happened that when I was first in Pai in November 2001, it was the perfect place to watch the Leonid meteor shower. This event happens every 33 years and occurs when the earth passes through the tail of the comet Tempel-Tuttle, the trail of dust and debris showing up as shooting stars. In this part of Asia and at this time, 8000 stars an hour raced through the night sky like a gigantic fireworks display. We had a celestial space party - it was certainly something to celebrate. Cosmic man.

Many come to Pai for meditation; me included, getting a little Banana Dhamma Instant Karma. *'DISCOVER the secret law of nature found in the complete voluntary enlightenment of Buddha the translocation of all beings from the cycle of rebirth'* was the message. Sounds like a corporate mission statement, doesn't it? Donning the white robes of the ascetic I first discovered the four foundations of mindfulness: body, suffering, mind, dhamma. Then the practice of standing meditation, walking meditation and, with legs crossed, sitting meditation - most uncomfortable. *'Practice how you concentrate mindfulness. How you protection your mind. How you protection suffering. How you come to tranquillity. How to use meditation for in your day life.'* If you don't understand any of this, it's because it's all in Hermit Speak.

But that wasn't all - now it was the Body Twist - the Hermit's Art of Controlling. *'Self-Exercise following the ascetic's patterns consists of many practices that stimulate all the movement organs from head to toes if the exercises are practiced properly and regularly the blood circulation in those muscles will be better include all the joints will be able to move easily and efficiently'* etc. etc. A bit like yoga for beginners. The best one was standing on one leg with your arms over your head, and pointing to the sky.

The retreat culminated in massage techniques and healing methods. Lower back to shoulder with thumbs, massage shoulder slowly and gently and back two times. Sit inside, lock ankle, one palm hand-massage leg both sides. Cross legs two times, hands lock feet at heels two times. Lock hands and arms two times, sit on feet, hold body and shoulder two times. Twist hand around neck two times up and down. And finally twist the body, fix and pull up body. I told you it was mind boggling, didn't I?

There were two options for continuing my journey to Mae Hong Son, the most north-westerly town in Thailand: by bus or river raft - no choice really, it had to be by river. Two days of white-water rafting down the River Pai visiting a waterfall, a fossil reef and hot springs. All food and gear included, and staying in the jungle in an overnight camp. It started off peacefully enough, until we got to the rapids and I got trashed as usual. They were only grade 3, not like the 5 on the Nile (that's another story) but still exhilarating enough. The lush forest with eagles swooping overhead, diving kingfishers, and lizards in the undergrowth more than made up for it. Swimming under the Suza waterfall, I got swept away by the current and not for the first time. But I did have my life-jacket on.

My travelling companions were mainly Dutch and one looked strangely like Burt Reynolds - angular facial features, broad shoulders and hairy chest, and with the same macho outlook on life. Then it dawned on me. River, steep wooded banks, gorges, rafting, rapids. Deliverance 2 here we come. *"Now let's you just drop them pants."* Whoops, I'm getting a bit carried away.

A bamboo shelter was our home for the night, and my tired and aching body soon fell into a deep slumber. Dawn arrived soon enough, with a chorus of crickets and croaking frogs. The second day passed without incident, except that one of the guides (who was wearing a bandana) picked up some floating weed, and placing it nonchalantly to his chin, exclaimed 'Osama bin Laden!' There was quite a likeness. It was just post 9/11 and obviously still very topical. I roared out with laughter and even one American friend (though he was from Hawaii) thought it was funny.

Mae Hong Son is another wonderful place, though there is less to do than in Pai. It has an end of the world feel to it - the mountains are really closing in on you here. I have a postcard of Wat Phra That Doi

Kong Mu poking its whitewashed spires through the mountain mist, with a backdrop of rugged grey peaks in the distance. When I was there however, the air was clearer and you could plainly see the town hundreds of metres below. It seemed quite odd watching planes from this vantage point, landing and taking off from the airport.

I got my timing wrong. After I had climbed the steps to the top, I discovered to my horror hordes of lazy fat bloated *farang* - mainly French on this occasion, who had been transported up in minibuses. Don't you just hate it when that happens? Bloody tour groups. Much more fun watching the local people bringing in food and offerings for the monks. 'Too many *farang* spoil the wat'. In the centre of town is a small picturesque lake (Nong Jong Kham) with two more interesting wats built in the Burmese style. If you're around in March you can watch monk ordination ceremonies here, or in October the Jong Para Festival consisting of folk theatre, dance and processions.

It was from Mae Hong Son that I decided to organise my hill-tribe trekking. In Chiang Mai it was far too commercialised like some awful package tour, and at the time of visiting, there was not much on offer in Pai. Go with the flow I say - you have to be very flexible when travelling and what will be will be. The hill-tribes of northern Thailand (Chao khao or mountain people to the Thai) all have their own unique language, customs, attire and spiritual beliefs. They originated from Tibet, China, Myanmar and Laos over the last 200 years or so. Belief systems are varied, but nearly all have elements of animism - a belief that souls and spirits inhabit all objects - and some ancestor worship. Buddhism and Christianity are treated like added extras. A lot are heavily into opium-growing, for home consumption as well as for trading.

The main groups are Akha (you'll see the women all over the streets of Chiang Mai and Banglumpoo, in their bead and feather headdresses and dangling silver ornaments, trying to flog off 'ethnic' jewellery), Lahu, Lisu, Mien (Yao), Hmong and Karen. The last two are the most numerous and most visited hill-tribes. The Hmong are characterised by their simple black jackets and indigo or black baggy trousers, while the Karen, split into several groups including the Long-Necks, wear thickly woven V- neck tunics of various colours, unmarried women wearing white.

So off I went to see the Karen and Maew (Hmong) tribes, trekking through the jungle and fields full of cabbages (a cash crop) to their little villages. Watching children play 'takraw' (a cross between volleyball and soccer) with a woven rattan ball, and throwing a live chicken around. Not so good. Staying overnight in the family's bamboo hut on stilts (to protect against flooding), shared with cats, dogs, chickens and pigs… I'm not kidding, though the pigs were kept at ground level. What a menagerie. Maybe how our medieval forbears lived. No electricity, gas or running water. Actually it was all very comfortable once we were tucked up in our sleeping bags and under the mosquito nets. It rained during the night (even though it was the dry season) but we were bone-dry thanks to the patchwork of palm leaves on the roof. Amazingly waterproof. And the guide got drunk on Thai Whisky - just as well he'd sobered up by morning.

Next day it was to a camp by a waterfall, back and forth over a fast flowing river - nearly up to our waists at times. Some tricky scrambling over rocks and up and down bamboo ladders. Luxuriant forest growth with banyan (strangler fig), teak and mango trees in profusion, and I saw my first gibbon in Thailand. And the number of rats was unbelievable. Who put the rat in the ratatouille? They were everywhere. 101 uses of bamboo. Answers on a postcard please. Here are some to start you off. Ladders of course, housing, fences, bridges, poles, furniture, hats, baskets, cooking and eating utensils, walking sticks and an instrument of torture - apparently one is strapped to a bamboo bench over living bamboo which is allowed to grow through your body - Ouch! A speciality of the Chinese. The guides made for us spoons, cups and bowls from bamboo - it really is an amazing material. Three days and two nights - all for about £25 - not bad.

Returning to Chiang Mai, I sorted out my Laos visa for the next leg of the journey. Christmas was approaching - you can't escape it anywhere in the world. The decorations, lights and Christmas trees go up - it's what the tourists expect. I remember once in a hotel in New Delhi, they even covered some bushes with a cotton fleece to resemble snow. And turkey with all the trimmings. Get me out of here. I headed to Fang and Tha Ton, a one horse town on the Mae Nam Kok River. Walked to the Burmese border - a low-key affair, but plenty of soldiers around. And climbed the hill to Wat Tha Ton with its Chinese shrine and large temple bell. Apparently this is rung every morning at 4 and then 6am, but I never heard it. A bit too early for me.

From Tha Ton it was by long-tail boat (so named because the propeller is mounted at the end of a long drive shaft extending from the engine) to Chiang Rai, stopping at various hill-tribe villages and hot springs en route. Plenty more trekking here if you're up to it. I think I stayed about one day in Chiang Rai, as the place doesn't offer much for the traveller. It is known as 'The Gateway to the Golden Triangle' but I was soon on my way to Chiang Khong, the legendary Mekong River and the Laos border.

Chiang Khong is a small market town and trading post, and important for two things: the ferry crossing to Huay Xai in Laos, and the Plaa Beuk or giant Mekong catfish. Growing to three metres long and weighing up to 300 kg, it is probably the largest freshwater fish in the world. Considered a delicacy in Thailand and Laos, most of the fish are sent to Bangkok, where they command high prices in restaurants.

Now on the endangered species list, there is a breed and release program to encourage regeneration. Though probably the greatest threat is the blasting of river rapids in China where the fish spawns. Stop the fishing altogether I say. I only stayed the one night here - there was a heavy rainstorm and I dreamt I was floating down the Mekong in my bed. Obviously too many Beer Chang. I've heard it contains amphetamines. The next morning I was on the little ferry boat. A new country and a new set of experiences awaited me.

CHAPTER 6

POWER TO THE PEOPLE

I had arrived in The Peoples' Democratic Republic of Laos, or The Land of a Million Elephants. Laos is a landlocked country sandwiched between Thailand and Vietnam, with China and Burma to the north and Cambodia to the south. It is about the size of the UK but only has a population of 5.8 million. Most of the country is mountainous - in the west the Mekong River is the most dominant feature. It has the most pristine forested environment in S E Asia; about two-thirds of the country is forested. It is also one of the poorest, and the roads, especially in the north, are appalling. It has the distinction of being the most bombed country in the history of warfare as a result of the American/Vietnamese War. There are bomb casings everywhere being used for steps, containers, posts, pathways and bridges. 101 uses of bomb casings. And yes, they celebrate Christmas - the French connection.

One of the first people I spoke to in Huay Xai was a tour rep. He had spent six years in Germany and spoke fluent German, French, English, Thai, Lao and a little Russian. And so open and welcoming. Really put me to shame. Actually I grew to love the unsophisticated and rustic charm of Laos, a country years behind the West, locked in a time warp of Communist domination. Though I don't suppose the people who lived there had quite the same appreciation. In particular, Hmong groups have been fighting a rearguard action since the Communists came to power in 1975. They had been supported by the United States; now they were being hunted down for being on the losing side.

My next destination was Luangnamtha, to the north-east, in exactly the opposite direction to the battalions of backpackers (it wasn't quite like that) who were heading down the Mekong by boat - the Cannabis Cruise as some call it. But for me it was an amazing eight hours in a songthaew over a very bumpy, rutted, dusty and sometimes muddy road, across fords, over rocks and through fields and forests. I didn't think the suspension would take it. The scenery very much reminded me of Uganda and Malawi, with heavily forested slopes and banana plantations. Children with happy smiling faces from small villages shouted out "Saibadee" - "Hello". Animals were everywhere, especially chickens and pigs - Squeal lika pig. About halfway through our journey we met a group of bikers. It's strange who you meet sometimes in the middle of nowhere. They were doing something like a trans-Asian tour. I must admit despite all the privations these are the sort of trips I love. Not at all touristy.

It was pitch black when we finally arrived - the power had been turned off. So after eating a meal by candlelight - how romantic - it was off to bed - if you could find it. Unfortunately, despite being shattered, I did not get a good night's rest. I heard lots of splashing sounds beneath me - bad plumbing maybe, and then scratching in the roof - more rats. The stuff of nightmares. When the first light of dawn came, I looked out of the window and to my astonishment, I discovered that my room was built over a duck pond. Wonders never cease.

For breakfast I ordered cheese with a crusty baguette and coffee. Traditional Lao food? Well it is now. Something good the French introduced. And freshly baked - as soon as you've ordered the waitress goes off to the market to collect it. In the meantime, you can put your feet up and watch the schoolgirls cycling past in their blue patterned skirts, with parasols to keep the sun off. Now don't get too excited.

I had arrived with a New Zealand girl. A great travelling nation, the New Zealanders - it is said that a quarter of them are out of the country at any one time. She was looking for a friend who had gone missing in Muang Sing, a market town to the north. I'd heard lots of bad vibes about the place - robberies, drugs busts by the police, an Aussie guy with his face slashed over his involvement with a local girl, and a mysterious death that was hushed up. Probably over-sensationalised - these things often are, but there must have been a grain of truth.

That evening we went to the local dance - at least they had their own generator with lights, a sound system and the coldest beer in town; well, at least it wasn't lukewarm like in Egypt. Then the excitement began. The band was like something out of the early 1960s - the Tremeloes or Gerry and the Pacemakers. It was all stiff backs and sideburns, guitars held rigidly to the chest, sharp suits and drainpipe trousers. When they started playing, couples took to the floor in a very regimented fashion in what could only be described as a waltz. As a tribute to a bygone era it would have been difficult to beat.

Now for one of those strange coincidences that one encounters every so often. I had just organised another trekking expedition and was walking down the main street (actually there's only one), when I spotted one of my travelling companions sitting in a café. I went over to talk to her. She was chatting to a man who seemed strangely familiar.

Then it dawned on me. It was only the same guy I'd travelled with in Africa four years before - up Kilimanjaro, down the Nile, to the gorillas of Bwindi and the beaches of Mombasa. And to meet up with him in this remote corner of Laos of all places. He was coming to the end of his travels - India, Nepal, S E Asia - I was only just beginning. I paused to reflect on the situation. The travelling community is like a city which is on the move every day. Sooner or later you're going to bump into somebody you know.

Next day we set off trekking together to see the Black Tai (formal dress only please), Lanten and Hmong hill-tribes in the National Biodiversity Conservation Area. The Black Tai are renowned for silk production and weaving, and the Lanten for indigo-dyeing and papermaking (from bamboo) and the Hmong - weren't they the ones with the white bandages on their legs and shaven eyebrows. Can't remember. Like in Northern Thailand the hill-tribes are amazingly diverse and it gets very complicated after a while. The jungle, with its twisting lianas and gnarled strangler figs, allegedly contains tigers and elephants, but you will be lucky to see more than the odd bird or butterfly. The leeches were bad - for some anyway, who were constantly stopping to mop up the blood. I find 100% DEET (insect repellent) helps, but it's not too good for the skin.

Again we stopped off at a local village, went for a swim in the river and watched girls pummelling rice with huge wooden pestles. As long as we didn't stray too far away past a Ta-laeow, a trellised rattan structure placed as a keep out sign. We didn't want to go upsetting the spirits. I could not stomach the hill-tribe diet of sticky rice - an unpalatable glutinous mass with soggy greens and beans, though some people swear by it. The rice grains are rolled into a ball and then dipped into an appalling meat stew. To be washed down by Lao Lao (rice whisky) - at least it would take away the taste. And when it was time for bed, this time we did have the luxury of a single light bulb, courtesy of solar energy, excellent for remote locations.

It was the parting of the ways once again, and I continued my journey southwards by bus to the village of Nong Khiaw. The only travelling companions I had this time were a load of dead squirrels and birds, very disconcerting to a vegetarian. This kind of scenario was going to crop up quite often. From Nong Khiaw, it's a long-tail boat ride along the Nam Ou River through rapids, past sandbanks and limestone outcrops. Temporary markets are set up on the shore, where people from far-off villages come to load heavy bags of rice into the boats.

We disembarked at Muang Ngoi Neua, one of the most amazing places I have ever been. It was just like a film set - the quintessential South-East Asian village you see in the movies, in travel brochures, on posters, almost untouched by the modern world. Surrounding this tropical Shangri-La and protecting it from outside influence, are huge limestone monoliths covered in forest. There is no traffic, save for the odd bicycle - the main street is just sand, lined with coconut palms, bamboo huts, restaurants and guest-houses.

Grizzled old women stooped double, wiry old men sipping Lao Lao in ramshackle bars, and children carrying firewood from the river - some looked only five years old. More pigs, chickens and turkeys - even the occasional water-buffalo made an appearance. Lighting is minimal - kerosene lamps and some electricity provided by generators in the evenings: the sound is deafening. And when they go off there is silence, and on a cloudless night you get a fantastic view of the stars. Then you can sit back and relax with your bottle of Beer Lao, hopefully chilled.

Swim and bathe in the river, paddle a boat or kayak, play with the children - as in Thailand, takraw is a national sport - go hiking and visit more hill-tribes, or walk to some caves. Leaving the village behind you walk across a school playing field, where you will probably be accosted for money - an admission fee (just a few pence); then through bushland and secondary forest to Tham Kang and Tham Pha Kaew. The first cave you can wade into, the second has a small stone Buddha image.

My accommodation in the village was very basic, to say the least. A simple bed with mattress on a concrete floor in a bamboo hut. A refreshing shower consisted of scooping out water from a trough and throwing it over your head. But for 30 pence a night I could hardly complain. The cheapest night ever. Pineapple and banana pancakes came in at 10 pence each. And when you order food in a restaurant the owner's daughter has to stop doing her homework and start the cooking. Economics again. Home economics. Sexual economics, something which I will elaborate on when we come to Luang Prabang.

Whilst on the subject of food, I would say the Lao eat almost anything - like the Chinese proverb which mentions eating everything on four legs except the table. For example, wild boar, bear, deer, lizards, snakes, squirrels and of course dogs – that would stop the damn things yapping I suppose. And a nine-inch centipede in a jar - used in Lao Lao I think. Better stick to the pancakes and 'France Fried' (French fries), as the Lao call them. And to round the day off a little Lao light entertainment - a musical evening with a xylophone and a violin with a body made from a coconut.

It was time to make my farewells, with hugs all round from this little village that time has forgotten. But all this could come to an end if the planned road construction ever goes ahead. Laos is slowly opening up, with major new road projects crossing the country. Are the people ready for such 'progress', and will it bring more bad than good - the dangers of disease, drug and people trafficking, environmental destruction and economic exploitation. Will that override the benefits of better communication, access to markets and more tourism? We shall have to see, but nothing is more constant than change, for better or for worse. As for me, it was time to hit the road - all the way to Luang Prabang.

This city is the architectural jewel of Laos, famed for its French colonial buildings and historic temples, and it also boasts the magnificent Royal Palace Museum. It has a pleasant setting on the confluence of the Nam Khan and Mekong rivers, and a spectacular mountain backdrop beyond. UNESCO World Heritage Status has been given in recognition of this, and might go some way towards preserving the best the city has to offer.

Most of the attractions are situated on or near the peninsula created by the two rivers, and a walking tour can be quite leisurely. I will concentrate on just one. Dating back to the 16th century, Wat Xieng Thong is Luang Prabang's most magnificent temple, and it has largely escaped the ravages of time. Built in the classic Luang Prabang style with layered roofs sweeping low to the ground (likened to the wings of a mother hen guarding her chicks), it is similar to designs in Northern Thailand. On the rear wall of the sim (ordination hall) is a brilliant tree of life mosaic, showing birds and animals in glorious hues of silver, lilac and green on a vermilion background. Inside there are decorated wooden columns and golden stencils. Stupas house Buddha images in various poses; in the Red Chapel there is a reclining Buddha that was displayed in Paris for many years until its return in 1964. At the eastern gate with its elephant mosaic pillars, stands the Royal Funerary Carriage House containing a dragon-headed funeral carriage and gilded urns.

For a great view of the city and surrounding area, climb to the top of Phu Si hill - sunsets are brilliant from 24-metre high That Chomsi (Large Stupa). The vista reminded me somewhat of Doi Kong Mu in

Mae Hong Son, but with far fewer farang, or falang as it is in Laos. Just to the south is Wat Aham, formerly the residence of the Supreme Patriarch of Lao Buddhism. Devotees come to make offerings at the spirit shrine under the banyan trees, but what I liked were the depictions of Hell inside. Just watch out for the machetes.

The Royal Palace was built in the early years of the last century, and conveniently located next to the river. It was converted into a museum at the time of the revolution; the royal family were exiled and all died a few years later. The building blends both French and Lao styles displaying royal religious objects and Buddha images. There are also busts and portraits of the monarchy, gilded and lacquered Ramayana screens, wall murals of traditional Lao life, musical instruments, masks … and elephant tusks engraved with Buddhas. Some of the royal apartments, including the bedrooms, have been preserved as they were when the king departed.

Well, that's enough of culture and architecture. Luang Prabang has to be the culinary capital of Laos. Eating out is excellent with all tastes catered for; the two Indian restaurants are superb, pizzas and pastas are delicious, risottos, omelettes, crêpes, fresh crusty baguettes, pastries, great coffee, shakes and yoghurts. And of course not forgetting some local vegetarian dishes such as foe (noodles), eggplant and mushroom soup, watercress, egg and tomato salad, and stir fries. With such a varied vegetarian choice, at last I didn't have to worry about bits of animal in my food. I think all the best chefs in South-East Asia must have gravitated here. So why not make a pig of yourself. I did.

From food we move onto sex, and it's time to tell you a funny little tale. But first here's some background information on the subject. Co-habiting, and indeed any form of sexual relationship between foreigners and Lao citizens, is deemed illegal by the authorities, unless a marriage permit has been applied for. I suppose Big Brother comes into the bedroom to check up on you. There are frequently notices in hotel rooms saying "No Sexual Girls in Rooms." Though similar signs are seen throughout Thailand and slightly different rules apply there. Does this mean only frigid women are allowed? Most amusing of all are pictures showing two white legs on top of two brown legs sticking out of a bush with a large cross marked over them.

Anyway the gentleman in question, is living with his Lao girlfriend in this guest-house in Luang Prabang they run together. All seems hunky-dory until he decides to put up a satellite dish in his garden somewhere and play loud music (loud for the Lao). So his neighbours shop him to the police and he goes on the run, somewhere around Vientiane. They soon catch up with him, but at least he's given a choice - marry the girl or be deported. So now he's a married man, and they get on like a house on fire. When I was there it was party night and what a slanging match, and didn't the crockery fly. Yes, the brides really are getting restless.

The easiest and probably the best way to get to the Plain of Jars is to fly to Phonsavan. I say probably, because I haven't actually done the trip myself - something for next time, so I'm relying on the experience of others here. When travelling, you can never see everything first time round, nor should you - a return visit usually gives you a more enlightened perspective. The modern town of Phonsavan is the capital of Xieng Khuang Province, a state much blighted by UXOs (Unexploded Ordinance), and as the plane descends you will notice the innumerable bomb craters that pockmark the landscape. There are still around sixty casualties a year, quite often children.

The Plain of Jars consists of five major sites surrounding Phonsavan, with jars that weigh from 600 kg to six tonnes. I wonder how they weighed them. There are various theories as to their origin - sarcophagi, wine fermenters or for rice storage. They are made mainly from sandstone, though some are granite, and thought to be at least 2000 years old. Research into the jars is currently being undertaken, so hopefully the enigma of their origins and purpose will soon be solved.

From Luang Prabang it's about a five or six-hour journey south by songthaew to the caving and karst centre of Vang Vieng. But first I was headed by boat to the Pak Ou Caves. These are about 25 km from Luang Prabang along the Mekong River, and contain would you believe yet more Buddhas in all shapes and sizes, but mostly standing ones. There are two caves in the limestone cliffs; the lower one, known as Tham Ting, can easily be entered by a series of steps from the river. Deeper in the cliff, Tham Phum requires a torch for viewing. At the time of my visiting there was quite a queue of boats disembarking, so be warned.

"Road not recommended for nervous persons," warns a Lao tourist magazine about the route from Luang Prabang to Vang Vieng, adding vaguely "there may be issues." Meaning breakdowns, punctures, overcrowding, ambushes by Hmong bandits (several people were killed by gunmen in 2003) and driving off the road into a vast ravine. Well at least I only suffered from the overcrowding. Out came those tiny plastic stools, and we were crammed in the aisle for what seemed an eternity. Legs and arms aching and a really sore bum were the result as the bus hurtled at breakneck speeds round zigzag bends; no chance of admiring the spectacular scenery now.

If you're into caves and caving, then Vang Vieng is the place to be. The great stegosaur-backed mountains here are honeycombed with passages, tunnels and caverns with ample opportunities for exploration. The most famous of the caves is Tham Jang, known for some unexplainable reason as Snail Cave (though probably because there's a stalactite that resembles a snail), which extends for some 3 km into the mountain. At one time it was used as a refuge from the marauding *jiin háw* (Yunnanese Chinese).

The best thing was swimming by candlelight in a cool spring at the foot of the cave. Tham San or Elephant Cave contained unbelievably a stalactite elephant, a few Buddha images and a Buddha 'footprint'. Most of the caves contain Buddhas scattered throughout their cavernous depths if you have the inclination, but when you are Buddhaed out there is black-tubing down the Nam Song River. You float gently down the river (it usually isn't white-water) in a huge tractor tyre inner tube past bemused locals as they go about their daily chores. I wonder what they really think of the lazy falang drifting by without a care in the world. My only concern was a rather large river snake swimming past me - I was lucky it didn't bite.

How's this for Lao efficiency. Public buses at 0530, 0550, 0610, 0700 and the next one not until 1300. Must be for the markets. But luckily for me a pick-up soon turned up and this time I got a reasonably comfortable seat for the four-hour journey to Vientiane. And no falang to join me - a truly 'ethnic' experience. Vientiane must be the quietest and most laid-back capital in all South-East Asia. The name translates as 'Sandalwood City', and it is a city of tree-lined boulevards and old temples strung out along the Mekong River. Vietnamese and Chinese shop-houses are juxtaposed with French colonial buildings, and then the more modern socialist architecture. The Hammer and Sickle still flies from many buildings; I even saw one over a monastery. How bizarre is that. I wonder what other countries still fly these. There seemed to be a preponderance of four-wheel-drive vehicles. No doubt owned and driven by the aid agencies, ex-pats and wealthy Thai businessmen. I can't imagine many Lao owning them.

The Patuxai or Victory Gate, built in 1962, is I suppose the focal point of the city, although a victory over what I'm not too sure. It is very reminiscent of the Arc de Triomphe in Paris, but having four instead of two archways. The ornate archway ceiling is decorated with carvings of apsarases or heavenly nymphs, and the structure is capped with a temple-like ornamentation. There are superb views of the city from its battlements. Its actual purpose is to commemorate the Lao who died in pre-revolutionary wars. *Power to the People.*

I only stayed in Vientiane for a couple of days, but that was enough for a quick walking tour of this city in miniature. There are three important wats to see. Pha That Luang, or Great Sacred Stupa, is Lao's national symbol, and one of its most revered sites. It consists of a cluster of pointed stupas constructed in three levels, with stairways between and built on a square base. Rising up from the middle of a bowl-shaped structure is the 45m-high central stupa. Prayer gates are positioned in the surrounding walls. The wat was originally constructed in the 16th century, but damaged considerably in the 18th and 19th centuries due to Burmese and Siamese incursions. It was not until the 1930s that restoration work brought it up to more or less its current condition.

Wat Si Saket sits opposite the Presidential Palace, and is famous for its thousands of silver and ceramic Buddhas, many placed in arched niches. Then there's a Buddha seated on a coiled cobra, a flowered ceiling (inspired by Versailles) and *jataka* murals. The wat is surrounded by dozens of stupas containing the ashes of temple devotees. Thankfully it was spared by the Siamese as they found the Thai style too beautiful to destroy.

Also in the central area is Wat Ong Teu, renowned for its Heavy Buddha, made of bronze and weighing several tonnes. It is flanked by two standing Buddhas. I think I might also mention Wat Si Muang, the spiritual home of the guardian of Vientiane. The legend goes that a pregnant woman was sacrificed by being crushed beneath the laying of the city pillar, thus sanctifying the chosen site for the temple. The That

Luang Festival which takes place in November involves a procession from Wat Si Muang to Pha That Luang. It is the largest temple fair in Laos with offerings of flowers, alms-giving and firework displays.

But Vientiane has a lot more to offer - parks, memorials, museums. The Haw Phra Kaew Museum, once a royal temple, used to contain the famous Emerald Buddha - it's now in Wat Phra Kaew in Bangkok. Another example of Thai/Lao rivalry. Why do neighbours never get on? Buddha Park (Xieng Khuan), 24 km south of the city, with its collection of Buddhist and Hindu sculptures in amongst shrubs and trees is definitely worth a visit. Shiva, Vishnu and Arjuna as well as Buddha are all represented here, showing the religious roots of the country. And there's a huge concrete pumpkin you can climb up on spiral stairways. There are three levels, said to represent Hell, Earth and Heaven. So you can say you've visited Hell and Heaven on Earth.

And now for something completely different. I'm going to copy out verbatim a little tale I heard from an Irish girl I was travelling with in Africa. We have kept in e-mail contact for many years, and this story about the properties of Tiger Balm on her travels in Laos makes for a very interesting read.

"Me again. Well I made it to smelly Bangkok after having the best time in Laos. I'm sitting in this Internet Café near the Khao San Road, where the dog keeps bringing in this dead rat off the street and the female owners keep screaming their heads off, while the fella chases the dog around the shop and the dog is yelping its head off, cos it has no idea what it's done wrong. Crazy place... never a dull moment. What can you do but laugh!!! Spent the last week in Don Det in the Four Thousand Islands which was really great - perfect place to relax before hitting the road again.

"OK so now my Tiger Balm story... this is unbelievable... Was on a bus from Pakse down to the landing point for Don Det Island with two girls

from Dublin and a Canadian girl. I ended up sitting next to this really old man who had apparently been carried onto the bus (I didn't know that at the time or I sure as Hell wouldn't have sat next to him). Anyway we head off for Don Det and he falls asleep and rests his head on my shoulder which was fine…his wife turned around to shake him off me, but he was so old I said leave him be so that was grand. Ten minutes later I feel his whole body weight completely collapses on me…I start to get a bit worried…shake him a little bit…his wife turns around from the seat in front and starts shaking the living daylights out of him - no response. I can't find a pulse anywhere. He's drooling out of the side of his mouth and his body is completely limp on his left side. Very much like a stroke victim. The bus is stopped. Chaos. This man is dying if not already dead and I'm starting to freak out big time.

"*His wife produces a jar of Tiger Balm ointment and starts rubbing it on his face, neck, arms…anywhere there's a bit of skin. He's making a few noises now, but I'm still convinced he's dying. Three Hail Mary's. The Tiger Balm treatment continues. I get out of the way. Then the wife starts rubbing a coin along his arm, then someone bites his big toe and they lay him out on the seat. Twenty minutes and a load of commotion later they take him off and put him on the back of a pick-up going to Pakse. The man is sitting up, completely conscious and talking to people. I could not believe my eyes…the miracle of Tiger Balm!!! I'll be stocking up on some before I leave.*"[3]

Perhaps if the makers of Tiger Balm read this, we'll get a commission.

My travels in steamy, exotic, mystical and laid-back Laos had now came to an end, as I crossed over the Friendship Bridge and the Mekong River to Nong Khoi in Thailand. I was headed back to Bangkok by bus. A Bad Karma Day to say the least.

It all started with frequent visits to the toilet resulting from the consumption of a rather hot green curry the previous night. Then the bus journey. On first impressions fine, until I was told I was on the wrong bus. The 0700 to Bangkok was a total wreck, patched up with filler, broken windows, window frames coming apart, and the door almost falling off. The seats inside were absolutely filthy and the foam full of holes and coming away. They also smelt distinctly of urine. So I sit down and start my wonderful nine-hour journey. The bus goes exceedingly slowly as it's overheating. The solution - just spray the radiator with a jet spray and on we go. That's if the driver knows where he's going. He keeps braking and stopping and then going round in circles as if he's trying to find the right way. The bus is full of mozzies and cockroaches. The air-conditioning doesn't work - can't open the windows - it's like an oven. He finally stops at a repair yard for about an hour - more spraying, and we finally arrive in Bangkok about four and a half hours late.

But that's not the end of the story. Getting off the bus, I gash my leg on one of the seats that has a bare metal arm protruding. I am tired, pissed off and not a happy bunny. So I start wandering around the Khao San Road about nine pm - can't find any single rooms, and they've all hiked up their prices for Christmas. The Khao San Road Hotel showed me one room where someone had just wet the bed. I told them quite clearly where to get off. I finally tracked down somewhere but it's like a prison cell - striped curtains and sheets, bars at the doors and windows and so dark. Worst of all it's half tiled all the way round the room. Like a psychiatric unit. Very claustrophobic. Where's the straitjacket and by the way, Merry Christmas.

CHAPTER 7

KHMER TODAY, GONE TOMORROW

Cambodia is famous for two things: Angkor Wat and the Killing Fields. The first is arguably the most monumental architectural achievement of man; the second is man at his most destructive and depraved. Seven hundred years separate them: it was the Ancient Khmers who built the Angkor temples between the 9th and 13th centuries, and it was the Khmer Rouge who decimated more than two million of their fellow citizens in the 1970s. Creative genius and the flowering of a civilisation, versus the genocidal madness of Pol Pot and his fellow psychopaths. Strange bedfellows indeed. And proof again of the impermanence of all things.

Part of the excitement of a trip to Cambodia is getting there in the first place. You could fly to Siem Reap (the airport for Angkor Wat) direct from Bangkok. But that's not very adventurous. Go by bus and endure fifteen hours of hell I say. After all, that's the joy of travelling - you wouldn't see much of the country from a plane seat. The journey from Bangkok to the border town of Aranya Prathet is straightforward enough, but when you arrive you know you're going to be in for a special treat. THUP THONG KUM says the hotel sign - I wonder what the English translation is? I certainly wouldn't want to stay there.

Once through the border you're in for a long wait at Poipet until the pick-ups and buses are full - it's the usual story I'm afraid. Make sure you get a couple of crusty baguettes from the street kids - you're going to need them. Once aboard make sure you wrap up well - not against cold, as it's bloody hot and humid, but against the dust - clouds of it, thick, choking orange dust that gets everywhere. Put your sunnies on to protect your eyes and wrap a krama (Cambodian scarf) round your face and off you go.

Huge stretches of the dirt road are not even graded and frequently washed away in the wet season. Potholes were everywhere, and there were diversions through paddy fields to avoid the worst stretches, or where bridges had collapsed. Along the roadside were numerous electioneering posters for the Sam Rainsy Party, Cambodian Peoples' Party and the Funcinpec Party. I suppose in such a fledgling democracy as Cambodia these symbols and identities are very important. Which one would you vote for?

We arrived in Siem Reap to the somewhat foreboding greeting of "Severe Epidemic of Haemorrhagic Dengue Fever." That's nice to know. The guest-house we got taken to was crap, but you don't have to stay there. In general the accommodation in Siem Reap is pretty good value for money, but you had to shop around. It's just part of the experience.

Siem Reap means Siamese Defeated (Reap of the Siamese). Quite an appropriate name, considering Thailand and Cambodia have been fighting each other for centuries, although it was the Thais who were the ultimate victors. It is the gateway to Angkor and even now there are tensions - this time over alleged comments by a Thai actress that the temples belonged to Thailand. Hundreds of Cambodians attacked the Thai embassy and businesses in Phnom Penh, the Cambodian capital. Many Thai citizens left the country, the ambassador was recalled and the Thai Prime Minister even threatened to send in troops. There have been regular border disputes and complaints about Thai companies exploiting Cambodian natural resources. Things have calmed down a bit now and normal relations resumed. Just another little brawl in the history of S E Asia.

The temples of Angkor are one of the most incredible sights I've seen in the world: the first glimpse is truly breathtaking. Built at a time when the Khmer civilisation encompassed huge areas of present day Thailand, Laos and Vietnam to Yunnan in China, they are the largest religious complex ever constructed. Scattered over the ever-invading jungles, the hundred or so temples cover an area roughly 25 km north to south and 35 km east to west, though there are some sites that extend well beyond this.

The temples were built purely as places of worship - the people lived and worked in wooden structures only, long since decayed. Angkor went into a slow decline from the 13th century onwards with Thai invasions, and was then totally abandoned. It was rediscovered by the French in the 1860s, and tourists started arriving in 1907. Major restoration work began in the 1920s and has been going on ever since, apart from during the Khmer Rouge era. Over the years many objets d'art have been lost to looting and smuggling, and a conservation body has been set up to research, protect and conserve the cultural heritage of the area. UNESCO World Heritage Status has been given, guards brought in to patrol the most important temples, landmines cleared and educational programmes set up. As director of UNESCO in Cambodia, Etienne Clement sums up, *"Cambodia's culture is very rich, but the country itself is very poor and weak. It's an ideal situation for illegal trafficking."*

At the centre is the most famous temple of all, Angkor Wat, and this is the best place to start a tour. If you hire a moto driver to get around, three or four days should be enough to see most of the highlights. So conquering my fear of motor-bikes (to be heightened again in Vietnam) we set off to explore. Sunrise at Angkor Wat is spectacular, vastly exceeding expectations. No photographer, however professional, could really do it justice. To stand on the sandstone causeway in the cool morning air, just before the crowds arrive, the beehive towers silhouetted by the rays of the rising sun, instantly transports you into another world.

At the time of the spring and autumn equinox, the sun rises directly over the tower of the central sanctuary. Of course, sunset is even better (if you forget the crowds) as the sun glistens on the royal lily pools creating a magical reflection framed by palm trees. Then as the sun sinks on the horizon, the stone is imbued with a warm pinkish hue, darkening as night falls.

Angkor Wat, often called Temple Mountain, is the finest and best preserved of all the monuments and was constructed in the 12th century to honour Vishnu, the Hindu deity. It is surrounded by a moat 190m wide, forming a rectangle measuring 1.5 by 1.3 km. The causeway crosses the moat from the main entrance and then leads into an avenue lined with naga balustrades to the central three-storied 55m tower. It represents Mount Meru (now known as Mount Kailash) in Tibet, and according to Hindu legend the very centre of the world and sacred abode of the Gods. This tower is enclosed by a square with interlinked galleries e.g. The Gallery of a Thousand Buddhas. Buddha images, ochre red, stand on the four sides of the central sanctuary, placed here when the Hindu Kingdom fell. Around the galleries are a series of carved bas-reliefs - some of very sensual women with narrow slanted eyes, heavy lips and full breasts. Others contain historical events, scenes from the Ramayana and Mahabharata, and Vishnu defeating demons.

My favourites are firstly Heaven and Hell, featuring from the latter such delights as beheadings, impalements and spikes thrust into the victim, creating an effect like a porcupine. I think something like this is reflected in Aztec culture, where arrows are fired into the victim's body. And then the Churning of the Sea of Milk, where the gods (devas) and demons (asuras) pull alternately on the serpent Vasuki, a five-headed naga, churning the sea to extract the elixir of immortality. The gods are victorious.

It's an extremely steep climb to the top - you literally have to scramble up - to make you in awe of all these gods. At the top were once bathing pools where devotees purified themselves before worshipping. Then it's the return journey. Just as well there's a railing down one of the staircases to help you, as there have been several fatalities. Pretty scary stuff. Lara Croft eat your heart out.

Coming a close second in its magnificence is the fortified walled city of Angkor Thom and its centrepiece The Bayon. There are five monumental gates 20m in height, with elephant trunk carvings, and crowned with the massive enigmatic face of the Buddha (or is it Jayavarman, the King responsible for the building). Statues of gods and demons from Churning of the Sea of Milk stand in front of the gates. Contained within are the Bayon, the Baphuon and the Elephant and Leper King Terraces.

The Bayon was built as a Mahayana Buddhist temple and is often full of saffron-robed monks making their devotions. It is mainly known for its cold smiling faces that seem to follow you around. There are 216 of them. Some say the smile can either be interpreted as compassionate or forbidding, depending on the changing light. Some scenes from Tomb

Raider were filmed here. The temple is full of low narrow corridors, precipitous stairs and more bas-reliefs including land and sea battle scenes, a circus and a woman giving birth.

The Baphuon is another representation of Mount Meru, and is currently being restored with financial assistance from the French Government. It is approached by an elevated sandstone walkway to the 43m central tower. The reconstruction work is enormous with huge cranes and earthmovers, as archaeologists attempt to shore up walls with concrete pillars. Just goes to show what a mammoth task it was in the first place without all the modern machinery.

The Terrace of the Elephants lies just north of the Baphuon entrance, with a bas-relief 350m long and a parade of elephants on either side. It was apparently the site of the king's grand audience hall. The Terrace of the Leper King with its nude figure of Shiva is further to the north, and was supposedly named after Yasovarman, who was said to suffer from leprosy. A long narrow trench excavated by archaeologists is decorated with apsarases (shapely dancing women).

About 400m to the south of Angkor Thom is Phnom Bakheng, a five-tiered temple mountain with seven levels, representing the seven Hindu heavens. Its main claim to fame is as a superb vantage point for the sunset view of Angkor Wat. Unfortunately you'll also be sharing the experience with many other camera-snappers and hordes of soft drink vendors.

Away to the east is the extremely romantic atmospheric ruin of Ta Prohm. This temple has been left to the jungle and the elements, looking very much like it would have done when the first French explorers arrived. Its crumbling towers and walls have been swallowed up in a strangled embrace of latticed branches and root systems. Thick foliage snakes around carvings and vast trunks have split the stonework, leaving jumbled piles of masonry scattered around the complex. The banyan trees, supported by huge flying buttresses, tower overhead, shrouding their hosts in the dappled gloom.

It is extremely difficult to negotiate some of the courtyards and corridors, what with all the rubble and stone blocks placed precariously above your head. In fact the whole setting reminded me of a scene from The Two Towers in Lord of the Rings - when Treebeard and the Ents were making an assault upon Isengard. *"They roared and boomed and trumpeted, until stones began to crack and fall at the mere noise of them... Round and round the Rock of Orthanc the Ents went striding and storming like a howling gale, breaking pillars, hurling avalanches of boulders down the shafts, tossing up huge slabs of stone into the air like leaves."* [4] I think the Ents were my favourite characters in Lord of the Rings. Unhurried and very thoughtful, and on a totally different timescale to man. And so it shall be in the present age, when the trees of the forest shall rise up and reign supreme over the crumbling temples of Mammon. Just goes to prove that man's grip on the natural world is so tenuous, a fleeting moment in the eons of time. Well that's a pleasant and sobering thought.

One thing you will notice around the temples of Angkor is the number of children and young people. They will be acting as guides, selling postcards, jewellery and soft drinks; working in rice and noodle-stalls, and riding oxen carts laden with food and provisions. I suppose in such a poor country as Cambodia they have to make a living as best they can, no proper schooling or welfare state here. And when so many of their elders were wiped out in the Pol Pot years, children under the age of 15 now make up half the population. They are amazingly well-educated for their tender years, many speaking almost perfect English, and not only that: one boy even knew that the UK consists of England, Scotland, Wales and Northern Ireland. There are probably some ten-year-olds in Britain who are unaware of that fact. The university of life is a great teacher.

But a sad thing happened when I was in Ta Prohm. I bought some postcards from a young boy and as soon as I was well away, a group of older kids robbed him of the money. This kind of thing goes on all the time unfortunately - worse still is when children are exploited by adults, as in sweated labour and the sex trade.

Getting away from the central area is where the motor-bikes really come in. The Roluos Group for example are found some 13 km to the east of Siem Reap. And for these more remote locations a guide is essential, not just for directions, but to avoid landmines. There are still plenty around. And mind you don't fall off on the dirt roads: it's easily done. The Roluos monuments are among the earliest constructed, dating back to the 9th century, and it's interesting to see how the architecture evolved over time. Bakong consists of a five-tiered central pyramid with eight towers and some well-preserved stone elephants.

Some 30 km to the north of Roluos is Banteay Srei (Citadel of the Women). Just shows you how much travelling is involved, and you really do need to work out an itinerary first. Unlike me. This is one of the best preserved temples and the stone-carving is quite exquisite. It is a Hindu temple dedicated to Shiva with more scenes from the Ramayana, and voluptuous women holding lotus flowers.

I could use up several more pages describing yet more temples, but this is just intended as a taster. The whole experience will certainly overwhelm you, regardless of how much or how little you see. And do interact with the locals - chat to the children, help the monks with their English, eat at the local restaurants, buy some postcards or a souvenir, and you will be richly rewarded with smiles and gratitude. The temples of Angkor are the true icon of Cambodia as the national flag testifies: a symbol of pride, a place of pilgrimage and the country's best investment for the future. Go and enjoy them.

Watch your step…Cambodia has a landmine problem. Well that's what all the literature says. There are an estimated four to six million of them scattered about the countryside and as many as 45,000 Cambodians have lost limbs as a result, about 1 in 255 of the total population. Even after extensive awareness campaigns, mines still claim up to 120 victims every month. The cost to the country, psychologically and economically, is enormous. It costs just US$5 to purchase a mine, but US$500 to clear and destroy it. The cost of rehabilitating one victim alone over a lifetime is estimated at US$3,000. Because so much land is mined, this prevents farming in many areas, livestock are killed or injured and there are food shortages. But it is when you see the victims with your own eyes that the horror really hits home. And this is where Aki Ra's Landmine Museum, between Siem Reap and Angkor, comes in.

The museum helps rehabilitate children who have lost limbs, to clear mines and other UXO, and as a demonstration and education centre. Various rockets, mortars, guns, hand grenades, a B40 grenade launcher and of course mines are on display. A Pineapple Mine with trip wire - the casing breaks up into fragments when it explodes; a Bouncing Betty Mine from the USA; a Claymore Mine and a Mon-50 - a Russian mine which would be strapped to the body of a suicide bomber and detonated by remote control. There were also leg mines - designed to maim, not kill, anti-tank and anti-truck mines.

"Take that look off your face." - Smoking Can Kill! A small detonator and ball-bearing is placed in a cigarette. As the cigarette is smoked, the detonator is ignited, the victim's face is blown off and the ball-bearing is fired through the back of the skull. Biopics of the land mine victims were pinned up on the hut walls, and then some of the casualties were walking around, which made for a very disturbing, but worthwhile experience.

The story of Aki Ra, growing up under the Khmer Rouge and later the Vietnamese, is quite extraordinary. He lived and worked with about ten other children, ploughing the fields and surviving on little more than rice soup. On one occasion, his father was given rabbit droppings as medicine, and a man was disembowelled for stealing a banana. Crying was forbidden and those who were considered bad had their throats cut with palm fronds. At the age of five, his parents were killed by the Khmer Rouge and he was fully indoctrinated into their way of thinking, singing 'patriotic' songs and wearing the uniform of black shirt and trousers. At the age of ten, Aki Ra was given his first gun - an AK47, and taught to use rocket launchers, mortars and bazookas.

He was captured by the Vietnamese army during the invasion. They had many camps in the Siem Reap area and were responsible for much damage to the temples at Angkor, killing animals and felling the forests. When they left in 1989, Aki Ra was then conscripted into the Cambodian army and joined the UN peace-keeping force in clearing landmines. He tells of the amazement he had when arriving in Siem Reap, at seeing roads and concrete houses for the first time. And when the UN put up a huge cinema screen with tanks and cars moving across it, people ran away thinking they were going to crash into the audience.

Aki went to school, quickly learnt to speak English and worked for UN forces until they left Cambodia in 1994. He recalls a six-month-old child orphaned when his parents were killed as their ox cart hit an anti-tank mine near the Thai border. The child was saved by his mother embracing him at the moment of the explosion, which catapulted both of them into a minefield. It took three days for local villagers to clear the field and recover the bodies. Incredibly the child had survived by suckling on his dead mother's breast. He now lives with Aki Ra's family.

Aki continued to clear mines and collected many relics from the war during his work. He bought a small piece of land and decided to set up the museum in 1999. His tireless action continues to this day with the museum, a mine action gallery, education, training and rehabilitation programmes.

While we are on the subject of landmines, it seems appropriate here to introduce another character with an amazing story to tell. When I am travelling on buses, trains and planes or just waiting in a departure lounge somewhere, it's always great to read a little about the country I'm visiting. Its history, its geography, its culture, its religion, its politics. Well in Cambodia, the book I was reading was *First They Killed My Father - a Daughter of Cambodia Remembers*, by Loung Ung. She is now the national spokesperson for the 'Campaign for a Landmine Free World' and lives in the USA.

The book catalogues her life from being a five-year-old in the spring of 1975, when the Khmer Rouge tanks rolled into Phnom Penh, to her emigration to the States in 1980. Most of us would hardly remember a thing from our formative years, but to have such vivid memories, to write an entire book about it is really quite mind blowing. She tells how she and her family were transported from a modern apartment in Phnom Penh, with plenty of food, clothes, television, even a maid - to the horror of the Killing Fields. Four of her family were murdered by the Khmer Rouge, including her mother and father.

When she was six, Loung plucked the bloated corpses of rabbits from swollen rivers to eat, and when she was seven she grabbed a ball of rice left unguarded beside a dying woman. Having been split from her family, she ended up in a training and re-education camp and learned how to hack an enemy to death with a hoe. She would spend a fourteen-hour day in the rice paddies, her legs bloody with sucking leeches. And at nine, when the Vietnamese forces arrived, she witnessed the public execution of a Khmer Rouge soldier.

After six months in a resettlement camp, an American church group sponsored Loung, her oldest brother and his wife to emigrate. They arrived in Vermont in 1980. Loung graduated from St. Michael's College in Vermont in 1993. Since the Khmer Rouge was ousted, Loung has returned to Cambodia several times. She's certainly an incredible lady. As a footnote and I hope I'm not being too presumptuous here, I had my picture taken in Ta Prohm under the banyan tree, just like she did, the temple that Loung's father said is the abode of the gods. To find out more about these extraordinary events go out and buy the book. A sequel has also recently come out, which I haven't got round to reading yet.

There was quite a shocking incident not so long ago, when a two-year-old Canadian boy was killed at an international school in Siem Reap. Gunmen had taken some thirty pupils and teachers hostage, and the child died as the school was stormed by police. The gunmen had threatened to kill them all, but fortunately the incident didn't have the same outcome as the events in Beslan in Russia. The motive for the attack wasn't clear, other than some financial demands, but acts of terrorism against the international community are thankfully very rare in Cambodia. But there are some desperate people out there and the huge stockpile of guns and other weapons isn't helpful.

The Tonlé Sap Lake is the largest in S E Asia and stretches some 120 km from Siem Reap halfway towards Phnom Penh. During the wet season (mid-May to early October) the water levels rise from about two metres to more than ten metres deep. And its surface area increases from 2,500 to 13,000 square km. This makes the lake one of the world's richest sources of freshwater fish, providing employment and sustenance for the local population. It is also very important for irrigation purposes. Unfortunately there are the threats of upstream dams and deforestation causing a build up of silt in the lake, and the future of this unique biosystem is uncertain. It takes about six hours by express boat to get to the capital - when the lake ends the rest of the journey is by river. The boat is usually pretty crowded and it's best to sit on the roof. But beware - take plenty of sunscreen to avoid burning, and during the early part of the journey you're liable to get pretty wet. Stock up on baguettes and soft cheese before you depart.

Phnom Penh was long considered the most beautiful of the French-built cities in Indochina, with its wealth of colonial architecture, splendid temples and palaces, and beguiling setting on the Mekong River. That was before the Khmer Rouge terror, but all is not lost. There is something of a resurgence going on. A lot of French buildings are being renovated, the Royal Palace has been spruced up, monks are out with their alms bowls, and restaurants and bars are once again packed with customers. And there are plans to build a park along the river-front. The city is certainly less frantic than Bangkok or Saigon, but the moto drivers are as persistent as ever. On my arrival, I noticed that there seemed to be a bigger concentration of ex-pats and NGO aid-workers than elsewhere in S E Asia and this is causing something of a boom. I think over the next few years there will be massive changes.

The Royal Palace, which is the official residence of the king, was built in the 1860s. It is most famous for the Silver Pagoda - so named because the floor is covered with over five thousand silver tiles. However, to me they looked more like stainless steel, and most are covered by a red carpet. Some sixty per cent of the Pagoda's contents were destroyed by the Khmer Rouge, but what remains is pretty spectacular. The Emerald Buddha - in fact a light, translucent green - sits on a gilt pedestal, whilst a life-size gold Buddha, decorated with 9,584 diamonds, stands in front in a glass case. There is a silver Buddha, a bronze Buddha and a marble Buddha, and bejewelled masks decorate the walls of the pagoda. A pavilion contains a huge Buddha footprint four metres long, and there is also an outdoor model of Angkor Wat. The most noticeable thing to me was how quiet and tranquil it was, certainly when compared to Bangkok's Royal Palace, and how immaculate and manicured the grounds and gardens were.

Each year, at the end of the dry season, there is a ploughing ceremony performed outside the palace to mark the beginning of rice planting. The oxen are offered a choice of rice, corn, beans, sesame, water, wine and grass, and what they consume is meant to predict the outcome of the harvest. A large consumption of water foretells drought and a failure of the crops. One year one of the cows declined to eat any of the dishes on offer and leapt backwards kicking over the food bowls. I am not sure what dreadful omen that is meant to convey, but it can't be any worse than Cambodia's recent history.

The great repository for the remains of Khmer culture is the National Museum. Here you will find Buddha images of course, and lots of Hindu deities - Vishnu, Shiva, Ganesh and a garuda with nagas. A standing Vishnu with eight arms looks almost Egyptian. And a statue of Yama, the god of death from the Terrace of the Leper King at Angkor. And as regards the bats in the belfry, are they still there - I didn't see any. Apparently there were more bats in the Museum than in any other man-made structure in the world.

Wat Phnom (Wat on the Hill) - though it is hardly more than a stunted knoll - is where Phnom Penh started. According to legend a woman called Penh found four statues of the Buddha here, washed up by the Mekong. An impressive staircase to the wat is guarded by lions and naga balustrades. There are lots of beggars and street vendors selling drinks - and birds in cages. You pay to set them free, but they are trained to return to the cage for the next sucker to cough up. I hasten to add, that's one scam I didn't fall for. It's such bad karma. Perhaps those concerned should have a look inside the wat at yet more visions of Hell. Crocodiles swallowing people, with only the head showing, somebody being axed to death, various liquids being forced down people's throats. And a guy being bitten in the bum by a dog, whilst trying to rescue a woman from a thorn tree. I'm sure I've seen that before. And a frightening precursor to the horrors of the Killing Fields.

CHAPTER 8

KAMPUCHEA, OUR MOTHERLAND

The National Anthem of the Angkar!

Bright red Blood which covers towns and plains
Of Kampuchea, Our Motherland,
Sublime Blood of workers and peasants,
Sublime Blood of revolutionary men and women fighters!

The Blood changing into unrelenting hatred
And resolute struggle,
On April 17th, under the Flag of the Revolution,
Free from slavery!

Between 1975 and 1979, Pol Pot and the Khmer Rouge murdered two million out of seven million Cambodians in what is known as 'The Killing Field' exterminations. The grand plan was to transform the country into a Maoist, peasant-dominated agrarian state with no room for intellectuals or professional people. Entire populations were moved from the towns to the countryside and forced to undertake slave labour for up to fifteen hours a day. Dissent was met with torture and execution. Cambodia was literally cut off from the outside world: currency was abolished, telephone and postal services halted, schools and hospitals closed and religion outlawed. The Year Zero had arrived.

In 1975 Tuol Svay Prey High School was occupied by Pol Pot's security forces and converted into the largest centre of detention and torture in the country. Over a period of three years more than 17,000 people held here were transported to the nearby killing fields of Choeung Ek and buried in mass graves. Called S-21, it has now been turned into the Tuol Sleng Museum of Genocidal Crime.

On a notice-board it says of the complex, *"It was surrounded with a double wall of corrugated iron, surmounted by dense barbed wires. The classrooms on the ground and first floors were pierced and divided into individual cells, whereas the ones on the second floor used for mass detention. Several thousands of victims (peasants, workers, technicians, engineers, doctors, teachers, students, Buddhist monks, ministers, Pol Pot cadres, soldiers of all ranks, the Cambodian Diplomatic Corps, foreigners etc.) were imprisoned and exterminated with their wives and children. There are a lot of evidences here proving the atrocities of Pol Pot clique: cells, instruments of torture, dossiers and documents, list of prisoner's names, photos of victims, their clothes and their belongings."*

Like the French and Russian Revolutions before it, the Cambodian Revolution was swallowing its own.

On the ground floor of the museum there are paintings by Vann Nath, one of the few survivors, and still alive today. They show prisoners being lashed and bayoneted; fingers cut off, babies smashed against trees - a real Buddhist Hell if ever there was one. Instruments of torture are on display - leg irons, axes, knives, spades and the gallows in the school playground, where victims were hauled up on a pulley and lowered into a barrel of filthy water. There is a photo gallery of the victims and of graves and mass burials. The first time I went a map of real human skulls and bones arranged in the shape of Cambodia was on display, but this has now been removed: it was considered too gruesome. In its place is a small gold-painted stupa and glass cases containing the skulls. To get an idea as to the mindset of the interrogators and the system they worked under, here is the list of security regulations.

1. You must answer accordingly to my questions. Don't turn them away.
2. Don't try to hide the facts by making pretexts this and that. You are strictly prohibited to contest me.
3. Don't be a fool for you are a chap who dare to thwart the revolution.
4. You must immediately answer my questions without wasting time to reflect.
5. Don't tell me either about your immoralities or the essence of the revolution.
6. While getting lashes or electrification you must not cry at all.
7. Do nothing. Sit still and wait for my orders. If there is no order, keep quiet. When I ask you to do something, you must do it right away without protesting.
8. Don't make pretexts about Kampuchea Krom in order to hide your jaw of traitor.
9. If you don't follow all the above rules, you shall get many lashes of electric wire.
10. If you disobey any point of my regulations you shall get either ten lashes or five shocks of electric discharge.

Right out of Nineteen Eighty-Four.

On arrival the prisoners would be photographed, their life histories recorded and then they would be stripped down to their underwear. They would be shackled in chains to iron beds or the floor, and slept without mats, mosquito nets or blankets. They would be woken at 4.30 a.m. for inspection, and had to ask permission to relieve themselves, otherwise a beating would follow. Bathing was irregular; there was no medicine and no hospital services. These extremely unhygienic conditions obviously led to the spread of disease. Finally, if they were still alive after all this ill-treatment and torture, they would be taken to the extermination camp of Choeung Ek and killed.

With the fall of Phnom Penh to the Vietnamese, only seven prisoners were found alive in S-21. In 1980 it was turned into a museum and the world slowly learnt of the culture of genocide under Pol Pot. Since then the entire complex has been slowly crumbling away - there are holes in the roof and much decay due to dampness penetration. Documents and photographs too are suffering in the tropical climate and the museum is desperate for continued funding. It is most important that this monument to 'crimes against humanity', like Auschwitz before it, is preserved not only to remember those who died, but as a poignant lesson for the future. And ending on a lighter note - just opposite S-21 is a Western-style café, complete with wicker furniture, pot plants, fresh flowers and soft, soothing music. A nice place for a coffee or a meal. I don't think the contrast could be more extreme.

But this is only a brief respite, for we are heading to the Killing Fields of Choeung Ek, just one of many scattered across the country. The remains of 8,985 people have been exhumed, and more than 8,000 skulls, arranged by sex and age, are now displayed behind glass panels in the memorial stupa, erected in 1988. Many of the victims were bludgeoned to death to avoid using precious bullets. Witness the knife and hammer wounds showing quite clearly in the skulls as the cause of death.

Our guide, a gentleman in his fifties, was quite visibly shaken when he showed us around (even though he must have done this many times before). He said that most of his family had been wiped out by the Khmer Rouge, but even now had no explanation for the psychotic insanity that had afflicted his country. What struck me was that these events occurred when I was a young man, with all the privileges and freedoms of the West and with very little knowledge of such horrors. But an accident of birth could have led to my picture being pinned to the wall, and to my being tortured and thrown into a mass burial pit. And walking on those hallowed grounds, with fragments of human bone and clothing still sticking out of the earth makes you think… "Yes, it could have been me."

A recent development which has caused some disquiet is the privatisation of Choeung Ek: a Japanese company has signed a thirty-year management deal to maintain the grounds and build visitor facilities. Of course the admission fee will go up and like Angkor, I doubt whether much will get ploughed back into the local economy. Phnom Penh Mayor Kep Chuktema said, "We need to beautify the site to attract tourists." But the current manager of the site, Neang Say, who lost forty relatives under Pol Pot exclaimed, "Justice has not yet been found for the victims, but at the same time their spirits have been traded for money."

An epitaph - "*Grievous voice of the victims who were beaten by Pol Pot men with canes, bamboo stumps or heads of hoes, who were stabbed with knives or swords. They have the human form but their hearts are demons' hearts. They had burnt the market place, abolished monetary system, eliminated books of rules and principles of national culture, destroyed schools, hospitals, pagodas and beautiful monuments, trying hard to get rid of Khmer character and transform the soil and waters of Kampuchea into a sea of blood and tears and drove it back to the stone age."*

Fortunately now all you can hear is birdsong and a crowing rooster.

CHAPTER 9

GOOD MORNING VIETNAM

*"And, it's one-two-three ...
What are we fighting for?
Don't ask me, I don't give a damn ...
Next stop is Viet Nam"*[5]

I Feel like I'm Fixin' to Die - Country Joe and the Fish

My introduction to Vietnam was not a pleasant one. Just as my bus was reaching the outskirts of Ho Chi Minh City there was a really nasty motor-cycle accident. It was a head-on collision. The bikes were hardly recognisable. One guy, quite obviously dead, lay sprawled out on the road, with a large pool of blood spreading from his head. The police, who were quite quickly at the scene, hastily draped a beach mat over his body. Not a pretty sight and a very good reason for not hiring a motor-bike.

There are close on three million motor-bikes in HCMC, and getting on one either as rider or passenger is dicing with death. Far, far more dangerous than say, white-water rafting, a bungee jump, or skydiving. There is very little in the way of traffic regulation and, like most S E Asian cities, Saigon is certainly not designed for pedestrians. Bikes and cars come at you from all directions. The general rule is biggest is best, so beware.

And another thing - beware also of motor-bikes with live animals strapped to the back of them - chickens and ducks are the favourites. Was this to be another bad karma day? Well, I did tell a girl trying to sell me some cigarettes that smoking would give her cancer. And another girl said she thought I was like a baby for eating ice cream. So I told her that she was a baby for wearing pyjamas with Teddy bears on them. At least they weren't the black variety worn by the Khmer Rouge. Then I might have been in trouble. It's good to interact with the locals, don't you think.

HCMC, henceforth to be called Saigon, with a population approaching six million is the largest of Vietnam's cities. It is chaotic, frenetic, hustling and bustling, not for the fainthearted and in the middle of a building boom. It is certainly a city of contrasts, of trendy new bars and pavement cafés, of luxury modern hotels, of parks, museums and churches, temples and pagodas, but also of run-down back alleys, busy street-markets, motor-bike repair shops and the persistent cry of cyclo-drivers vying for your attention. Except when you're loaded down with bags and really need them. And not forgetting the incessant clanking of the noodle knockers, iron rods being banged together to advertise the sale of noodles. Christ, I've got a headache.

I will start my city tour with the museums, and where better than the War Remnants Museum, better known as the Museum of Chinese and American War Crimes. The name was changed apparently not to frighten off the good old greenback. The Vietnamese always call it the American War, which is quite appropriate as like present-day Iraq, the

Americans did the invading. It's sad to say that the culture and legacy of war still predominates in both Vietnam and Cambodia, but there it is. I think it will take another generation for the healing process to finally succeed. But I remain optimistic.

On my arrival I was confronted by a rather aggressive beggar who wanted dollars from me as well as dong (Vietnamese currency). He was an amputee who had lost both arms, so I did feel guilty over his plight and gave him some money. But I certainly didn't appreciate having the aforementioned stumps being thrust into my face. I assumed his injuries were caused as a result of the 'American War'. One never knows.

The museum is the most popular in Saigon - especially with Western tourists who want to seek out the truth. Outside is the paraphernalia of war - armoured vehicles, artillery and infantry weapons, tanks, a helicopter and a small plane. There is also a guillotine on display which was used during the French occupation. Inside there are lots of pictures of napalm victims, cluster-bomb injuries, and the effects of Agent Orange. The latter is graphically illustrated by two deformed stillborn babies that are embalmed and on display in jars. There's a man being dragged behind a tank and another being thrown from a helicopter. Even more horrible, a GI lifting up a corpse by the hair, the face half missing. Then some pictures of bodies piled up during the My Lai Massacre, when 504 Vietnamese villagers were murdered. And finally, a picture showing four American GIs posing for the camera with two decapitated corpses.

A caption reads, *"The above picture shows exactly what the brass want you to do in the Nam. The reason for printing this picture is not to put down the GIs but rather to illustrate the fact that the army can really fuck over your mind if you let it. It's up to you. You can put in your time just trying to make it back in one piece or you can become a psycho like the lifer in the picture who really digs this kind of shit. It's your choice."*

Nearly eight million bombs were dropped on Vietnam by American forces, compared to about two million dropped by all sides in the whole of World War II. Three-hundred-and-fifty-two billion dollars were spent, fifty-eight thousand Americans and three million Vietnamese killed. Some horrifying statistics for a horrifying event. Yes, the insanity and madness of Vietnam, and of Iraq for that matter. Can you blame the Vietnamese for wanting the dollar and all the benefits the West has to bestow? I think we owe them so much.

Just one block away is the Reunification Palace, so named on that fateful day 30th April 1975, when the communist tanks arrived at the gates and a soldier unfurled the Vietcong flag from the roof. The palace was built in the early 1960s to replace the older Norodom Palace, which had been bombed. I wouldn't say it was a particularly attractive structure - I hate 'sixties architecture, all concrete and glass and no ornamentation, but it's very airy and light inside. Much more to my taste are the Central Post Office and, just opposite, the Notre Dame Cathedral. The Post Office is a huge iron-vaulted building, more like a train station, and was built between 1886 and 1891. There is a huge picture of Ho Chi Minh at one end above the clock and it is hard to avoid his perpetual gaze. Big Brother is watching you.

The cathedral - a smaller copy of its French model, was built slightly earlier. It has twin Romanesque towers topped with iron spires and still dominates the city skyline. The stained glass windows, which were a casualty of World War II, were never replaced. In front of the cathedral is a statue of the Virgin Mary. There are lots of museums in the city covering the communist struggle, the country's history going back to the Bronze Age, some heroic Soviet-style artworks such as flag waving scenes, and the Ho Chi Minh Museum, containing many of his personal effects. It was really all quite daunting, especially if you only have a couple of days. Was I flagging already?

There was just enough time to see the Jade Emperor Pagoda, although my journey was rudely interrupted by an extremely aggressive American, while I was trying to draw out some money from an ATM. It had taken me ages to find one which would take my card, a common problem when travelling. And he accused me of barging in front of him in my haste - I thought another war was going to start. I could almost hear the B52's flying overhead.

The Jade Emperor Pagoda is an extremely colourful and vibrant Chinese temple, filled with Buddhist and Taoist statues and wood-carvings. As you enter you will notice the pungent aroma of burning joss-sticks which pervades the air. The interior is dominated by an effigy of the Jade Emperor draped in luxurious robes, correctly addressed as 'Most Venerable Highest Jade Emperor Of All-Embracing Sublime Spontaneous Existence of the Heavenly Golden Palace.' A bit of a mouthful. He is flanked by his guardians, the Four Diamonds - and in front six more figures, the gods of the Polar Stars, Longevity and Happiness and their acolytes.

To the left of the Jade Emperor is Thien Loi, the God of Lightning, who slays evildoers. Through the door in another chamber is Thanh Hoang, the King of Hell, the gods of Yin and Yang, and four more gods rewarding the good and punishing the evil. He looks towards the 'Hall of the Ten Hells', a wood panelled Oriental equivalent of Dante's Inferno or a painting by Bruegel. Another room contains twelve female ceramic figures (and accompanying children), each representing a year in the Chinese calendar. They are presided over by Kim Hoa Thanh Mau, the protector of all women. Childless couples pray here to be granted a child. Fertility worship seems to very prevalent here. No wonder there are so many people in Vietnam.

There are numerous other temples and pagodas to see - you could spend weeks here, but I had other items on the agenda. Most importantly the Cu Chi tunnels, built by the Vietcong to outfox the Americans some 30 km from Saigon, and stretching to the Cambodian border. It's absolutely amazing how they constructed the tunnels using only hand-tools. Far too small for most Westerners to use - I crawled on my hands and knees along a 100-metre supply tunnel, and that had been enlarged for the tourists. You would really have to squirm on your belly through the rest, and probably get stuck in the process. Frightening, and certainly no good if you suffer from claustrophobia.

There are 250 km of tunnels in this district alone, and the network provided for living areas, weapons storage, hospitals, and kitchens, with concealed shafts connecting them to the surface. Even the actual command room from which the 1968 Tet offensive was planned. This provided an excellent communication strategy for the Vietcong and allowed them to launch surprise attacks on the Americans. Even though a large USA base was established here it took months for the Americans to discover the tunnels. After ground assaults proved to be ineffective, it was then that they resorted to massive air attacks.

Some ten thousand Vietcong died here in the extremely difficult living conditions, and many more civilians. But they prevailed despite all the odds. Cu Chi has now become a place of pilgrimage for many Vietnamese, and a place of learning for school children.

A guide clad in green battle fatigues will show you around the site. He explains how the tunnels were constructed and how they were camouflaged, and most important of all, will suddenly disappear down the most diminutive of holes - a trapdoor in the ground, just proving how impossible it was for the Americans. But not all the holes were entrances - some contained bamboo punji stakes, yet another use for that wonderful material. Or revolving traps with metal spikes. And trip wires were hidden in the undergrowth and primed to detonate a grenade - or release a box of scorpions onto their unsuspecting victim.

As if all this death and destruction wasn't enough, you're also invited to fire off an AK-47, a Colt 45 or a machine gun. Not my cup of tea, or noodle soup, I'm afraid. In conclusion, I will just quote from the accompanying video presentation. *"Cu Chi, the land of many gardens, peaceful all year round under shady trees ... Then mercilessly American bombers have ruthlessly decided to kill this gentle piece of countryside ... Like a crazy bunch of devils they fired into women and children ... The Americans wanted to turn Cu Chi into a dead land, but Cu Chi will never die."*

Now for something decidedly more peaceful - the Caodai Great Temple. Caodaism is a fusion of the secular and the religious, and of Eastern and Western philosophies. It combines Mahayana Buddhism, Confucianism, Taoism, native Vietnamese spiritualism, Christianity and Islam. The term Caodai, meaning high tower or palace, is really a euphemism for God. It was founded in 1926 by a mystic called Ngo Minh Chieu. The Caodai played a significant political and military role in South Vietnam up until the 1950s. But their power slowly waned, and when the communists came to power, their lands were confiscated and four of the sect executed.

Today they number about three million and are most prominent in Tay Ninh and the Mekong Delta. Like Buddhists, the Caodai believe in the concept of karma, wishing to escape the cycle of birth and rebirth; they believe in the existence of the soul and sometimes use mediums to communicate with the spiritual world. Many adopt celibacy and vegetarianism as a lifestyle. There is much emphasis on the duality of Yin and Yang, and the Ten Commandments get thrown in for good measure. The organisational structure closely mirrors the Catholic Church, with bishops, archbishops, cardinals and a Pope, although the latter position has been left vacant since 1933.

The Great Temple, situated 4 km east of Tay Ninh, to the north-west of Saigon, was built between 1933 and 1955. It is certainly hybrid in style, combining French ecclesiastical and a Chinese pagoda - a rococo fantasy in gaudy pinks, blues and yellows. What a combination. It has twin towers and a central dome, and inside has nine levels, representing the steps to heaven. Columns with multicoloured entwining dragons reach up to the all-seeing divine eye in the heavens.

Ceremonies are at 6am, noon, 6pm and midnight, and worshippers wear yellow (Buddhist), blue (Taoist), red (Confucian) or white (other). Women are seated on the left, men on the right. Visitors are confined to the gallery above. Chanting in a hymn-like fashion is accompanied by traditional Vietnamese music, and the services include offerings of incense, tea, alcohol, fruit and flowers. I went to see the mass at 12 noon - well that was when all the tour-buses turned up. Just goes to show I don't always travel independently. By the way, I think Caodai, as well as being quite wacky and exotic, is a very tolerant belief system. We in the West, especially the fundamentalists amongst us, would learn quite a lot from it.

To the south of Saigon are the extensive lush, green and fertile wetlands of the Mekong Delta, formed by the huge amount of silt brought down by the river each day. It is the rice basket of Vietnam - it produces enough to feed the entire country with some left over for export. Indeed Vietnam has become the second largest exporter of rice, after Thailand, in the world. The whole area is intensively farmed - there are also tropical fruit orchards, fields of sugar cane and coconut palms. Fishing is another important mainstay of the local economy. It is not surprising that flooding is a major problem, especially with the deforestation upstream in Cambodia. And from the sea with all the problems of global warming. Many have lost their lives, with homes and crops destroyed. There are thousands of canals, and transport is easiest by boat. In the southern reaches of the Delta, estuarine crocodiles can occasionally be spotted.

There are innumerable tours and excursions available, or you can travel independently if you so wish. One of the usual routes is first to Mytho for a boat trip to see bee keeping, an orchid garden and snake farm. Then to Ben Tre for the coconut candy workshop and the Vien Minh Pagoda with its large white statue of the Goddess of Mercy. Though not as big as the one I was to see later in Penang. Nearby is the San Chim Vam Ho Bird Sanctuary, famous for its storks. And so we come to Vinh Long and the Mekong River Islands, in particular the Cai Be Floating Market, with its exotic displays of fruit and vegetables. Visit the orchard, watch rice-paper making, go to the bonsai garden. Just outside town is the Van Thanh Mieu Confucian temple.

There are more colourful floating markets and a stork garden at Cantho. It's the largest city in the region, and it's here that the rice-husking mills are situated. Camau, much further to the south, lies in a swampy area infested by mosquitoes, and borders the U-Minh Forest, the largest mangrove forest outside of the Amazon. But its main claim to fame is as a wholesale animal market, where produce is frozen for shipment to Saigon. Over to the west and the border with Cambodia is Chau Doc, known for its floating houses, under which fish are raised in suspended metal nets. Nearby is Sam Mountain, where there are dozens of pagodas and temples, many set in caves. It's hardly a mountain at 260 metres, but the view of the flat plains of Cambodia stretching into the distance is most impressive. There is a military outpost on the summit, highlighting the conflict between the two countries. The summit road has been decorated with ceramic dinosaurs; this type of kitsch offering was going to be repeated many times.

These are just a few of the places to visit in this fascinating area. The Mekong Delta is rich not only in its culture and history, but in bird and plant life as well. It conjures up images of women in conical hats stooping to plant the flooded paddies. Of grizzled old men ploughing seedbeds with their water-buffalo. Of young girls in their *ao dai* (traditional long white tunics) cycling over rustic bamboo bridges. Of brown carpets of rice spread along the roadside to dry. Of storks and cranes feeding in the mangroves. Of boats full of the exotic shapes of longan, jack-fruit, rambutan, durian and mangosteen. And of colourful and ornate temples, pagodas and churches dotted across this verdant landscape.

Yes it is all this, but there is a downside. It is definitely overpopulated and over-polluted, but that happens in many places. What really turned my stomach were the animal markets. Monkeys in tiny cages, the bars dirty and rusting, a rabbit and turtle crammed into the same cage with not enough room to turn round, live birds pinned down by their feathers. A fellow traveller told me she'd seen a frog being skinned alive - I'm glad I didn't see that. And of course at the snake farm the snakes are bred for eating. At an outdoor restaurant I asked why small bags of water were tied to overhead beams. "To keep away the flies," I was told. Well it would have helped if they didn't have caged birds with containers full of live maggots to feed them. Unfortunately the cruelty is so in your face.

The recent outbreaks of bird flu and SARS throughout South-East Asia are of course directly related to animal welfare issues. From eating endangered species like the civet cat to the appalling and unhealthy conditions animals are kept in prior to slaughter. Millions of animals and birds have now been culled in an attempt to control these viruses. But one must address the root cause; namely eating habits and a change in animal husbandry.

I must confess I have very little sympathy with the human fatalities that have befallen those responsible. Now I think I know why the

Khmer Rouge and other factions got away with torturing and killing so many. It is only one step from the abattoir to the Extermination Camp.

I have to say a little about some of the scams. It has been official policy to charge foreigners between two and five times as much as what the Vietnamese pay, though this has been changing. So that sets the scene. The foreign exchange bureau tried to diddle me out of about three pounds. Actually that also happened to me not so long ago in Peru. And crossing borders and changing currency in central Africa is an absolute nightmare. A guest-house in Saigon charged me five dollars for a room when we had previously agreed on four. Why didn't she charge me five to start with? I wasn't going to complain.

A young boy tagged along with me in a small village, then another, then a couple of girls. Was this just friendliness, an eagerness to meet visitors, or was there an ulterior motive. As I waited for the bus, I decided to buy myself a drink from a street vendor, only to discover I was unwittingly paying for my new 'friends' refreshments as well. Fleeced again, though it didn't cost that much – but it was the principle that mattered.

However, later on my trip, there was something that happened in Hanoi that humbled me and made me a little less cynical. And you can hardly blame the Vietnamese for trying to get a small share of the cake - probably a very large share if I was an American.

GRAND PALACE, BANGKOK, THAILAND, MAY 2003

ON THE DEATH RAILWAY, KANCHANABURI,
THAILAND, MAY 2003

WAT THAWET LEARNING GARDEN,
SUKHOTHAI, THAILAND, JUNE 2003

VILLAGE LIFE, LUANGNAMTHA, LAOS, DEC 2001

CHILDREN AT ANGKOR WAT, CAMBODIA, JAN 2002

THE ABODE OF THE GODS, TA
PROHM, CAMBODIA, JAN 2002

GUARDIAN DRAGON LION, SHWEDAGON
PAYA, YANGON, MYANMAR, NOV 2003

CHAUKHTATGYI BUDDHA, YANGON,
MYANMAR, NOV 2003

BALANCING BOULDER STUPA,
KYAIKTIYO, MYANMAR, NOV 2003

ORANGE SELLER, KYAIKTIYO, MYANMAR, NOV 2003

CHAPTER 10

SAME, SAME, BUT DIFFERENT

Dalat is Crazy. Crazy House, Crazy Monk, Crazy Cowboys, Crazy Chicken, Crazy Motor-bikes, Crazy People, a Crazy Place. But then that could apply to all of Vietnam. The city is situated in the Central Highlands, a mountainous area renowned for its cool temperate climate with countless streams, waterfalls and lakes. There are many hill-tribes in the area, still known by their French name of Montagnards (mountain people). A lot of the forest cover has gone, removed in large part by the effects of Agent Orange. Agriculture is also making inroads, in particular market gardening and flower-growing. Animals have hardly fared any better, with many being stuffed as trophies. Dalat itself was once called Le Petit Paris, complete with a miniature replica of the Eiffel Tower. It has become a magnet for artists and bohemian types and is also the country's most famous honeymoon spot - more kitsch I'm afraid.

Right, let's start with the Crazy House. This Alice in Wonderland (or is it Flintstones) creation, with its concrete caves and tree trunks, tigers and giraffes, giant wire spider webs and a naked lady is in fact a guest-house. The Hang Nga Guest-house and Art Gallery is the proud possession of Mrs Dang Viet, a long haired hippie type dressed in 'sixties garb and burning incense. It helps that she's the daughter of Truong Chinh, Ho Chi Minh's successor. Otherwise I don't think planning permission would have been granted. The fanciful architecture towers up several stories, its branches twisting and turning around bizarrely-shaped windows and walkways. The courtyard outside is noisy with the cacophony of caged birds, the sense of disarray and confusion is quite palpable.

Known as the Crazy Monk, Vien Thuc is the only inhabitant of Lam Ty Ni Pagoda. He can speak six languages and has apparently produced more than 100,000 works of art, which he sells to tourists. He is a keen gardener - witness the miniature Japanese garden complete with bridge - and has built much of the garden furniture. Now he is reckoned to be the richest man in Dalat - the hermit monk has become the business monk. There is always a steady stream of visitors to his pagoda - he's a popular man. I asked him, as I do many monks, why are they not all vegetarian. And why is there so much animal cruelty in Vietnam. He answered quite simply, "Because they are hypocrites." Just because someone professes to be a Buddhist, or a Christian, or a Muslim, doesn't mean to say they believe in their faith or follow it without reservation. It's sometimes just a badge of convenience or belonging. Not so crazy after all.

Crazy Cowboys...and girls. What sort of image does that conjure up? Of Vietnamese guys and gals dressed up like Howard Keel and Doris Day in Calamity Jane. And guiding you on horseback round the lake in the Valley Of Love. How tacky is that. And you have to pay for it. A picture maybe. More money. Rent a canoe, a paddle or motorboat. Then it's shop 'til you drop in the souvenir-stalls. It has to be seen to be believed. What I can't understand is one assumes the

Vietnamese were raised on a surfeit of these rubbishy Westerns, and had role models like John Wayne and Ronald Reagan, when these very same people were bombing the shit out of them. Or have I lost the plot. Crazy Cowboys definitely.

Some 17 km south of Dalat on the Nha Trang road is Chicken Village, home to the Koho, hill-tribe people who traditionally lived in stilt houses and believe in ancestor and spirit worship. The village is named after a huge concrete statue of a chicken. Explanations are many and varied, but there appear to be two main schools of thought. Firstly that it was built in honour of a local girl who died for love, and secondly as a memorial to chicken farmers. A popular local alternative to a statue of Ho Chi Minh. And a crazy idea whatever way you look at it.

Crazy motor-bike riders are everywhere in Vietnam. In Dalat they're called the Easy Riders. They've been given a great write-up in Lonely Planet and on several websites. They can be hired by the day or more to get off the tourist trail and into Vietnam proper, as one girl I spoke to put it. No more organised tours. I have been told they are pretty safe (for Vietnam anyway), and the experience can be the highlight of your trip. I must confess I was tempted, but caution got the better of me. Visions of that accident in Saigon were still fresh in my mind, but don't let me put you off. If you have the urge, go for it.

A final crazy incident happened in a Vietnamese restaurant. A lot of people rave about Vietnamese food, though it's not as unique or varied in my opinion as say Indian or Thai. This is probably quite a biased statement as being vegetarian, I'm not into seafood, which is very much a mainstay of the Vietnamese diet. Though up-country you might get served dog, rat, frog or snake - they all taste like chicken evidently. Anyway, there was a large family group next to me and didn't they make a mess. The table linen was dripping with spilt soup and sauces, rice was scattered everywhere, and the floor beneath was covered with lumps of meat and bones. On their departure, the waitress just swept the whole lot into a corner and invited the next group in. I dread to think what the kitchens were like.

It had seemed a lifetime since I last swam in the ocean, but now here it was, the warm inviting waves of the South China Sea lapping at my feet. I had arrived in Nha Trang, probably the best beach resort in Vietnam. It's a great party place (though thankfully not quite on the Magaluf model) with plenty of bars, cafés and restaurants catering for all tastes. There are probably more than a hundred hotels, many situated along the palm-fringed beachfront. It's superb for snorkelling and scuba diving in the clear turquoise waters, and you can take a boat to some nearby islands. Most of the time I just chilled out on the beach, as I needed a rest after so many weeks on the road.

When I was feeling a little more active I decided to go on one of the boat tours. There are an amazing seventy-one offshore islands, so plenty to choose from, as were the tour operators. The main contenders appeared to be Mama Linh or T M (Trouble Makers) Brothers. Both seemed to encourage the virtues of drinking alcohol and deck-side dancing, but T M did seem to have the edge with their Boy Band. I can thoroughly recommend the 'Floating Bar', consisting of a barmaid in a rubber ring, serving drinks from a crate positioned alongside. Sun, sea, sand and…whatever.

After all that, I'm surprised I had any energy left for night-time revelries, but I did. I first had a bite to eat - Nha Trang is excellent for vegetarian food. Why not try the 'Good Morning Vietnam' or 'Same, Same, But Different' cafés. (That expression has become something of a byword in Vietnam, with bar owners, guest-houses and tour operators all trying to outdo each other). Followed by a couple of games of pool and some drinks on a hotel roof top bar overlooking the ocean.

Then finally to the Rainbow Bar on the beach for a nightcap. And what a nightcap. The Finns were in town, so out came the cocktail buckets - whisky or vodka mixed with Red Bull and Coke. There was no stopping them. I was totally trashed by 4am, but they were still in full flow. Is it not true to say that Finland; along with the Republic Of Ireland has one of the highest per capita consumption rates of alcohol in the world? Not so. Luxembourg and Romania are much, much higher. But then you don't meet many people from these countries travelling.

All good things must come to an end - and I steeled myself for another torturous fifteen-hour bus journey, Cambodia style. I was headed to the attractive riverside town of Hoi An. In its heyday the town was a prominent trading port for Dutch, Portuguese, Chinese and Japanese vessels. Its development quite closely mirrors Melaka in Malaysia, with its Chinese temples and shop-houses, pagodas, assembly halls and chapels. Hoi An Old Town is another UNESCO World Heritage Site; fortunately it largely escaped the ravages of the 'American War.' Restoration work is in progress - some of the French colonial buildings are a little faded, and the town is becoming a repository for Vietnamese cultural history. It's a great place to browse and buy souvenirs, in particular wood-carvings, ceramics and textiles. Hoi An is alive with the whirring of sewing machines. If you're into fitting out your wardrobe, check out the more than 200 tailors. "What's your name - where you from - you want suit special price." Same, same, but different.

Probably the most famous structure in town is the Japanese Covered Bridge, erected to link the Japanese and Chinese communities across a stream. A small temple in the northern part of the bridge commemorates the monster Cu, who was held responsible for floods and earthquakes. The two ends of the bridge have guardian defenders

- monkeys and dogs. The tale goes that the bridge was started in the year of the monkey and finished in the year of the dog.

West of Hoi An, around the city of My Son, are the most important remnants of the ancient kingdom of Champa. This Hindu-influenced kingdom flourished from the 2nd to 15th centuries, and was in direct competition with the Khmers to the west and the Vietnamese to the north. It was eventually swallowed up into Vietnam. Extensive damage was caused during The American War by aerial bombardment, but the Vietnamese authorities are slowly restoring what they can. My Son is to Vietnam what Ayuthaya is to Thailand, Angkor is to Cambodia or Bagan is to Burma. Such a tragedy then that so much of Vietnam's cultural inheritance has been lost.

I did not stay in Danang, called by the Americans the 'Saigon of the North' with all the connotations that entails. It is Vietnam's fourth largest city and marks the limits of the tropical zone. In winter, travelling north from here the temperatures plummet. I was travelling in January - the winds come down, the sun disappears behind a leaden sky and you might as well be in London. Its principal attractions are the Museum of Cham Sculpture, the Cathedral and the Caodai Temple, the largest outside Tay Ninh.

China Beach, made famous as a R&R centre for American soldiers, stretches away to the south. I saw a programme on TV recently about the American evacuation from Danang in 1975 - it was anything but R&R. As one plane took off it ran over several people on the runway. Others were so desperate to leave, they were clinging to the wheels and stairway. Soldiers were shooting at them and seven men fell off the plane. One lady fell off at 3000 feet and quite bizarrely, according to CBS cameraman Mike Marriott, waved goodbye as she plunged to her death.

Staying on a cultural theme Hué, about 100 km to the north, also did not fare well with the war. It was the setting for one of the bloodiest battles of the 1968 Tet Offensive, and huge areas were laid waste by both the US and the Vietcong. Lying astride the less than aptly named Perfume River, Hué is divided into two sectors. To the north, the moated Citadel is a massive brick-built structure with walls six metres high. It contains the Imperial Enclosure and Forbidden Purple City, the home of the Vietnamese Emperor.

Entry is gained by ten fortified gates, topped by highly-decorated pavilions with colourful tiled roofs. Once inside, you can marvel at Dien Thai Hoa, the Palace of Supreme Harmony, used for coronations, official receptions and other important ceremonies. Built in 1803, it contains a large hall with ornate timbered ceilings supported by carved and lacquered columns. The Forbidden Purple City itself is a bit of a disappointment, as it was almost totally destroyed and has largely been given over to vegetable plots. Thien Mu Pagoda, twenty-one metres and seven stories high is just outside Hué and overlooking the river. It was built in 1844 and is regarded as something of an icon of the city. Next to the tower are two pavilions; one containing a massive marble turtle representing longevity, and the other an enormous bell.

The DMZ or Demilitarised Zone marks the old North/South Vietnam border at the 17th parallel on the Ben Hai River. It was established back in 1945 with the defeat of the Japanese and remained until reunification in 1975. The legacy of minefields throughout the area continues to maim and kill - over five thousand since hostilities ended. Tours of the zone can be organised from Hué and a visit to the Vinh Moc Tunnels, like Cu Chi, but still in their original state. You might say 'Same, same but different.'

CHAPTER 11

HALONG HAS THIS BEEN GOING ON

I was going to call this chapter 'Hassled in Hanoi', which would have been quite an appropriate title for the first part anyway. Hanoi has been referred to as the Paris of the Orient with its lakes, parks, tree-lined boulevards, ornate French colonial buildings and coffee-shops giving it a Gallic charm. Indeed you could almost imagine yourself to be in the City of Lovers, with the smell of freshly baked baguettes and roasted coffee-beans wafting past. If only there weren't the motor-bikes. Worse even than Saigon in a way, for as soon as I stepped out of my hotel door onto the street, my heart was in my mouth, and my nerves shattered. But then I suppose we all have our phobias and I have to confess I haven't been to Paris recently. Maybe it's just as well.

It didn't help when one guy actually followed me for maybe twenty minutes on his motor-bike and even rode up on the pavement. "No, I don't want to rent a motor-bike, or buy postcards or tacky souvenirs." And another pulled at my jacket as I was attempting to cross the road. He too had some postcards. And a German lady I was travelling with had her breasts grabbed in an attempt to close the deal, though I don't think it was a sexual thing.

One of the hardest things I have had to come to terms with on my travels was this lack of privacy, the concept of personal space. What George Orwell termed 'Ownself' in Nineteen Eighty-Four. And nowhere was it more marked than in Hanoi.

The American War of capitalism and colonialism has obviously had an indelible effect on the Vietnamese, but so has the reverse of the coin - communism. Decades of repression, the creation of a police state and human rights abuses. The age-old conflict of individuality versus the collective and West versus East. But things are changing rapidly. Market reforms are being embraced, but not so much the politics - to a certain extent the mindset of minder still prevails. Investment is flowing in along with the multinationals and everyone wants a piece of the action. The dollar is king - has America finally won the war via the back door.

I was staying near the Hoan Kiem Lake, not far from the Old Quarter. So one dreary morning, I made my first tentative steps onto the damp city streets. It was raining intermittently as it does at this time of year, a mist of cold drizzle falling from a battleship-grey sky. The temperature was about 12°C, but the wind chill made it feel much colder. I was freezing - and finding it very difficult to adapt, having spent so much time in the tropical heat. North Vietnam's winters are not very long, but they are pretty miserable.

The Old Quarter with a thousand-year-old history, is a maze of some fifty streets and alleyways with shops selling silks, jewellery, paintings, Buddhist altars and statues, herbs and spices, ao dai dresses and water puppets. There is a walking tour you can do from Ngoc Son Temple at the northern end of Hoan Kiem Lake, taking in not only temples and shops, but monuments, bridges, the Water Puppet

Theatre, cafés, restaurants and the St Joseph Cathedral. The temple is surrounded by trees, and stands on an island reached by a red wooden bridge. It is a riot of colour, whitewashed walls juxtaposed with bright red shutters and beams, gold-painted carvings, embroidered silver dragons on a backdrop of greens and blues. Enough to pierce the doom and gloom and lift my spirits. The lake itself - Lake of the Restored Sword is named after a giant mythical golden tortoise that came up from the depths to return the sword to its heavenly owners. There are tortoises in the lake - one that died back in 1968 weighed 250 kg and was over two metres long.

Water Puppetry was begun by rice-farmers over a thousand years ago. The puppets are made from water-resistant fig-tree timber. As well as human characters there are also figures in the shape of domestic animals, dragons and unicorns. At the Water Puppet Theatre a tank of murky waist-deep water is used to float the puppets with a system of long poles. The performances depict scenes from rural life - rice-farming, fishing and legends with fire-breathing dragons and fireworks. Over to the west the St Joseph Cathedral, built in 1886 in neo-Gothic style, is famed for its twin square towers, elaborate altar and stained glass windows. I ended up in a coffee-shop somewhere, enticed by the freshly cooked pastries and aroma of ground coffee. But I had hardly got into my seat when a guy came in from the street, crawled under the table and started to polish my trainers. I thought he was going to rob me.

Hanoi is packed with museums - very handy for those rainy days. The Vietnamese Museum of Ethnology is probably the finest, with its dioramas of tribal village life, long and stilt-houses, village markets, funeral ceremonies and videos to match. There is a map showing the location of the fifty-four different ethnic groups, along with photographs and artefacts. There's also a history museum with a sculpture garden, a Museum of Vietnamese Revolution (hardly surprising), a Fine Arts Museum and a Women's Museum (namely the International Women's Movement against the American War). Plus an Army Museum with battlefield models, various weaponry, a Soviet MiG-21 jet fighter and the T-54 Tank, the first to break through the gate of the Presidential Palace in Saigon on the morning of April 30th, 1975. Not forgetting the Hoa Lo Prison Museum back in the Old Quarter, built by the French and containing various instruments of torture and a guillotine. It was known as the 'Hanoi Hilton' by American POWs imprisoned there, including Pete Petersen, who later became US Ambassador to Vietnam when diplomatic relations were restored in 1995. So if you're into war, history or culture you certainly won't be disappointed in Hanoi.

I'm saving the best till last, which is of course the Ho Chi Minh Mausoleum to the west of the Old Quarter. This huge concrete bunker of a building supported by square columns, contains the glass sarcophagus housing the embalmed remains of Uncle Ho. White-uniformed guards stand in defensive posture over the wispy-haired yellowing corpse, as ranks of Vietnamese devotees pay their respects. The whole setting is quite surreal, echoing a scene out of a James Bond film in the Cold War era. Ho was following his predecessors Lenin and Stalin in this macabre adulation, though his own wish was to be cremated.

The long line of visitors snaked around the building: some were crying, others trying to suppress an awkward smile in an outpouring of respect for this liberator and revolutionary patriot. Too much idolatry for me I'm afraid. During the country's major national holidays, the General Secretary of the Communist Party, the Prime Minister and the President line up in front of the Mausoleum to review parades of the ethnic minorities, rolling tanks and goose-stepping soldiers. That would be a sight to see.

Behind the Mausoleum is the Stilt House where Ho lived from 1958 until his death in 1969. It is a very simple and modest structure built to traditional Vietnamese designs. Inside is elegantly crafted with lacquered and polished wood. Such a contrast to the nearby Presidential Palace, a French Colonial Baroque edifice, much decorated with elaborate columns and balustrades. Just proving his egalitarian principles I suppose.

And there is one more museum - the Ho Chi Minh Museum no less, with an enormous statue of our hero, his hand raised in the symbolic gesture of learning with the sun rising behind. Still, I suppose it's better having Uncle Ho as an icon than Colonel Sanders or Ronald McDonald, like we do in the West. In fact, I believe there was a plan to have something like a chain of KFC Restaurants in Vietnam with a HCM logo, due to the passing resemblance between him and the Colonel. I wonder if it got off the ground. There are some great websites that take this a bit further, purporting they were twins - both born in 1890. More to the point, an activist for PETA (People for the Ethical Treatment of Animals) was fined US$15 by the authorities in Ho Chi Minh City back in 2004, for protesting outside a branch of KFC. Good on him - bring these multinationals to book. And Long Live Ho Chi Minh and the Socialist Republic Of Vietnam.

Halong Bay is in my opinion, and many others', the most scenic and picturesque part of the country. It has over 3000 islands rising majestically from the Gulf of Tonkin and has been compared to the limestone landscapes of Guilin in China and Krabi in Southern Thailand. A bit warmer in Thailand though. In 1994 it was designated Vietnam's second World Heritage Site. The bay covers an area of 1500 square km, and the islands are dotted with beaches, cliffs and caves. The popular vision is of a junk with huge brown bat-wing sails, drifting slowly past a monolithic limestone stack reflected in the clear emerald waters. On my visit, unfortunately the weather had not improved - it was still rainy and cold with poor visibility. But I didn't allow that to interfere with my enjoyment of the occasion.

Ha long translates as 'where the dragon descends into the sea.' The story goes that a great dragon came down from the mountains, with its thrashing tail taking huge chunks out of the coastline and creating all those islands, inlets and caves. A dragon-like sea monster called the Tarasque has been sighted by sailors on several occasions in the area. There are boat trips across the bay to catch a glimpse of this Vietnam Nessie, and the creature has spawned an enterprising local tourist industry. The waters and islands of the bay are host to a great diversity of ecosystems including offshore coral reefs, freshwater swamp forests and lakes, mangrove forests and sandy beaches.

Hang Dau Go (Grotto of Wooden Stakes, Driftwood Grotto), or as the French call it, the Cave of Marvels, was named after bamboo poles that had been stored there. They were used to impale the invading Chinese fleet on the receding tide. The grotto consists of three chambers and reached by ninety steps. The stalagmites in the first hall resemble gnomes. In the middle of the chamber there appears to be a monk draped in a long cloak, with his right hand clasping a cane. Moving into the second chamber, a mysterious light glows on the limestone and in the third the visitor is greeted with a panoply of elephants, horses and men in some kind of battle scene. At the deepest point of the grotto, a 'royal garden' appears around a clear pond and a backdrop of mountains. So much for the imagination.

Hang Sung Sot (Cave of Awe) also has three chambers, in the second of which is the famed 'pink penis rock', regarded as a fertility symbol. Actually there are lots of rock penises in the cave, of all shapes, sizes and colours. It brings a whole new meaning to the expression 'getting your rocks off.' Although I thought it was more noted for its penguin trash cans.

Hang Trong (Drum Grotto) is named for the drumming sound the wind makes as it blows through the stalactites and stalagmites. There are lots of other fanciful names for the topographical features throughout the bay. Man's Head Island, Dragon Island, Swan Islet (a bit like Chicken Island in Krabi, Thailand), Toad Islet, Dog and Cat Islet, Sphinx or Egypt Islet. But I will leave it to the local tourist literature to sum up. *"Not only beautiful within range of traveller's vision, but also within their profound mind win respect to the far-off past and changes of nature and cultural history."*

Back in Hanoi I was planning the next leg of my journey. I had decided not to go to Sapa on this occasion, a former hill station in the north-west, renowned for its spectacular scenery and trekking with the hill-tribes. The weather seemed colder and damper than ever and if it was like this in the city, god knows what it would be like in the hills. I was desperate for sunshine and warmth. So I chickened out.

Some months later I remember reading on the BBC News Website about a fire that had engulfed a disco, shops, a restaurant and offices in Saigon. I think about sixty people died and as many were taken to hospital. At the time a wedding reception was in progress and it took three hours for fire-fighters to get suitable ladders. An eyewitness said, "I heard lots of screaming and shouting from inside the building. I saw lots of people jumping from windows. It was a bloody scene." Strange how these incidents happen just after I leave a place. But I have had closer shaves than that. And looking back, I did scald myself in the shower in the guest-house in Hanoi.

I was in a contemplative mood. So, I'm going to tell you about the young girl I met working in my favourite café in Hanoi. She was in her mid-twenties, very pretty with warm brown eyes and long lustrous hair. But she told me she had lost most of her hair due to illness and her lovely locks were false. She wore a hat to cover the top of her head. She worked 12 hours a day from midday to midnight, six days a week, and had to cycle to and from work - a 24-kilometre round trip. She was studying hard at college in English and other subjects as well. I went into that café several times - it was my haven away from the Hanoi traffic, and she was always smiling and helpful. A lesson in humility I think.

Everyone kept telling me I should have gone on the motor-bike tour at Dalat, I should have gone by train and forget the tour-buses. And a nagging thought kept entering my mind: "Be more independent." Bearing that in mind, I purchased my ticket to Manila and the adventure continued. There were no direct flights from Hanoi, so I had to go via Saigon. I was just about to go through the boarding gate, when I was told I needed a return ticket from the Philippines (I prefer to buy one way only). I wasn't quite sure whether this was a requirement of immigration at Manila or a bureaucratic hurdle to be overcome with Vietnam Airlines. Anyway a return ticket (to Bangkok) was purchased for something like US$450 (a ridiculous amount) and off I went. But I was told most emphatically this could be refunded on my arrival.

Although travelling is generally a pleasure, there can be a lot of mental and physical strain to go with it. Yin and Yang. So sometimes I am quite a shitty traveller. But now, whenever I feel angry or pissed off, critical or judgmental, irritated or miserable, that young girl comes to mind with an immediate calming effect. My situation doesn't seem so bad after all and I can look at things from the other person's point of view. This isn't entirely altruistic - I don't want to be saving up any bad karma for my next incarnation. Was this my road to Damascus?

CHAPTER 12

HEY JOE

On the flight from Saigon to Manila there were very few Westerners - businessmen and guys looking for brides very probably; certainly no backpackers. And this was going to be very much the pattern for the next three weeks. The first thing that hit me was the heat and sunshine. Walking on Sunshine. I was back in a tropical climate. And I wasn't asked for my onward ticket at immigration, but I still had to get that refund. The taxi-driver who took me from the airport to my hotel in Ermita was very friendly and chatty and spoke perfect English - the American influence.

I must confess I was very wary, hearing of all the tales of Manila's taxi-drivers fleecing Westerners. But I negotiated a fair price and it was what he had to say next that staggered me. Maybe he was just humouring me, but quite casually offered me his sister as a partner. Whether this was a proposal of marriage or just a one night stand, I wasn't too sure. If you think Thailand is into sex tourism, come to the Philippines. This kind of thing was going to happen often.

The Philippines is an archipelago of more than 7000 islands to the east of Vietnam and north-east of Borneo. It is home to some eighty-three million people. In some respects it is a microcosm of South-East Asia, with its mix of modern and ancient, its colonial past, its hustle and bustle, its crowded streets and markets, its towering mountains, volcanoes, coral reefs, white beaches and rice-terraces. But in other ways it is totally different. For a start it is a predominantly Catholic country - the influence of the Spanish and then there are the Americans. Can you imagine anyone else in Asia playing basketball; the love of fast food is obsessional and the film industry the most prolific in the region. And then there are the festivals - Jesus and Mary Parades, Crucifixion Carnivals and Passion Plays all acted out with the fun-loving exuberance that only Filipinos know how to achieve. Very much out on a limb, in some ways the country has developed in isolation from its neighbours. Yes, the Philippines is a bit awkward to get to, it doesn't really cater for backpackers (mass tourism doesn't exist at all), the hotels are more expensive, it's time consuming getting around …but isn't that part of the appeal.

What else is the Philippines famous for? Imelda Marcos and her shoes, political corruption, Muslim insurgents bombing buses and shopping-malls, sinking ferries, cock-fighting, pop bands (Filipinos are great singers) and violent tropical storms. In December 2004 during the Typhoon Season, a series of devastating storms hit the country, leaving over a thousand dead or missing. Close on a million people were directly affected. Back in 1991, 8000 people died and 50,000 made homeless on the island of Leyte. What makes it so much worse are the landslides and flash-flooding. And what causes these? Logging. Nearly 3000 square kilometres of forest are lost each year. I've seen it so many times before. Just look at the news headlines.

Some recent examples include Nepal, Italy, Columbia and Scotland. No trees means nothing to anchor the soil. It's hardly rocket science, yet people never learn. Philippines President Gloria Arroyo promised to clamp down on illegal logging, saying that those responsible should be prosecuted in the same way as terrorists, kidnappers or drug traffickers. But the Philippines is a poor country, and if we can't get to grips with the problem in the West, how can we expect them to.

Time to have another go at Britain, I think. Look at the state of the Scottish Highlands, bereft of trees and wildlife. All turned over to deer and sheep-grazing and grouse moors. It's terrible what's happening to the Amazon Rainforest; it's terrible what's happening to tigers in India and rhinos in Africa. But we Brits destroyed the Caledonian Forest and killed off the wolf, the bear and the lynx, and are not doing much about their return. Let's get our own house in order first.

Mount Pinatubo, the volcano to the northwest of Manila was also in the news not so long ago. It blew itself apart in a huge eruption in 1991, losing 300 metres in height, and causing ash clouds, rock storms, mud flows and earthquakes. Since then a volcanic lake has formed, and locals were scared it might overflow. So a channel has been dug down the side of the volcano to drain some of it off. It seems to have been a success, though like coastal defences I feel it can only be a very temporary solution.

What does the image of Manila conjure up? *"A splendid, fortified city of wide, cobbled streets and regal townhouses"* as described by 19th century traveller Fedor Jagor. Sadly no, most was destroyed in World War II and now it is a vast urban sprawl surrounded by shanty towns. But amidst the huge American-style shopping malls, high-rise hotels, shabby apartments and street markets there is the colourful Chinatown, some historical buildings have been left standing and there's a great city park and gardens. And then there's the Jeepney, that brash gaudy transport icon of the Manila streets. Based on the US Army Jeep with benches in the back, the rainbow-coloured Jeepney is festooned with badges, chrome horses, horns, aerials and mirrors. They also sport such great sayings as 'Praise the Lord' and 'Jesus Loves You'.

The first day I had in Manila was perhaps the most entertaining I have ever had - and all for free. It started in Rizal Park with a wander around the 3D model map of the Philippines. This fantastic edifice immediately focuses the mind on the complexities and varied landscapes of the Philippine archipelago. From the central cordillera and rice-terraces of north Luzon to the Chocolate Hills of Bohol, the tropical palm fringed beaches of Panglao and Borocay, the perfect conical shape of Mount Mayon and the coral-reefed jungle-clad island of Palawan. I think every city should have one.

The park is named after Dr José Rizal, the Philippine national revolutionary hero, who was executed by the Spanish colonial authorities here in 1896. The actual site of the execution is marked by a tableau of life-size bronze statues as he faces the firing squad. Very moving and theatrical. Nearby is the Rizal Monument, symbolising Philippine nationhood and freedom. There are some very pleasant Chinese and Japanese Gardens and a forest park.

Filipinos use the park to walk and jog, picnic, play and sing music, and to chat. I was amazed at the number of people who said "Hello" or "How are you" or just smiled and waved courteously. And no sales pitch. You certainly wouldn't get that in Hyde Park. And its here that the "Hey Joe" comes in, a throwback to the World War II days of GI Joes. Men said it many times, but it was never voiced in an irritating or obtrusive manner. Well, it never got on my nerves like the "Hey Mister" cult of Indonesia. I was very impressed with the number of litter bins, people sweeping the park and children collecting cans for recycling. It may only have been a token effort - I did see plenty of rubbish elsewhere, but it was a start.

In the early evening I went to the Concert in the Park (free of course), a mixture of Filipino, Indonesian and Spanish music and dancing. That's what I love about the Philippines - it's not just one culture, but an eclectic mix of styles branded in an exotic Filipino fashion. The arrangement was entitled 'Bayanihan', which roughly translated means 'a communal spirit achieving seemingly impossible feats through the power of unity and co-operation.' Though I'm not too sure as to the connection. Night-time was falling and as I looked out over Manila Bay lit by the reddening hues of the setting sun, something quite spectacular was about to happen. It was the Jesus and Mary Show.

A huge array of floats with Jesus and Mary statues, bedecked with flowers and festooned with flashing fairy-lights, was heading to the Quirino Grandstand. Great throngs of people came dressed in their finery, many looking like American evangelists. Dancers in beaded and feathered headdresses with blacked-out faces and garish costumes, and young boys banging away on drums, in a Rio-style carnival atmosphere. The Philippines version of Mardi Gras. The participants went on stage and the floats lined up in front of the stadium. Then began the singing and the dancing and the drumming in this other-worldly celebration of life. Statues of the Virgin Mary were held high (strangely they were all white-skinned with curly blonde hair) as speeches were made and incantations recited.

During the performance I went up on stage - well, to one side of the stage - and looked out at the huge crowd of thousands before me. Apart from a couple of invited dignitaries, I think I was the only white person there. Yet I didn't feel alone or isolated, I was on a bit of a high really. It was only on returning to the UK that feelings of alienation crept in. I wonder if all travellers think like that. So the carnival went on with rapturous adoration and I looked on in wonderment. What a great introduction to this amazing country.

This extravaganza, and the Ati-Atihan festival like it in Panay, is a homage to Santo Niño, an image of the Christ Child. This was given by Ferdinand Magellan, the maritime explorer, to the newly-baptised chief of a Cebu tribe in April 1521. Magellan led the first circumnavigation of the world, but he never made it himself as he was killed in fighting on the island. Out of some 250 of his men, only 18 survived to return home after the three year long expedition. But like a lot of Christian festivals, the Ati-Atihan has its roots in earlier pagan rituals, in this case a peace settlement with the Negritos tribe three centuries before. Ati-Atihan means 'pretending to be aboriginal', hence the blackening of the faces and bodies. I thought it looked very African, but in fact it has a lot more to do with Papua New Guinea. A throwback to the time when all of South-East Asia was populated with aboriginal tribes.

Next day I came back down to earth. It was the usual tour of museums, churches and colonial buildings. Many historical monuments are contained within the old walled Spanish city of Intramuros to the north of the park. This city was built on an old Muslim settlement back in the 16th century and has known many incursions from the Chinese, Dutch, British and Japanese. However, it remained pretty intact until the Americans bombed it in the Second World War. Those pesky Americans again.

Over recent years many of the walls, gates and ramparts have been restored and the place still has a sense of history to it. San Agustin Church was the only building left intact after the city's destruction and is one of the oldest churches in the Philippines. The vaulted ceilings are painted with Italian frescoes and the crystal chandeliers are from Paris. The remains of Miguel Lopez de Legazpi (Spanish conquistador and builder of the city) are contained in the chapel to the left of the main altar. Manila Cathedral rose from the ashes in 1951 in a Romanesque style with a splendid cupola dome and tower, the sixth church to be built here. It is noted for the 4500-pipe organ in the choir loft, and stained glass windows. The Plaza de Roma outside used to be a bullring. Fort Santiago, once the seat of Spanish military domination, is now a memorial to José Rizal, who was imprisoned here before his execution.

In the evening I decided to go for a pizza, one of the few places I could get anything vegetarian. Even when I used to eat meat, I would not have touched such Filipino 'delights' as 'balut' - a chicken or duck embryo. The occasion was uneventful; apart from the fact the guy cleaning up the plates was armed. This seems to be commonplace in the Philippines. The whole country was in a constant state of tension. This could be something to do with the kidnapping and beheading of tourists and others by Abu Sayyaf (Sword of God). This militant Islamic group has mostly been active in their southern strongholds of Mindanao and Sulu.

Apart from the kidnappings, they're also very adept at bombing shopping malls and ferries. But Abu Sayyaf is not the only group in revolt. There's the Moro and Islamic National Liberation Fronts who both want separate Islamic states in the south. The conflict goes back to when the Spanish first arrived all those centuries ago and the Muslims now think they're getting a rough deal from the government. Despite worshipping the same god and having virtually the same scriptures and prophets, Muslims and Christians are always squabbling.

Just before I arrived, the USA had sent in 1200 troops to help track down the militants. More have been arriving as America continues its 'war on terror.' There have been frequent protests outside the American Embassy in Manila against this deployment. And it didn't help matters when gunmen from the Communist New People's Army shot dead an American tourist and injured his German companion while they were climbing Mount Pinatubo. Though there are also those who support American involvement: one taxi-driver I spoke to even went so far as to say he thought the Philippines should become the 51st state.

I retired to a bar in Ermita. There was a Filipino cover band playing - four men and two girls blasting out hits by Mariah Carey and Whitney Houston. Actually they were very good - Filipinos are excellent imitators and they know how to entertain. One of the girls in particular had a fantastic voice. Would put 'Pop Idol' or 'X Factor' to shame. But then came the familiar chat-up lines from women sidling up to me: "Do you like the music, do you like the Philippines, do you like me? Would you like to buy me a drink???" Then, if I took the bait "Would you like to dance?" and afterwards who knows what. But maybe a more likely outcome would be "Would you like to buy my brother, sister, mother, friends a drink? Come to a party and have a spiked drink." And wake up in a bath full of ice with my kidneys removed. No, I jest. It was just another day at the office and I left the joint unscathed.

My last day in Manila was spent trying to track down the correct Vietnam Airlines office somewhere in Makati, the business district, for the refund of my ludicrously-priced ticket to Bangkok. And when the refund came through on my account, they'd knocked off a 12.5% admin charge. The final scam. I was pretty furious at the time. Though I have to say in all honesty it was also down to my own foolishness and stupidity. I should have put a bit of effort into research and preparation for the journey. And coming back to the UK, you soon realise that such scams pale into insignificance compared with what we have here. Something to which I am sure all mortgage, insurance and tax payers will testify. It was definitely time to leave Manila to explore some more of the archipelago.

CHAPTER 13

BAHALA NA

"You may have much gold and grandeur
Yet by God be reckoned poor;
He alone has riches truly
Who has Christ, though nothing more."

I decided to fly to Cebu, the most populated island in the Visayas Archipelago. Directly in the flight path is Mount Mayon, called the world's most perfect volcanic cone and a popular location for trekkers and photographers alike. I got a spectacular bird's eye view from the plane - the volcano was smoking (a filthy habit) and predicted to erupt at any time. For that reason the area was closed off and I never did get the chance to trek to the summit.

Mount Mayon is considered to be one of the most dangerous volcanoes in the world. In the eruption of July 2001, the lava flow miraculously formed in the shape of the Virgin Mary, and the once symmetrical cone was cracked. Ash was blown six miles into the air and tens of thousands had to flee their homes. Back in 1993 seventy-seven people were killed during a two-month eruption. The deadliest eruption was in 1814 when 1200 people were buried under a carpet of ash. And as recently as December 2006, Typhoon Durian swept through the area causing landslides of ash and boulders and wiping out several villages. It is reckoned over 1,000 have died in the Philippines from this calamity.

Also in the flight path are the towns of Legazpi and Donsol and the island of Masbate. I didn't stop off there, but I know a girl who did. Yes it's my mate Rose again. It's good to have a female perspective on things occasionally, and here's her story.

"Hi guys, I'm still in the 'pines suffering from typhoons, wind, rain and a lack of sun (December 2001). This has been my standard conversation for the past week, repeated on average 10-20 times a day.

My name is Rose.

No, I have no companion.

I'm 27...yes, still single.

No...No children.

No I'm not looking for Filipino husband...I'm actually a tourist.

No...I'm not from America or Australia.

I come from Ireland.

No IRELAND in Europe...not THAILAND.

Yes I can manage.

Salamat ho (Thank you).

"I'm sure they don't believe me when I say I'm not looking for a husband. I even get dirty looks from some women. What can you do...I've been here for almost two weeks and have not set eyes on another tourist - this is really strange but fun. The Filipino's are really friendly - I've already been put up in three different homes. Went to Donsol to see the Whale Sharks but no joy; only got to go out once thanks to the third typhoon in as many days.

Left Donsol this morning laden down with five homemade flower pots and a wooden carved whale shark. I'm now in Legazpi waiting for the clouds to shift from the Mayon Volcano so I can take a friggin' picture - still no tourists in sight - something is wrong.

"*Had a really mad December 8th (Feast of the Immaculate Conception). Was staying with this horrible woman in Masbate - got sent there by her lovely daughter as there were no hotels in Balud. Ended up pitching my tent outside her house much to the amazement of all the villagers. Never did I have such an audience from babies up to great grandfathers. I'll never forget the ooh's and aghhh's. Two local girls offered to take me into Balud for the festival. There's a statue of The Blessed Virgin Mary on a stage surrounded by multi-coloured balloons and flashing disco lights…Father Ted wouldn't have come up with this even…two huge speakers on either side and that 'eighties tune… "Hallelujah, It's Raining Men, Amen." It's pumping out at top volume. I do a double take…I really can't believe my eyes or ears.*

"*Tonight is the crowning of Her Majesty the Queen. Basically fifteen or so local girls take part in a beauty contest…very pagan…and there's the statue of Mary looking on. The songs got better (or worse) as the night went on. I just had to laugh - there were tears in my eyes from laughing so much. It's a pity Dermot Morgan passed away, for I could have written a new episode of Father Ted for him.*

"*So that's been my tale from the Philippines…lovely, beautiful, crazy country that it is. I wish I had more time to spend. Will definitely be back for another December 8th sporting plenty of glitter."*
[6]

Cebu City is the major entry point to the Visayas; it is the country's busiest port and oldest city, and is famous for Magellan's Last Stand. He finally met his match on the offshore island of Mactan, when the local chief Lapu-Lapu sent him packing with a spear to his head and a poisoned arrow in his leg. A stone rotunda opposite the City Hall houses a cross commemorating his arrival; shouldn't they have been celebrating his departure instead?

I was headed to Bohol and Panglao Island and the fabulous Alona Beach for some R&R, swimming and snorkelling. A fast ferry takes about two hours to get to the town of Tagbilaran on Bohol. Then it's over the bridge by motorised tricycle in a cloud of exhaust fumes to Panglao, through coconut groves and banana plantations. It really is a great place to rest your weary body after months of travelling. I'm not into diving, having a bit of a phobia with all the clobber you have to put on and obviously being in such an alien environment. I would probably forget to breathe. So I stuck with the snorkelling - but beware of the sea urchins.

After a couple of days it was back on the road to Bohol and the Chocolate Hills. In the centre of the island a range of 1268 near-identical hills lies scattered like boulders on the beach. Local legend tells that they are the solidified teardrops of a lovelorn giant, but in reality they are the weathered remains of ancient coral reefs. The name arises from the colour of the carpet-like vegetation, which turns a rich chocolate brown in the dry season from December to May. Bohol is also famous for the Philippine Tarsier. With its huge searching eyes, rotating head, bat-like ears and spindly fingers it was the inspiration for Steven Spielberg's ET. Unfortunately I didn't see any.

How's this for a bit of nonsense. Ferry from Hagnaya (northern tip of Cebu Island) at 7.30am to Bantayan Island. Okay, so it's a small boat because there are not that many passengers; then in mid-channel we are conveyed to a larger boat which then goes back to Hagnaya to pick up more passengers. Finally leave for Bantayan at 9.30. And why are they dishing out all these life-jackets? Well, ten days before, ten people had been drowned when a similar boat capsized. Most reassuring. With all those islands, the Philippines rely very heavily on shipping for transportation. Unfortunately some boats are ridiculously overcrowded, maintenance leaves a lot to be desired and the seas can be pretty rough, especially in the typhoon season.

Back in December 1999, the MV Asia South Korea sailing from Cebu City to Iloilo, sank in these very waters. Over fifty people died, including some foreign tourists. Twelve years earlier over four thousand died, when the ferry Dona Paz collided with an oil tanker and sank off Mindoro, in the world's worst peacetime shipping disaster. I had escaped by a whisker again. It was a case of Bahala Na. A combination of 'God will provide' and 'Come what may.' What will be, will be and just go with the flow. Remember, 'To be rich in God is better than to be rich in goods.'

My most vivid recollections of Bantayan Island are mainly related to ex-pats running restaurants, guest-houses and bars. One place I stayed in was run by a Danish guy (actually maybe Swiss) who was wheelchair-bound. He had three Filipino girls at his beck and call, seeing to his every need. There were packs of condoms everywhere, so presumably he was active in that department. Concubines and condoms. Next door the bar owner was married to a Filipino. She was fed up with Bahala Na (it's basically a male preserve as the women end up doing all the work???) and that's why she married a Westerner. That's why thousands of Filipino women work as domestics, carers and nurses all around the world - to escape the grinding poverty and resignation to fate of their spouses. Another abiding image was the litter and the irony of a sign on the beach which read 'LET'S KEEP SANTE FE CLEAN AND GREEN.'

The adventure continued. A motor-trike from Santa Fe to Bantayan Town, then a rowing boat, outrigger and another rust-bucket to Cadiz, a fishing port on Negros Island. And the Westerners just melted away. They all fly into the resorts. Then a bus to Bacolod with buckets of dead stinking fish and chickens, very much alive in baskets. I think they were off to the 'Six Cock Derby'. Sounds like a gay gang-bang. At least there was the impressive backdrop of the Mount Kanlaon volcano, with sugar-cane fields sweeping down before it. The city of Silay, known as the Paris of Negros is en route, and remarkable for its old ancestral homes, two of which have been turned into museums. It also has the majestic silver-domed Church of San Diego surmounted by a crucifix.

The island of Negros is as the name suggests home to the Negrito people, the original aboriginal inhabitants of the island with dark skins, wiry hair, flat noses and bulbous lips. In fact they were not far removed from the aboriginals of Australia and must have borne a common ancestor. I saw several throughout the island, mainly mothers with children. Though now they are thought to number less than 20,000 in the whole of the Philippines. Another endangered species. I picked up a catamaran to Iloilo on Panay and I've never been nearer to being seasick in all my life. The trip from Georgetown to Medan in Sumatra came a close second. The boat was extremely unstable (as are all catamarans in my opinion) and I was sincerely regretting eating the Purple Yam Pie.

I arrived in Iloilo after dark, something I hate doing in such places, but it's occasionally unavoidable. I headed to a hotel called the Centercon, which was charging between five and eleven pounds per room. Too expensive, but I wasn't going to fuss. Until I saw the room and the cockroaches. There were just a couple to begin with, until I opened the wardrobe and then a whole army marched out - twenty or maybe thirty appeared. This was an infestation. The receptionist said, "Are you scared of cockroaches?" to which I replied heartily, "No, but I don't want to sleep with them."

The next hotel was several pounds more expensive, but I had no choice. And only a couple of dead roaches here. They must have been busy with the insecticide. From now on Iloilo will be known as 'Cockroach City.' And why are there so many cockroaches here? I think it's because people eat rice in their rooms and the spilt grains are never cleaned away. Those eating habits again.

Iloilo also has its fair share of ancestral homes and churches. St Anne's Church, a twin-towered Gothic-style domed structure and the Jaro Metropolitan Cathedral, famed for the Nuestra Senora de la Candelaria (Feast of Our Lady of Candles), are further examples of Catholic devotion. Iloilo also has its own Mardi Gras, the Dinagyang Festival, held in the fourth week of January. Outside the city, if you have the time there are opportunities for rock-climbing, mountain-biking, caving and kayaking as well as visits to tribal groups. But time was catching up with me and I was soon on the bus headed to Caticlan.

Apart from the usual assortment of villagers, tribal peoples, mothers and babies et al, this time I had for company an Australian guy called Tony (or was it Bruce). He was the stereotypical wife-hunter down to a T. Early fifties, swept back greying hair, tattooed arms, open-necked Hawaiian shirt and sporting a hairy chest with a hanging medallion. He confessed to me he'd already been stung once. The prospective bride had run off with the rent money - some had been given to her brother to buy a motor-bike. But Tony was hooked and he was on the pull again.

We passed the town of Kalibo, famous for the Ati-Atihan Festival, the best and biggest in all the Philippines. A week-long street party of dancing and singing in magnificent costumes sadly missed. You have to book weeks or even months ahead for accommodation. That reminds me of a few places in Malaysia. At Caticlan we boarded a bangka for the short sea crossing to the fabled white beaches of Boracay.

An international jet-setting playground of sun and pleasure-seekers, the island is a mere nine kilometres long by one wide. Along the beach is strung all the paraphernalia of a tourist resort - bungalows, bars, restaurants and tour operators. And all human life is here - not just Westerners, but Japanese, Chinese and Korean - it's their playground too. What with the American troops arriving, there was a hint of paranoia amongst some ex-pats. Two Israelis had been stabbed and I heard that there was going to be a revenge attack. And a girl I was talking to at the bar was convinced she was being pursued by plain-clothed policemen.

The island is a magnet for touts, scam artists and sex-workers. I can say from personal experience the ladyboys are a speciality. Philippine men are a bit smaller than say their Thai counterparts (I think it's all to do with a poorer diet), so the transformation is all the more convincing. Some even go so far as reducing the size of the Adam's apple. You try telling the difference after a few beers and cocktails at four o'clock in the morning.

And what became of Tony you might ask. Well I forgot to mention he was a born again Christian and took quite a liking to me (although not in the Biblical sense, I hasten to add). So much so I was cajoled along to a prayer meeting and prayers were said for my soul. "Cast out those demons, Lord!" Was I ready for conversion? We were joined by some American guy (and his Filipino wife of course) in the deliberations and the expectation that Tony too would soon be happily married to a girl less than half his age. However all was not in vain as I got my own back by giving those assembled a lecture on vegetarianism.

But don't ask me about the 56-year-old German alcoholic from Hong Kong who kept falling over and was in love with Glenda, aged 22, but whose best friend was Rommel the Rooster. The mind boggles.

More seriously sex tourism, especially the exploitation of juveniles, is a major problem. There are an estimated 400,000 prostitutes in the Philippines, up to a quarter of them children. Prostitution really got off the ground with the arrival of the Americans, with girlie bars growing up around naval and military bases. Let's blame the Americans again. Angeles, to the northwest of Manila, is the sex capital of the country, nestling in the shadow of Mount Pinatubo, which back in 1991 almost completely destroyed it. God's vengeance. The paternalistic mentality of home, hearth and heaven is still very strong in the Philippines - the cult of the virgin mixed with the whore of Babylon, the unwholesome legacy of Spanish Catholicism.

As the Philippines seem to be so imbued with religious fervour and fanatical about its festivals, I thought I would finish on the Crucifixion Carnival of San Fernando (Pampanga) in Luzon. Every Good Friday, the village of San Pedro Cutud is host to the bizarre ritual of crucifixion re-enactments. Penitents clad in loincloths, are first whipped by gangs of flagellants until they bleed. Just as in Biblical times, they carry their crosses in the baking sun from the village centre to the recreated mound of Golgotha. Then the 'executioners', dressed as Roman Centurions, rope and nail them to the crosses as the crowds gather to watch the grisly spectacle. The crosses are hoisted upright and bedded into the ground with a jolt. The pain must be unimaginable, but there are plenty of volunteers. It's all seen as atoning for one's sins over the past year, a form of cathartic exorcism, a big 'Thank You' to Jesus. Many penitents have been doing it for years and the event is becoming a major tourist attraction. I wonder how many Hail Mary's a crucifixion is worth.

The Philippines is the one country which I feel I didn't do justice to, and it just begs to be revisited. The rice-terraces of Banaue, trekking up Mount Mayon, the forests and reefs of Palawan, the Kalibo Ati-Atihan Festival, the crucifixion re-enactments and Mount Pinatubo. Why didn't I make time to go to these places, why didn't I extend my visa? Was I too shattered, going over my budget and running out of vegetarian food? Probably. And you need a lot of time to get around the Philippines. But as General Douglas MacArthur (I wonder whether Ellen is a relation) is famous for saying *"I will return."* Although I prefer Arnold Schwarzenegger's expression *"Hasta la vista baby - I'll be back."*

CHAPTER 14

THE GOLDEN WONDER

Burma, or Myanmar as it is more properly called, is generally off the tourist itinerary. Ever since the British left in 1948, the country has been in turmoil with infighting between the various ethnic groups. In 1962 a coup brought the country under military rule with a huge catalogue of human rights abuses. So there is a great debate as to whether one should visit or not.

Reasons for going include the income gained from tourism, influencing the government, increased economic development and liberalisation, and having witnesses to the oppression. Reasons for not going are giving approval and resources to the government, the wishes of Aung San Suu Kyi (pro-democracy leader held under house arrest) to boycott the country, and forced labour being used to construct some of the country's tourism infrastructure. I think it is very much an individual choice. Like say the issue of abortion or euthanasia, there is no black or white here, only grey. I decided to go and I'm glad I did. As a country it is unique, a brilliant, vibrant photogenic land full of colour and surprises. A truly golden wonder in every sense of the expression.

Myanmar has been likened to a parrot facing westward. In that case it would be a parrot sitting on the elephant's head of Thailand. To the north along the border with China and India, the eastern end of the Himalayas reaches almost 6000 metres. In the centre are the sun-baked plains around Mandalay and Bagan, rising to the Shan Plateau in the east. To the west of the capital Yangon are the floodplains and delta of the Ayeyarwady River, and stretching down to the south a long coastal strip and the Myeik Archipelago. There are still huge areas of forest covering perhaps forty per cent of the land surface, mainly teak and cherry wood. But like other South-East Asian countries, excessive logging is a problem, especially considering the corrupt state of government. The country is also rich in fish, gems, minerals, natural gas and oil - all big money spinners for the regime in the international market place. I'm surprised George Bush hasn't launched an invasion force.

The current population stands at around fifty million, although firm statistics are hard to come by in such a closed society. The people are made up of various ethnic groups; not just Burmans, but Shan, Chin, Kachin, Karen, Kayah, Mon and Rakhaing. Hence the name Myanmar to encompass them all. Around seventy per cent live in rural areas. Tourists are pretty thin on the ground, maybe 200,000 per annum (apart from the day-tripping Chinese), a fraction of the six million who visit neighbouring Thailand. And then it's mainly other Asians - Taiwanese, Japanese and Thai. Visitors from the UK came in under five per cent, so I was very much a rarity. Just the way I like it.

I had company. A French/Italian girl who lived in Switzerland and told me she worked in the film industry, knew Al Pacino and Sean Connery, kept saying "Ooh La La" and had a huge suitcase full of clothes. Not a typical backpacker at all. She was to be one of those 48 or 72-hour friends that one so often meets travelling. We were the only

Westerners on the plane, a Bangladeshi Airlines flight from Bangkok. I was keen to see the Golden Dot of Shwedagon Paya that is supposed to glitter outrageously as you approach Yangon Airport. But it was getting dark and I missed it. However, the view from the taxi window after leaving the airport more than made up for it. The floodlights had just come on and there it was, a glittering golden dome 98 metres high and piercing the sky.

Yangon is so much quieter than Bangkok; it is full of trees but thankfully not so full of cars. British colonial architecture sits cheek by jowl with Buddhist stupas, Hindu temples, Christian churches and Muslim mosques, giving an exotic perspective to this most unusual South-East Asian City. It is certainly stuck in a time warp with frequent power cuts, men dressed in longyis (Burmese sarong), and none of the multinationals which usually deface the urban scene. Very conservative (with a small c) and traditional in a nice, unassuming way. The women often wear their lovely glossy hair down to the waist and have sunblock on their faces. There's breadfruit on sale everywhere (a bit like grapefruit), durian (not as bad as the rumours make out) and baskets full of cockroaches balanced precariously on women's heads. And although driving is on the right hand side of the road, most of the cars are right hand drive. Well that makes sense. This is Burma, sorry Myanmar.

If you thought that Thailand was full of Buddhas and stupas, then you will be totally gobsmacked with Myanmar: there must be millions of them. Let's start with the greatest of them all, the Shwedagon Paya, what Kipling called *"a golden mystery…a beautiful winking wonder."* This great golden dome was originally built by the Mon people some time between the 6th and 10th centuries, but has been rebuilt many times, most recently in the 18th century. There is a legend about two merchants enshrining eight of the Buddha's hairs at this site accompanied by rays of light entering Heaven and Hell, the shaking of Mount Meru, winds, lightning and earthquakes. Myanmar is very prone to earthquakes, hence the rebuilding. Once enshrined, the casket was covered with a golden slab and over this a golden stupa was built, then a silver one, then tin, copper, lead, marble and finally brick. Apart from earthquakes, the Shwedagon Paya has undergone abandonment, British occupation, pillaging and fire, but it's now as grand and awe-inspiring as ever.

The Shwedagon is approached by four covered stairways with chinthe (half lion, half dragon) deities guarding the entrances. These stairways are lined with shops selling flowers, paper umbrellas, Buddha images, books and incense-sticks. But watch out for the caged birds - again! I think there is a parallel here with the state of the nation. Once on the main platform you are confronted by a bewildering array of stupas, temples, prayer halls, statues, images and pavilions.

The central stupa is truly an incredible structure. First it is ringed by smaller stupas on a raised platform, then it rises up in octagonal and circular terraces and capped by the bell, banana bud formation and umbrella (or hti). The seven-tiered hti is 13 metres high, plated with gold and weighs five tons. It is hung with gold and silver bells and jewellery of all kinds. The top-most vane, which turns in the wind, is studded with 1100 diamonds. And finally an orb containing another 4351 diamonds, upon which rests the 76-carat apex diamond. The stupa or zedi is regilded each year. There are reputedly over fifty three metric tonnes of gold-leaf on the structure.

Around the base of the stupa are shrines and planetary posts, each day of birth represented by a planet and animal sign. I was born on a Monday, so mine would be the Moon and a tiger. In the Bell Pavilion is housed the 23-tonne Maha Ganda Bell, which was taken by the British in 1825 and accidentally dropped in the Yangon River. The Burmese eventually retrieved it by floating it to the surface on logs and bamboo. Nearby are two banyan trees, one supposedly grown from a cutting of the Bodhi tree in India where the Buddha gained enlightenment. A great view over the Yangon River towards Thanlyin and the Kyaikkhauk Paya is afforded from this position.

When I was there the Offering of the Matho Robe ceremony was underway; speed weaving of robes for the Buddha on handlooms throughout the night. Teams of young women furiously weave away on the saffron cloth, with friends and family singing and chanting encouragement. Passers-by donate 1,000 kyat notes (worth about 80 pence), which are pinned to the weavers' blouses. Hundreds of families set out mats to sleep here so they can rise and pray at dawn. And as evening fell and the setting sun cast its rays on the great dome, the gold turned to amber, the lights came on and the whole place became a magical fairyland.

Just opposite Shwedagon's southern gate is Maha Wizaya Paya, sometimes called Ne Win's Pagoda. Built in 1980 from public donations, it commemorates the unification of Theravada Buddhism in Myanmar. The King of Nepal contributed some sacred relics. Apart from the usual pictures of the Buddha's path to renunciation there are also some of other paya throughout the country e.g. Bagan, Bago and Mandalay. The central area has trees sculptured in concrete, complete with leaves and fruit. The connection with Ne Win is that he had the paya topped with an 11-tiered hti - no doubt as kutho (Buddhist merit) for his next life. He died in 2002, aged 91.

Ne Win ruled Burma, as it was then called, with an iron fist from 1962 to 1988, when he retired at the time of the pro-democracy uprisings. He is widely reputed to have ordered the assassination of Bogyoke Aung San (father of the Independence Movement and Aung San Suu Kyi) in 1947. A devotee of Marx and Stalin, obsessed with numerology - his lucky number was nine - Ne Win was said to bathe in dolphin's blood to regain his youth. The date of his 'retirement' - 8th August 1988 - unfortunately heralded a new crackdown with some 3,000 demonstrators killed. Aung San Suu Kyi was placed under house arrest, where she remained until 1995. The 1991 Nobel Prize for Peace was awarded in her absence. At the time of writing she was under detention again. The Burmese remember him as the man who took them from prosperity to poverty - a Ne Win situation.

A visit to the Bogyoke Aung San Museum was in order. This was the family home in Yangon and you can see some old pictures of a trip to England, of his wedding, in military uniform, with his wife and three children and the house at Natmauk where he lived as a child. There is a Buddhist altar on the top floor with a view of Shwedagon Paya, but it was closed to visitors. A reading room contains books on Spanish Civilisation, the French Revolution, India, military history, engineering, aircraft and warships. Then there was *Psyche-Analysis and the Unconscious*, *Health and Longevity through Rational Diet* and an interesting, very prophetic *Can America Prevent Frightfulness from the Air*, J M Spraight, 1939. In the bedroom, Suu Kyi's was the only bed with bars on the side - was this foretelling the future? His son Aung San Lin drowned in a pond in the garden in 1953. The other son lives in Chicago and occasionally visits Myanmar.

Throughout Myanmar, Bogyoke is regarded as a heroic martyr, even by the generals. There is a Bogyoke Market, a Bogyoke Street, a Bogyoke Road, Bogyoke banknotes and of course a Bogyoke Museum. But mentioning his daughter in public is almost taboo.

But I will mention his daughter now. Aung San Suu Kyi is currently being held under house arrest at no 54, University Avenue Road, south side of Inya Lake not far from the Sedona Hotel. Ironically, her opposite number Ne Win lived on the north side in self-imposed exile. At Check Point Charlie (no 30) they have a double roadblock. Most cars and pedestrians were being diverted, but some went straight through without being checked. They certainly didn't let me through, even though I asked them nicely - I wonder why? Around the area there were 'No Photograph' signs - I think that's what the English translation was. Shortly before my visit, an Italian photographer had his camera confiscated and was immediately deported.

Suu Kyi was re-arrested in May 2003 after clashes between her NLD (National League for Democracy) supporters and pro-government forces in Depayin, northern Burma. In September 2007, many thousands of people, led by monks and nuns, took to the streets of Yangon. Some were even allowed through the roadblock to see Suu Kyi. It was the largest anti-government protest since 1988. Things may be changing at last.

Right, back to the Buddhas - for the time being anyway. At Chaukhtatgyi Paya there is a reclining androgynous Buddha 216 feet long, in a large metal-roofed shed with lots of lipstick, heavy eye make-up and large lashes. The 108 distinguishing marks on the soles of the Buddha include the Sun and Moon, mountain ranges, flowers, animals, the dragon king and royal barge, representing the animate, inanimate and conditioned worlds. Bamboo scaffolding has been used for renovation and painting, but doesn't look very safe. The Ngahtatgyi Paya contains the five-storey Buddha. A more appropriate name would be the Spock-eared Buddha. You have to take your shoes off walking through the complex, but cars are allowed to drive through - shouldn't they take the tyres off first? And is the driver wearing shoes or sandals?

The Sule Paya in the centre of the city is another receptacle of the Buddha's hair. No wonder the guy was bald. It's 46 metres high and looks almost as majestic as Shwedagon. A great meeting-place for the locals - no Westerners there at all. Near the jetty on the Yangon

River is the Botataung - yes you've guessed it - Buddha's Sacred Hair Relic Pagoda. Actually I've got a theory. If Buddha was shaved all over, presumably apart from one place, it must have been a pubic hair. The hair in question was found in a golden cylinder after the pagoda was bombed by the RAF in 1943. When the pagoda was rebuilt, the centre was left hollow to allow people to enter. It contains a mirrored maze of Buddhas and pagodas and other artefacts, protected by bars and padlocked, just like the people of Myanmar. The Gilded Bronze Buddha image was returned to Myanmar from Britain (Victoria & Albert Museum) in 1951, 66 years after it was removed.

My city tour was completed by a visit to the Thway-Hsay Lake (The Washing-off Blood Lake). 'Here in this lake, Myanmar heroes cleaned their blood-stained swords after going into battle during the first and second Anglo-Myanmar wars.' Bogyoke Aung San said the Burmese struggled like bullocks under the British and were treated like dogs by the Japanese. Then they get independence and treat each other like rats.

CHAPTER 15

A BALANCING ACT

It was back to some hardcore travelling as we boarded the bus from Yangon to Kinpun to see the Balancing Boulder Stupa of Kyaiktiyo. Totally exhausted after five hours - cramped, hot and sweaty, and I was suffering from a sore throat. Must have caught it on the plane from that damn child coughing and spluttering. One of the cabin crew had wiped the child's snotty face with her sari. How yucky is that. I had a cold sore for weeks afterwards. From Kinpun it's about another two hours up a steep winding road on a large open truck, with tightly-packed benches for seating. I have to confess on this occasion I went for the soft option and paid a bit more to sit in front (both ways!).

The tiny stupa - such a contrast to Shwedagon - is just 7.3 metres high and sits atop a massive gold-leafed boulder on the edge of a cliff at Mount Kyaikto. Like Shwedagon it is revered as one of the most sacred Buddhist sites in Myanmar. It is said that the boulder keeps its perilous balance due to a meticulously placed Buddha hair in the stupa. So if the boulder were to fall off the cliff, it would be a case of hair today, gone tomorrow. Ha! Ha!

There is a small bridge for men only to gain access to the boulder to enable the fixing of gold leaf. (I think there is something in Buddhism that says if women perform good deeds in this life they will be reincarnated as a man in the next). Apparently if you wedge a small piece of wood or bamboo beneath the boulder, you can see it flex as the boulder rocks back and forth. A terrace below enables you to look up at the spectacle. Another boulder nearby is called the Stone Boat Stupa, which according to mythology was used to transport the balancing boulder from the sea to its current position.

Surrounding the various rocks and shrines is a huge piazza, which was packed with pilgrims making their devotions. A good time to come is at sunrise or sunset, when the horizontal rays of the sun create a magical scene, with lighted candles and monks who spend the whole night in meditation. Craft shops and restaurants line a stairway down into the local village. Among the things for sale were cockroaches and cicadas. One minute they were flying around, the next impaled on sticks and loaded into baskets on women's heads. Then crunch as a girl pops one into her mouth. And now I know what those bits of wood are used for - not for sticking under the balancing boulder at all. They come from the Thanakha tree (*Limonia acidissima*), being ground down to make a paste and applied as a sunblock or skin conditioner. The paste is very aromatic and used to make intricate patterns on women's faces. In January 2004, twenty people died and more than thirty were injured, when a fire engulfed shops and stalls at the pagoda.

It was now time to see the Old Bago Lady. On the journey, the bus was forced to stop by some cows crossing the road. Or rather children dressed in pantomime cow costumes. And elephants. They came up to ask for donations - it was some kind of celebration. I think it was the festival of Kahtein, at the end of the Buddhist Rains Retreat, when money is offered to the monasteries. The Kyat notes (Myanmar currency) were folded and stapled into floral patterns on wooden 'trees' called padetha and held aloft by the children. How often have you heard that as an excuse for being late to work: 'There was a cow on the road.'

Bago is only 80 km from Yangon and I was stopping off to get the bus up to Mandalay. Though Bago is certainly worth visiting in its own right. The city owes its position to the alleged sighting of a female swan standing on the back of a male. An auspicious omen. Ever since then it seems men in Bago have the reputation for being hen-pecked, or is it swan-pecked (by the Old Bago Lady). Bago is perhaps most famous for the huge reclining Shwethalyaung Buddha, at 55 metres the second longest in Myanmar and the world. It beats Wat Pho in Thailand by 9 metres, but is still 19 metres short of the one in Dawei, in the south of the country.

The image is 16 metres high; the small finger alone measures 3 metres, and the eyebrow, eyelid, nose, lip and neck all come in at 2.29 metres. The head rests on a bejewelled cushion. Along the back there is a tableau depicting the conversion of 'heathen' worship into Buddhism and the building of the Buddha, completed 994 AD. At one point the Buddha was abandoned to the jungle, and was only rediscovered in the 1880s.

Outside, the Guardian Dragon Lions look more like Pig Lions with pointed pig ears, snout noses and curly tails. It really was "Squeal lika pig" as a guy rode past with a boar strapped to the back of his bicycle. How the rider managed to keep his balance I'll never know. Then I just escaped from a coach-load of package tourists - they make up about 90% of the visitors to Myanmar. Mainly Germans, who else!

Shwemawdaw Paya, at 114 metres is even higher than Shwedagon, with the former hti embedded in its base. It fell in 1917, the result of one of the frequent earthquakes. The stupa was completely levelled in 1930 and reconstruction work not finished until 1954. There are pictures showing a moral tale - a frog swallowing a cobra, a goat pursuing a tiger and a calf being suckled by its mother. A subtle message to the military junta no doubt. And a drugs-free school - drugs are obviously a major problem here - the government is financed by them.

Behind the Shwemawdaw, the Hintha Gon Paya contains statues of the nine emperor gods with buffalo heads and holding fishes. There was a bit of a knees-up going on here with dancers, drums and cymbals and Chinese/Burmese music. When one of the dancers smiled at me on completion of the performance, his lips dripped with blood-red betel-juice. A popular pastime chewing those betel-nuts, though they are a carcinogen.

At Mahazedi Paya I had to climb up the stupa in my bare feet - the Burmese insisted. Women are not allowed to climb to the top at all. God it was hot, but with a great view of all the other stupas in the distance. No package tourists will be coming here, that's for sure. So many dogs (bitches) wandering around with huge elongated breasts and nipples, from suckling all those pups no doubt. A guy with a huge protuberance on his face was begging. Beggars, amputees and those with physical deformities seemed more noticeable than elsewhere in S E Asia, apart from Cambodia maybe. And more people staring vacantly and aimlessly into space - I expect they have a horror story to tell at the hands of Tatmadaw (the military junta).

Back in town I went to the '555' restaurant - I wonder why '555'- which had some rather peculiar specialities on the menu. 'Goat fighting balls' - or goat testicles to you - would go nicely with the cockroaches and cicadas. I'm sure I saw one woman eating them.

Actually I have a theory - 555 was Adolf Hitler's membership number to the German Workers' Party or DAP (*Deutsche Arbeiterpartei*). Could be a connection. I think it should be called the '666' restaurant, don't you? And early next morning I was woken by the call to prayer - why do they always place mosques so near Western hotels? There's definitely a conspiracy going on here. And getting back to the Old Bago Lady, some Burmese women don't age very well - mainly the effect of the sun, as exemplified by a wizened, wrinkled toothless old crone smoking a cheroot. There are several cheroot factories in Bago.

By the way, Hitler hated smoking, just like me. And he was vegetarian.

CHAPTER 16

THE ROAD TO MANDALAY

Rudyard Kipling never took the Road to Mandalay - and I'm not surprised. It was another fifteen-hour epic of cramped legs and an aching back with the obligatory break for repairs. Though not nearly as bad as the journey from Inle Lake back to Yangon. That really was an epic. Mandalay was the capital of the last Burmese kingdom before the British invaded; today it is an important cultural and monastic centre much influenced by a large Chinese presence. George Orwell said of Mandalay in 'Burmese Days' that it is hot, dusty and renowned for pagodas, pariahs, pigs, priests and prostitutes. I don't suppose much has changed. The city itself is laid out on a grid system, and is dominated by the huge walls and moat of Mandalay Fort. The walls of the fort are some 8 km long, and every so often there is a red and white signboard written in Burmese and English with the following rousing battle cry.

OUR THREE MAIN NATIONAL CAUSES:
Non-disintegration of the union.
Non-disintegration of national solidarity.
Consolidation of national sovereignty.

Even better THE PEOPLE'S DESIRE:
Oppose those relying on external elements, acting
    as stooges, holding negative views.
Oppose those trying to jeopardise stability of the
    State and progress of the nation.
Oppose foreign nations interfering in internal affairs of the State.
Crush all internal and external destructive
    elements as the common enemy.

I trust the reader is suitably impressed.

In 1942, during fierce fighting between the British and Indian troops and the Japanese, the Royal Palace within was completely gutted. A new concrete construction is rising from the ashes, built by convict labour for the benefit of tourists. A 33-metre watchtower gives a commanding view over what seems little more than a prison complex. In the meantime the Burmese soldiers stationed here tend their vegetable plots to supplement meagre wages. It is indeed a most dispiriting and soulless place.

Near to the fort is the Golden Palace Monastery (Shwenandaw Kyaung), a traditional Burmese wooden monastery. It was originally part of the Royal Palace, but was dismantled in 1880 and so the wonderful *jataka* Buddha and Ramayana carvings have been preserved for posterity. Next door is the Sandamani Paya, where the teachings of the Buddha have been inscribed on 1774 marble slabs by Ukhan Ti the

Hermit. An extreme case of OCD (Obsessive Compulsive Disorder). But wait for this. The World's Biggest Book at Kuthodaw Paya with 729 tablets containing Buddhist texts enclosed behind bars in mini stupas. More internment.

The last in this cluster of temples is the Kyauktawgyi Paya, famous for the huge seated Buddha carved from a single block of marble. It took 10,000 men to transport it here from the mines of Sagyin in the mid-19th century, a popular time for Buddha-building. Some more moralistic tales - a crow amongst hens, a goat chasing a leopard, four bulls charging each other, a dog (or is it a bear) pissing in a pot and a gambling/drinking den.

In the centre of town these parables are continued in the Shwekyimyint Paya. There's an interesting diorama of dogs eating a carcass, a man holding his severed right hand with his left - must have been a Muslim transgressor, a guy dying from snakebite, a topless woman waving - usually Burmese themselves cover up. Then a baby being carried off by a bird of prey, a man sitting on a crocodile and a man falling off a cliff - must have been me. Which I did in Australia and broke my ankle. Another man appears to have bitten off his arms and legs and was arguing with his wife, and a man was being scalded by monks. Demons were falling down before the Buddha, and again the portrayal of the impermanence of life - from youth, to love and romance, marriage, parenthood, old age, then death. The rich tapestry of the human existence.

At Mahamuni Paya, southwest of the town, I got roped into applying gold leaf to the Buddha at a cost of another dollar. Pilgrims have applied so much gold; it's apparently 15cm thick on the image. Monks clean the face and teeth of the image at 4am every day. Various Khmer figures - lions, Shivas and Airavata, the three-headed elephant, were taken from Angkor Wat by the Thais, then stolen by the Burmese and installed here. Now all worn down by constant rubbing. A case of giving and taking away. In the same complex is the Maha Buddhavamsa Museum with a map of the Buddhist world in concrete, complete with an ocean full of fish. From Japan to Sri Lanka and Pakistan to Japan there are pictures of the various temples and images. And a huge gong.

'LONG LIVENESS WILL BE PREVAILED IF YOU BE WITH MANDALAY HILL 8/7/2003'. So says the sign at Sutaungpyai Pagoda, especially if you go barefoot. And there are some rather incongruous pictures of the generals visiting - and praying - they have this at a lot of stupas. There are far-reaching views over the floodplain of the Ayeyarwady River - the sunsets are stunning. Much beloved by French and Italian package tourists - but no British. I think news of the tourist boycott is only known in Britain. One Burmese girl was wearing a T-shirt with the message "Gimme Head" with a picture of a pint of beer underneath. I'm sure she didn't understand the double meaning.

Close to the top of the hill is a standing Buddha image (Shweyattaw) pointing with an outstretched hand towards the Royal Palace. The Buddhist version of 'Christ the Redeemer.' According to legend this is where the Buddha directed the town to be built. And since then Ukhan Ti, the hermit guy, seems to have been responsible for building many of the images around the hill. The military importance of the hill was highlighted in 1945, when the British retook it in fierce fighting with the Japanese. The military connection continues with the posting of Burmese army sentries in some of the monasteries.

If you want a bit of evening entertainment, I would recommend the Mandalay Marionettes with dances from the zat pwe (Buddhist *jataka*) and Yamazat (Ramayana tales). These dances are accompanied by traditional music on drums, pattala (xylophone) and cymbals. A little more risqué (it doesn't take much to be risqué in Myanmar) is the Moustache Brothers and their A-Nyeint Pwe entertainment combo - dances, comedy, satire, music and marionettes. A celebration for all ages and all occasions. It has been called Guerilla Street Theatre or Moustache Mayhem and is often politically motivated.

At their home in Mandalay where performances take place, there are pictures of Aung San Suu Kyi when she visited in 2002. Support has been received from fellow comedians as diverse as Frank Carson, Eddie Izzard and Hugh Laurie. The imprisonment of U Par Par Lay, one of the brothers, was mentioned in the film *About a Boy*, starring Hugh Grant. He was making fun of the generals - *"My hat is so large it protects all Myanmar"* - referring to the star-topped hat that is the symbol for the National League for Democracy. He got six months in jail for that comment.

He was imprisoned again from 1996 - 2001 and sentenced to hard labour. The Moustache Brothers are no longer allowed to perform outside their home in Mandalay, so they perform inside instead. They want tourists to visit, because that protects them from arrest - a no show situation would soon be communicated across the world.

'THE MOUSTACHE BROTHERS ARE UNDER SURVEILLANCE. POLYGAMY, MONOGAMY, PHILOSOPHER'S STONE, ELIXIR HERB, ROOT HAREM, MALE FEMALE EUNUCH,' say the notice-boards to give you an idea of what's on offer. Par Par Lay, his brother Lu Maw, 'the men with moustache', and Lu Zaw perform most evenings to the small groups of tourists who crowd into their front room. Lu Maw translates the show into English, explaining the graceful, costumed dances performed by his wife and sisters. She is dressed as a princess in a long lilac gown with flowers in her hair and overflowing with beads (it could be the Roaring 'Twenties) and holding the Lonely Planet guide with her picture on the cover.

And then the political jokes told by Par Par Lay, one of which I will repeat here. 'A man caught a fish, and asked his wife to grill it. She said "You silly man, how can I? The government has put up the price of charcoal and cooking oil so much that I cannot afford them!" So the man returned the fish to the river, whereupon it leapt out of the water and shouted its thanks to the generals that had brought the country to such ruin.' The show ended with everyone sipping green tea (how civilised) and Lu Maw saying it was tourist pressure that led to Par Par Lay being let out of prison 18 months early. It was originally a seven-year stretch. So spread the word.

Scattered around Mandalay are the ancient cities of Amarapura, Inwa/Ava, Sagaing and Mingun, each one taking turns as capital of the country after the fall of Bagan in the 14th century. A new king, a new reign, a new palace and a new capital to highlight the Buddhist philosophy of impermanence. Amarapura just to the south means 'City of Immortality', another reference to the transient nature of things - it was only capital for forty years. There's not much left of it now; the city walls were torn down to be used in road and railway building, with the wooden palace buildings dismantled and carted off to Mandalay.

It is mainly famous for U Bein's bridge, at 1.2 km the longest teak span in the world. The twisting and rickety structure crosses the shallow Taungthaman Lake, supported by 984 teak posts salvaged from Inwa palace, though some have been replaced by concrete. It has been standing for two centuries and today is popular with children posing for pictures with flowers in their hair. Indeed it is quite a thoroughfare as cyclists, monks and women laden down with fruit-baskets venture back and forth. An almost idyllic rural scene that just begs to be captured on film.

At the start of the bridge is the Maha Ganayon Kyaung Monastery, a centre for monastic study and strict religious discipline. It is home to some five thousand monks. If you arrive at about 11am you can watch them going for their morning meal and they are extremely well behaved. Unlike some of the package tourists who not only took pictures in their dorm but of them having a shower as well. Is there no privacy? And this must happen every day. As most of them were novices their robes were white, but it's not always as simple as that. A general rule of thumb is saffron for Mahayana, red for Theravada (dark red means fully ordained), pink for women, and white for boys. But in Thailand it's saffron for Theravada and white for women. Same, same, but different.

I spoke to one older monk Ashin Kelasa, who had his own room. His mother died when he was nine years old. He has written several dissertations in excellent English entitled *Tolerance with Wisdom*, *What Life Needs*, *Tears through Compassion* and *How Meditation Can Help*. We discussed various topics e.g. G W Bush, Iraq, Israel, Palestine, Tibet, Aung San Suu Kyi and vegetarianism. He said Mahayana Buddhism = vegetarian, Theravada Buddhism = non-vegetarian, which I thought a little simplistic, but he's the expert. *'May the whole mankind be prosperous, healthy, happy, peaceful and free from any danger in new year.'* A very uplifting and informative discussion.

Sagaing lies to the west of Mandalay and was the nation's capital for a few short years during the 14th and 18th centuries. The area supports many monasteries and nunneries. On Sagaing Hill, Umin Thounzeh (30 caves) contains 45 Buddha images in a crescent-shaped colonnade. There are steps and walkways to a profusion of stupas and temples amongst the trees over the entire hill. It really is mind-blowing. A sign in one of the temples - 'BE KIND TO ANIMALS BY NOT EATING THEM - MANDALAY VEGETARIAN SOCIETY. PEACE TO ALL BEINGS - BUDDHISM IS DEAD, USELESS AND OF NO VALUE UNLESS IT IS LIVED. THE LORD MANU ON MEAT EATING:

He who consents to the killing, he who strikes, he who slays, he who buys and sells, he who cooks, he who serves, he who eats, they are all murderers.' That's all I needed to know.

Mingun is to the north on the Ayeyarwady River and is renowned for what might have been the world's largest stupa. It was begun by King Bodawpaya in 1790 with the aid of thousands of slaves and POWs. His death in 1819 brought work to a halt, leaving a brick base with sides standing 72 metres high. The completed stupa would have stood 150 metres high. In 1838 an earthquake split the monument creating perhaps the world's biggest pile of bricks. Although I think that honour must ultimately lie with Bagan as you will see in the next chapter. Mingun is also famous for having, at 90 tonnes, the largest working bell in the world. It used to hang beneath an exquisitely-carved wooden roof with figures of yawning monks. Now they have disappeared, probably stolen by art thieves, and the roof is in disrepair. No-one has any interest in restoring the structure, instead preferring to donate to the new glistening white concrete stupas that line the distant hills.

After the conquest of Myanmar by the British, the town of Pyin U Lwin to the east of Mandalay became a colonial hill-station. It lies at an altitude of 1070 metres and was ideal in the stifling heat of summer for escaping the oppressive humidity. In winter it can get quite chilly. There are still plenty of well-preserved colonial buildings, many of which have been turned into hotels. Though there is also a proliferation of modern Chinese developments.

The town was originally a Shan Danu village, but there are now some fifteen thousand Indians and Nepalis, descendants from colonial immigrants. So at least you can find a decent curry-house. Woollen knitting is a popular pastime for the women in town - for those cold winter nights. And the area around Pyin U Lwin is important for growing temperate-climate fruit, vegetables and flowers - in particular roses, dahlias and chrysanthemums. Travelling by horse and cart is still commonplace - in the style of a Wells Fargo stagecoach and you will no doubt be taken to your lodgings in this fashion. An important landmark in town is the Purcell Clock Tower which copies the chimes of Big Ben and just opposite the lime-green mosque - you can't miss it. Chimes versus chanting.

About 3 km to the south of town are the immaculate National Kandawgyi Gardens, with swamp, bamboo, rock, orchid and croton gardens, plus an orchard, pine, oak, eucalyptus and a natural rainforest. There is an aviary with various types of fowl and pheasant, and a golden stupa in the centre of a lake with swans and ducks. The gardens were set up in 1917 with help from Kew. There is a large temperature range from 2°C to 36°C, so it is very interesting to see what can survive here. I was very impressed that the garden was so well-managed - one of the best I've seen.

Back on the road to Mandalay are the Anisakan Falls, set deep in the forest. The falls have been created in five separate sections and there are more falls on the cliff opposite. It was a bit like a circus with the locals trying to act as 'guides' and vendors selling drinks from their backpacks. Some people were carried up and down in hammocks, so perhaps it was a kind of pilgrimage to reach the falls. I'm not quite that infirm - yet!

The next part of my trip was going to be by train to Hsipaw for one night, returning the next day. I wanted to go on to Lashio, but my month's visa was running out and I didn't really have the time. The highlight of this journey was going to be traversing the Gokteik railway viaduct. This viaduct was built in 1900 by an American company for Burma Railways to connect the north-eastern part of the country. It was the second highest railway bridge in the world at that time, and a massive engineering feat.

The trains go very slowly over the bridge to avoid putting undue stress on the ageing structure - maintenance schedules are not what they could be. However it means you can take some decent pictures, though the train guard tells you not to - there is a military camp underneath the bridge with armed sentries. And minefields. The best pictures can be obtained from a distance when you can get the whole viaduct in. Its presence amidst the green of the jungle and towering cliffs is quite surreal - the immense silver edifice striding like a giant across the huge gorge. Seemingly incongruous with its environment, yet at the same time a great wonder to behold.

My time in Hsipaw was all too short - I didn't even have time to see the Shan Palace and certainly not the Bawgyo Paya or go on the many walks, boat trips and river tubing. Next time. Another place I wanted to go was Katha, north of Mandalay on the Ayeyarwady, but it would have taken too long to get there. Time is always a problem.

The town is famous as the setting for George Orwell's *Burmese Days* - he was stationed here as a colonial police officer during 1926 and 1927. The British Club and the adjacent tennis court are still there, having metamorphosed into an agricultural co-op. And also the police station, jail, some red-brick mansions and the hospital where Orwell spent time recuperating from dengue fever. *Burmese Days* is a brilliant indictment on colonial hypocrisy, racism (we white men must hang together) and human psychology in all its rawness. You must read it.

Meanwhile I was back on the railway station at Hsipaw for the return journey. Young boys on the platform were sitting on their haunches, like they were going for a crap. I think they actually piss this way, as they are restricted by their longyis. But the longyi shall soon be no longer. Trousers (and shorts) are catching on big time, especially in the north with the influence of the Chinese. Longyis are not really practical in the modern world - no pockets, they get filthy and constantly have to be re-adjusted.

Wrinkled old men were riding their bikes back and forth, children playing hide-and-seek, railway staff smoking cheroots and girls cradling babies. Perhaps they were all contemplating 'The People's Desire'. But when the train pulls in, there is suddenly a rush of commotion. An army of vendors appear with bowls of bananas and oranges on their heads, baskets full of buns, cakes and nuts and clutching bundles of chrysanthemums.

When I arrived back in Mandalay, I just missed out on a share taxi to Bagan and the boat was fully booked. I think touts buy up all the tickets. But one of the ferry services (Myanmar Travel and Tours) is government-sponsored and best avoided anyway. I kept hearing the 'Westminster Chimes' and 'Auld Lang Syne' coming from hotels, shops and restaurants and it's not even the New Year. And I'm so glad I didn't hire a driver guide, as one or two people recommended. Far too expensive at US$50 a day, or US$30 if you hire them for 20 days or more. What's more they're always on your tail - one couple even had a guide escorting them round the Botanical Gardens. They drive with you, eat with you, sleep with you - it's like having a conjoined twin. Still, one man's poison.

So for me it was an eight-hour journey to Bagan by bus, taking much less time than the ferry. And it was a year since I broke my ankle in the Blue Mountains in Australia. So perhaps this book could also be called 'Backpacking With A Broken Ankle.'

CHAPTER 17

BRICKS IN BAGAN

Mingun may have been the biggest single pile of bricks in the world, but surely Bagan must hold the title for the largest number of piles. From the 11th to 13th centuries, when it was overrun by the Mongols of Kublai Khan, the building of these huge temples continued unabated. After that, the area was occupied by bandits and the warring ethnic groups - Shan, Mon and Bamar. Bagan was not populated again until the arrival of the British. An earthquake in 1975 shook the monumental structures, adding to the damage already caused by looting, war, occupation and the weather. A restoration project sponsored by UNESCO has been going on for many years.

The thousands of stupas and pahto (temples) cover an area of some 40 square km on the east bank of the Ayeyarwady River. Such a huge area can obviously not be covered on foot - a bicycle or horse and cart are the preferred options. With limited time it is also better to concentrate perhaps on Old Bagan and the immediate vicinity.

Most visitors like myself will probably stay in Nyaung U, 5 km north-east of the main archaeological site. I got a really clean en-suite room with BBC World on TV for just US$5. Pretty good value. It's a nice place to chill out at the end of a hard hot dusty day on the road. Lots of shops and restaurants with a variety of local and international food, a colourful market and souvenir-stalls at the nearby Shwezigon Paya. This beautiful bell-shaped stupa rises up on three terraces and contains four bronze standing Buddhas dating back to the 12th century, the largest in Bagan. Shwezigon is also important as a pre-Buddhist nat (guardian spirits) site - there are 37 nat figures here, and more of the Hindu God Indra. As for the Buddha himself, he resides over the garuda, naga serpent, elephant, tiger, snake, crocodile and eagle all paying their respects. The golden stupa looks absolutely spectacular when lit up at night.

Next day it was time to explore, so I was off on my bike, as Norman Tebbit used to say (remember him). As there are so many temples, I am going to be extremely selective. Starting from the south and overlooking the River Ayeyarwady, Manuha Guphaya is home to three seated, rather squashed Buddhas, one 46 feet high and two 31 feet high. There's a huge alms bowl out front and there was supposed to be a recumbent image 91 feet long next door, but I couldn't find it. Must have woken up and Buddhaed off. Further up the riverbank, Mingalazedi (Blessing Stupa) still has some glazed *jataka* tiles around the terraces, though many have been damaged or stolen. It is the westernmost monument at Bagan - ideal for the sunset viewing of Ananda and Thatbyinnyu Pahto.

In Old Bagan Gawdawpalin Pahto (Platform to which Homage is Paid), suffered bad earthquake damage, and although restored you can no longer climb to the top for those sunset pictures. What struck my eye was a poster in a nearby café for the government-owned Myanmar Airways, which has not got a good safety record. Since 1989 there have been at least eight fatal crashes. It looks like the plane's about to crash into a stupa. The caption reads *'You're safe with us.'* Mahabodhi Paya is modelled after its namesake in the Indian town of Bodhgaya, where the Buddha attained enlightenment. It has an unusual pyramidal shape and I was fascinated by watching squirrels clamber up and down the brickwork.

Just outside Old Bagan, Shwesandaw Paya has the distinction of having one of the highest accessible terraces, so you will have to share it with the hordes of package tourists at sunset. They were crawling over it like flies on a pile of dung. I made a quick escape. The hti was toppled by the 1975 earthquake and can be seen lying below. A new one has replaced it. To the north, Ananda Pahto is one of the grandest, best maintained and most venerated of Bagan temples. It is set in a beautiful courtyard full of bougainvillea and acacia trees. Built in the early 12th century, it reminded me very much of a Greek Orthodox Church with the Greek Cross structure, dark maroon and gold contrasting with whitewash. In 1990 the spires were gilded to celebrate the temple's 900th anniversary.

The base and terraces are decorated with glazed *jataka* tiles with four teak standing Buddhas, almost Christ-like, teaching the Dhamma. Even the monks' dissertations were a bit like Gregorian chanting. Staying with the church-like feel, Sulamani Pahto (Crowning Jewel) to the east has frescoes on the plasterwork and some glazed plaques. Stupas stand at the corners of each terrace. There are red Buddha images facing the four cardinal points. It was almost dark when I left and the motor-cycle vendors were making one last attempt to sell me their cloth paintings. They didn't close the deal.

Comparisons of Bagan with Angkor Wat are obvious - it's difficult to decide, but I have to say that Angkor is just that bit more unique and impressive. And it was really tough on my bunions, this barefoot lark. And how many bricks are there in Bagan - I wonder if anyone's counted.

Heading to the south-east you will see a solitary peak rising from the hot dusty plain. This is Mount Popa, the core of an extinct volcano, the Mount Olympus of Myanmar. It took about two and half hours in a pick-up to get there from Bagan. At the base of the rock is the Mahagiri Shrine, home of the 37 nats, and a major pilgrimage site. These were mannequin-like - some adult, some children - riding horses, holding fishes, sitting on tigers. There are two tigers at the entrance to the shrine. The tiger is quite an important image in Burmese nat culture - a shame they were all wiped out. Together with the elephants, rhinos and sambars that used to inhabit the dense forests here.

Nat worship pre-dates Buddhism and is still widely followed, the area around Bagan being very much its cultural centre. This animistic reverence of the natural landscape e.g. animals, trees, lakes and hills has evolved into a spiritual guardian that holds sway over places, persons and experiences. Shrines were built to placate the 'Guardian Nats', later to be called Spirit Houses which were placed just outside newly-constructed dwellings. Offerings of food, incense and flowers would be offered up daily.

These shrines are common throughout Myanmar and neighbouring Thailand - just look in the grounds of hotels and guest-houses. Larger shrines would be dedicated to important personages like the king. Animal sacrifice to appease the nat was commonplace, though the eating of pork was said to offend the spirit world. So that's why some Buddhists still eat meat, it's the influence of the nat. It is said that the Burmese love the Buddha, but fear the nat. I knew a Burmese guy living in the UK a few years ago and his girlfriend was called Nat. Now I know why.

Nat festivals or *nat pwe* consist of loud music with gongs, drums, xylophones, music and drama. The spirit medium or *nat-gadaw* (nat wife), a transvestite, becomes possessed in a trance-like state. The original trance music and dancing. Then I suddenly realised what that guy in Hintha Gon Paya in Bago was doing. For there is a nat called Big Brother Kyaw, a drunkard nat given to provocative dancing - can create quite a stir in 'conservative' Myanmar. And Big Brother - well that is appropriate. Those possessed sometimes have to be exorcised by trained Buddhist monks. In the hierarchy of things, Buddha comes at the top of the tree, followed by Hindu then Bamar nat. The greatest nat festival at Taungbyone, 20 km north of Mandalay, is a riot of drinking, dancing, wild music and spirit possession. Something to look out for.

It was another barefoot climb to the top - 777 steep steps with two sets of near vertical metal ladders. Comparisons with the knife blades at the Vegetarian Festival in Phuket could certainly be made. Perhaps a slight exaggeration. There were macaque monkeys everywhere - somebody was bitten quite badly on the hand. And you have to avoid treading in monkey poo - not very nice squeezed between your toes. At 4981 feet above sea level, Mount Popa is higher than Ben Nevis, although nowhere near as cold. Refreshing I would say, a relief from the hot sweltering plains.

There are great views back towards Bagan and the landscape is surprisingly well-forested. This is due to the fertile volcanic soils and heavy rainfall in the vicinity of the mountain. Tiny shacks snake up from below on winding paths and at the top you are surrounded by a panoply of monasteries, stupas and shrines. You will also be surrounded by pilgrims making their devotions. And woe betide you if you wear red or black, curse, criticise others, or have a ham sandwich in your lunch box as the residing nat will not be happy. I didn't see the Yeti, a hermit monk wearing a tall peaked hat - don't they live in the Himalayas?

CHAPTER 18

CANOES, CATS, CAVES, CHURCHES AND CHEROOTS

Cramped, compressed and constricted would be suitable adjectives to describe the opening of this chapter as I embarked on the twelve-hour journey to Nyaungshwe (Golden Banyan Tree) and Lake Inle, although that did include the pick-up and an hour's delay. I wrote in my notes there were only eight inches between seats, though I don't remember having a ruler with me. Whatever it was they were going for the Guinness Book of Records and I shouldn't have been surprised. I always head for the back seat for the legroom and this time I got it. Though it could be that being over the back axle was not always the most comfortable of positions, as you're bouncing all over the place.

FOREST ARE FOREVER read the roadside notice board from the Forest Department Thazi, just beyond lots of clear felling and truck-loads of teak logs. Makes you realise how many trees have been removed. And then a sign saying 'For Livestock Farming'. It will soon be a desert of scrubland, eroded soils and dust. Myanmar contains 75% of the world's teak, though one wonders for how much longer. There was also extensive mining for granite chippings used in road construction. On the way down to Lake Inle they were dynamiting the cliffside to widen the road, creating clouds of choking dust. Development continues unabated.

My first night in Nyaungshwe was spent in the 'Bright Hotel', which hardly lived up to its name. My room was dark and dingy with grime, mould and peeling paintwork. The bed was far too small, with a really thin blanket. Torn and taped lino on the floor completed the depressing picture. I rarely change hotels, but this time I had to make an exception. What a contrast to the place I had in Bagan and both hotels charged five dollars a night.

At Yadana Man Aung Paya, the oldest temple in town there were more Buddhist dioramas. THE FOUR GREAT SIGNS OF THE OLD, THE SICK, THE DEAD AND A SERENE MENDICANT MONK, MADE PRINCE SIDDHATTHA PONDER ABOUT THE UNSATISFACTORINESS IN LIFE AND RENUNCIATION. A dead guy is being pecked at by crows and a vulture and pig were looking rather hungry. PRINCE SIDDHATTHA IS LOOKING AT HIS NEW BORN SON BEFORE RENUNCIATION. His wife lying with the child at his feet and he's off. A little hypocritical I feel, but I can understand his sentiments.

The Museum of Shan Chiefs is housed in a large teak and brick mansion, the former palace of Sao Shwe Thaike, first president of Myanmar, 1948-1952. He was imprisoned when Ne Win came to power in 1962, and died in jail. The exhibits contain a very dusty display of thrones (or rather just the pedestals), tables, beds, divans, cabinets and costumes with some old photos from colonial times. I think the best was a pair of handcuffs dated 1865. Downstairs is a huge empty room with bars at the windows and a cage in the middle, just like Anthony Hopkins' incarceration in *Silence of the Lambs*. Perhaps Ne Win tortured people here.

Just south of town is the village of Nanthe with the ruins of Kyaukhpyugyi Paya and its guardian chinthe (lion/dragon deities). The 700-year-old sitting Buddha must have had a recent makeover, as the bright red lip gloss testified. There was much commotion with a passing troupe of drummers and cymbal-bashers. I think it was all to do with a monk ordination in the nearby monastery.

Lake Inle is 22 km long, approx 11 km wide and 875 metres above sea level, with hills rising on both sides. Across the lake there are some seventeen stilt villages inhabited by the Intha people, who originally migrated from Dawei in southern Myanmar. They are renowned for their one-leg rowing technique - the leg in question is wrapped round the oar. It's easier to spot fish when standing up. The area supports a huge variety of flowers, fruit and vegetables. Many of these are grown on floating islands formed of water hyacinth and marsh, and secured by bamboo poles.

It was quite cold and misty when we started off on our motorboat trip at 7am. Non-motorised canoes carrying foreigners are no longer allowed on the lake itself following a drowning incident. Everywhere was a hive of activity. People were dredging the canals outside their stilt houses with buckets (that'll take a long time) and lone fishermen were putting out their cone-shaped nets. This leg-rowing business looks very laborious, tiring and slow but it must work. Many of the boats looked overloaded as we progressed slowly through the water hyacinth - you almost feel a hippo is about to surface, but this isn't Africa.

Our first stop was the Shwe Inn Thein Pagoda at Indein with its dilapidated stupas, before heading to the lakeside market of Thaung Tho Kyaung. So many souvenir-stalls and boats. Then to the gold, silver and blacksmiths and an umbrella workshop. These umbrellas are for sun protection only and not waterproof. The paper is made from mulberry bark with patterns from the poinsettia plant. The handles and spokes are made from bamboo (another use). Silk woven longyis and Shan-style shoulder bags are produced on wooden handlooms, whilst stringing pearls and setting precious stones provides another occupation for these industrious people.

Phaung Daw U Paya is the setting for the festival of the same name, when four heavily-gilded Buddha images are ferried round the lake in the ceremonial barge, while one remains at home as guardian. The festival takes place in late September/early October, and monasteries around the lake are blessed by the arrival of the images. The Jumping Cat Monastery - Nga Phe Kyaung (or Monastery of Pouncing Pussies as I call it) sits on stilts over the lake. There are Buddha images in Shan, Tibetan, Bagan and Inwa styles enclosed in ornate wood and mosaic cases. The pussies in question are trained by the monks to leap through hoops.

The next day was a very relaxing canoe trip round the canals, with a lady rower. We first visited a cigar-maker - 600 a day were produced - must be a heavy smoker. The leaves (from the thanaq hpeq tree) which are used to wrap the tobacco are destalked and cleaned, then flattened under bags of stones. Very laborious. There was a school and pig-pens on stilts, and a nat shrine in the banyan-tree jungle opposite Nanthe, which has been left pretty much undisturbed. At another monastery I had a good chat with the resident monk, who not only had a skilful command of English, but also of world history. It was very peaceful apart from the roar of the diesel-engined boats in the distance, and I was presented with a water-lily necklace as a memento of my visit.

There are lots of good treks in the Lake Inle area. One excellent day-trek, lasting about eight hours, goes to Htut-Eain (Big Cave and Meditation Cave) and the Pa-O villages - Lwe-Kin, Nan-Nwe

(Monastery) and Kan-Daw east of Nyaungshwe. It's a big monastery for only two resident monks in such a remote place, but serves all the local villages for festivals and celebrations.

I walked with my guide up through the groves of mango, papaya, avocado and jackfruit, fields of sesame, sugar cane, peanuts and garlic. The locals were even trying to grow wheat in one field on a steep incline - but will it work. A lot of deforestation again, but some secondary growth as well. Fantastic views over the lake, canals and rice paddies could be enjoyed to the distant hills beyond. Just a little too hazy for decent pictures though. Inle, like Danau Toba in Sumatra, must be one of my favourite places.

Backtracking to Kalaw (Pine City), this former hill station at 1320 metres has very much the same atmosphere as Pyin U Lwin. Colonial architecture, churches, teashops, the railway and the train station all give the aura of the bygone era of the British Raj. Like Pyin U Lwin there is an abundance of Indian and Nepalese restaurants. The area is a centre for trekking and visiting the local hill-tribes. The pines were planted by the British, as they are not native to this area. If you want a good view of the town and the surrounding area climb up the steps to Thein Taung Paya.

Just over two kilometres to the south of town is Christ the King Catholic Church, very much linked to Father Angelo Di Meo who lived in Myanmar from 1931 until his death in 2000. He managed to stay in Myanmar despite the suspicions of the Japanese, British, and the Burmese military junta alike. The statue of Christ crucified at the altar was brought from Italy, and the picture of him rising on the clouds behind was painted by Father Angelo. At the back of the church there are more statues - St Anthony, St Teresa, Mother Mary and Joseph. Small tableaux on the side walls show the story of the crucifixion. A stone grotto next to Father Angelo's tomb is said to have curative powers. At the Baptist Church there was a Sunday school on a Friday. I don't know why. A biblical quotation read *"Blessed is he who comes in the name of the Lord." Matthew 21.9.* Is that why all Christians shout "Jesus" when they achieve orgasm?

I ended my tour of the town at Kalaw Station, the buildings in a mock-Tudor style with a waiting room and stationmaster's office. It was rather dilapidated, but must have been great in its heyday - a pity about the ugly white concrete structure over the tracks. On the way back to my hotel I passed a small fairground, which looked like something out of the Victorian age. A Burmese girl was singing cover versions of 'Candle in the Wind' and 'Yesterday Once More.' Two very sad songs, and it almost brought tears to my eyes. Suddenly and most poignantly it encapsulated the occasion, the situation in Myanmar and was definitely an emotionally defining moment.

Several villages in the local area can be visited on a day hike. I was told that overnight stays by foreigners in the longhouses had been stopped, due to them getting things like head lice from the children and bugs from the animals. I never had any problems in Thailand or Laos. I think there was a political motive at play here. On the way up the track we were met by Pa-O (Black Karen) and Palaung tribes coming down from the hills for market day. The Pa-O generally wear dark indigo costumes whilst the Palaung women are garbed in more colourful blue and red.

The traditional longhouse is about fifty metres long and houses eighty people, which seems to be mainly children. I was immediately besieged by ladies trying to sell me their wares - Shan-style bags, shawls, longyis, jewellery. It would certainly be very smoky in the evening when they're cooking food. We walked further up the hill through tea and sesame plantations to a viewpoint, where on a clear day you can see Mount Popa.

The whole area reminded me somewhat of the foothills of the Himalayas in Nepal, so it was quite appropriate that we had lunch in a Nepalese restaurant. Lentil and potato curry with heaps of chapattis. Yummy. Surrounding it was an English country garden with roses, marigolds, nasturtiums and sweet peas. Just to make me feel at home. I was chatting at length to a Sikh gentleman, who was guiding another party. His forbears had come over in colonial times and settled here. He said it would cost him US$3000 to go to India for a month, because of all the government taxes, passport and visa charges. Which would be bad enough for a Westerner, but for him totally prohibitive. Talk about rubbing salt into the wounds. He also mentioned that most people were not interested in politics anyway, and only watched international TV for the sport. We all walked back to town together through the forest and rice paddies. What a great day.

To the north of Kalaw are the fabulous Pindaya Caves, and if you want to see Buddhas in their thousands, over eight thousand in fact, this is the place to come. They're made of alabaster, teak, marble, brick and cement and laid out to form a labyrinth within the cave chambers. There are some smaller side chambers as well, accessible only on your hands and knees where people come to meditate. Notice at entrance to the caves:-

Whatever has the nature of uprising.
All that has the nature of cessation.
The giving up of all evil.
The cultivation of all good.
The cleaning of one's mind.
This is the teaching of the Buddhas.

The first Buddha is called 'Cutie-Sweetie', and there are Buddhas from the Narcotics Control Board and Suppression Bureau, Royal Thai Government and Police. And various other countries e.g. France, Germany, USA, Australia, Malaysia. Then the 'Perspiring Buddhas', though the only perspiration I saw was on the sweaty brows of German package tourists. Deeper inside the caves were the Fairy's Bathing Pool, Black Clay Hillock, Resonant Stalactite, Elephant's Mooring Post and Mythical Horses' Tethering Post. And suddenly all the tourists disappeared - were they unwilling to follow in my footsteps? Silence reigned, apart from the occasional drip of water. Wonderful.

And so I left Pindaya, with the apprehension of a pretty horrendous bus journey back to Yangon. It is therefore appropriate to let the reader know of the Causes of Ripening in Hell - including anger, cruelty, wickedness, tormenting, murdering of spiritual man, hermits and monks. Because of killing living beings by putting them into flames, boiling oil or water. Also patricide, matricide, murdering of arahats (Buddha's disciples), wounding of Buddha and destruction of bodhi tree and Buddha images.

The night-bus was Hell on wheels. Arrggh, I should have flown!!! Very little legroom, again, hardly any padding on the seat - so bad in fact that my back was bruised from constant rubbing on the metal frame. I was elbowed in the head by one guy, my feet were trodden on, a bottle of water spilled over me and finally a middle-row seat (yes, they cram those in as well) was pulled down on my leg. Get me off this bloody bus. I finally arrive battered and shaken with my nerves in tatters, sixteen hours later. Bus travel in Myanmar is not to be recommended. Will I ever learn, though I suppose it is the environmentally friendly option.

CHAPTER 19

A NE WIN SITUATION

"Virati papa, to refrain from sin; this
is the way to auspiciousness."

"All this needs to be known - Do not be frightened
whenever intimidated, Do not be bolstered whenever
flattered, Do not be softened whenever appeased."

"The New Light of Myanmar." (28/10/03)

There is a Burmese joke that George Orwell wrote three books about Burma. First, his debut novel, *Burmese Days*, which highlighted the hypocrisy and intransigence of the colonial administration in the backwoods of Katha. Second, his satirical novel *Animal Farm*, in which the animals overthrow the humans and take control of the farm, only to find that the pigs have transformed into men. The leaders of the oppressed becoming the oppressors. And third, his political masterpiece, *Nineteen Eighty-Four*, the classic Machiavellian tale of a soulless, reality-distorting dictatorship. *Burmese Days* obviously referred to the 1920s when Orwell was serving in the Indian Imperial Police Force. *Animal Farm* could be the take on Ne Win and the generals. *Nineteen Eighty-Four* must reflect the current political situation of economic mismanagement and social manipulation. The State Peace and Development Council is the perfect analogy for the Ministry of Truth. WAR IS PEACE. It is the 'People's Desire' to love Big Brother. That is the face of modern Myanmar.

The truth is out there - it may be whispered in the teashops, or in a taxi or at a market-stall. Many people I spoke to were only too willing to impart their views, albeit very cautiously or in private - guest-house owners, guides, taxi-drivers, monks, comedians! Many questioned the validity of sanctions and especially the US and British stance on tourist boycotts. The EC has a more pragmatic approach, trying to ensure the people of Myanmar suffer as little as possible, letting travellers make up their own minds. The military makes most of its money from oil, gas, gems and the illicit opium trade. The tourism boycott makes a minimal impact on them, but a huge impact on the half a million people who work in it. Fewer visitors mean fewer jobs and far less money. In fact tourism is one of the few industries you can ensure that most of the income goes direct to the people involved in it.

When Aung San Suu Kyi was rearrested in May 2003, the response by the United States was to punish the Burmese with new trade sanctions, in particular cancelling clothing contracts, putting tens of thousands of Burmese women out of work and - according to some critics of sanctions - into prostitution. I wonder how many arms contracts were cancelled. The British Government has come up with a number of reasons why tourism to Burma is 'inappropriate'. It says that Bagan was forcibly cleared of residents back in 1990, but nevertheless continued to help British companies trade with Burma.

Another argument concerns the widespread use of forced labour to construct tourist projects, but this too is a thing of the past according to the International Labour Organisation.

The most persuasive argument is Aung San Suu Kyi's call for a boycott of tourism under the government-sponsored Visit Myanmar Year in 1996 "as a demonstration of solidarity with the democratic movement in Burma." But this is not the whole story, as on several occasions she has simply said that tourists should examine their own consciences before visiting the country while the junta remains in power.

Myanmar is run very much on tribal lines, a system of medieval fiefdoms. If Suu came to power tomorrow, would she be able to hold the country together and end its tragic history of in-fighting? Or would Myanmar simply disintegrate into full-scale civil war like Yugoslavia? I discussed all these issues with a Burmese guy (now an Australian citizen) I met in Bukittinggi in Sumatra. Politics is not simple.

To explore these issues further, I found it most interesting reading *The Burmese Fairy Tale* by Ma Thanegi, a former aide to Aung San Suu Kyi. After her involvement in the pro-democracy demonstrations in 1988, she was imprisoned in Insein Prison in Yangon for nearly three years. She disagrees with Suu over her stance of discouraging foreign investment, withholding aid and imposing sanctions, as being counter-productive. It may have captured the imagination of the outside world, but did nothing for the average Burmese, just increased tensions with the government. In conclusion:- *"Put away the magic wand and think about us as a real, poor country. More isolation won't fix the problems and sanctions push us backward, not forward. We need jobs. We need to modernise. We need to be a part of the world. Don't close the door on us in the name of democracy. Surely fairy tales in the West don't end so badly."*[7]

Ne Win died in 2002, but his legacy continues. Aung San Suu Kyi is still under house arrest in her home in Yangon and the National League for Democracy seems as far away as ever from gaining power. But it was a similar situation in 1990 with Nelson Mandela, the other great freedom-fighter of the second half of the 20th century. He was released from prison in the February of that year after 27 years' incarceration, and four years later was President of South Africa. We all have our long walks to freedom, but some are more enduring than others.

I trust Ma Suu's long walk will shortly be reaching its conclusion. Never is an institution or organisation or body politic at its weakest when it seems at its most impregnable. As the collapse of the Roman and British Empires, Russian Communism and Apartheid have all testified. The collapse of the military junta in Burma is just a matter of time; all things must pass, all things are impermanent as Buddhism teaches.

UN Special Envoy Ibrahim Gambari has now met with both Aung San Suu Kyi and the junta's leader General Than Shwe. Some diplomatic pressure from China was at last forthcoming. But at the same time there has been a crackdown on demonstrators, with monasteries raided and monks beaten and imprisoned. An estimated forty people have been killed, but that is very likely a conservative figure. Myanmar, or Burma if you prefer, faces an uncertain future - let us all hope that this time there is some light at the end of a very dark tunnel. And that peace and prosperity finally prevail.

CHAPTER 20

FROM SAMET TO SAMUI

When I arrived back in Bangkok it was almost Christmas again; how I long to escape the frivolities of the festive season. I was up early as I was heading south for a few days' relaxation to Ko Chang, Ko Samet and Pattaya. Three very different locations but only a stone's throw from the city.

It's great fun people-watching on the Khao San Road; the hookers were looking bleary-eyed and sneering at each other. They kept pouting and combing their hair - perhaps they were still touting for business. The bin-men were doing their final round as the cafés and restaurants were opening up for breakfast. But I was soon to leave the busy metropolis far behind.

Ko Chang, like the beer, is big, the second largest island in Thailand after Phuket. The island has a rugged grandeur about it and is still mainly covered with rainforest. It has a wealth of wildlife including the stump-tailed macaque - saw plenty of those, civets, monitor lizards, pythons, cobras, deer and wild pig. I spent most of my time in the south and the quietest part of the island. It's great for hiking, although it's easy to get lost on the interconnecting trails in the jungle. There are also the usual activities of snorkelling, kayaking and mountain-biking. Or just rest on one of the island's beautiful beaches. Right, those were the good points. Unfortunately Ko Chang is steadily going downhill. It's being spoiled by unsympathetic beach development, with cliffs being blasted away to make room for luxury villas. I think the aim is to turn it into an expensive package destination. What finally ruined it for me was when I saw a monkey chained to a tree in the hot sun. I complained to the guest-house owner, but he didn't seem to care - maybe he will be reincarnated as a monkey.

So it was time to pack my bags and head to Ko Samet. This island is only about three hours away from Bangkok, so I was expecting the place to be quite commercialised. It is very popular with young Thais escaping from city life, and it can get very crowded during public holidays. That is what is so nice about the place; it is predominantly for the local people and not a tourist ghetto, like some places in Phuket and Ko Samui. Having said that, I did see several Westerners of the beer-belly variety on a weekend sojourn from Bangkok with their rent-a-brides. If you're into candle, or rather oil-lit dinners (with the rent-a-bride of course), it can be quite romantic, saying sweet nothings to each other at one of the beach-front restaurants as the sun goes down.

The beaches have pretty romantic names as well like Diamond Sand, Coconut Bay and not forgetting Candlelight Beach. I stayed just south of the mermaid statue on Ao Hin Khok, which was probably the most romantic of all. The mermaid in question helps a prince to escape from and defeat a lovesick female giant. So beware of any female ploy to ensnare you on this lover's island.

A popular Thai expression - "Solly no have", as in "Solly no have room, cold beer, pizza, shake" etc. etc. and finally "Solly no have woman." "No Woman, No Cry." Well it was certainly hard to find a room in Pattaya, Thailand's den of sexual iniquity - the worst of East meets West - the tackiest, seediest, most soulless place I have ever been. The ultimate creation of unrestrained market forces. And so many fat ugly men with huge beer-bellies. Yuck. I finally checked in after about twenty attempts. I didn't even want to be here - it was all for research. Pattaya is Thailand's busiest beach resort with over 12,000 rooms available in hotels, bungalows and guest-houses, and all packed to the gunnels. From November to March the town has around one million visitors, mainly from Europe, the Middle East and Russia.

It all began with the Americans back in 1959, with the Vietnam - sorry American - War kick-starting the development. Today, anything goes with a wide variety of races, colours and sexual orientations on offer. If you're really into ladyboys you'll just love the Alcazar transvestite and transgender show. *"Be entertained with music, lip-sings and dances played by many perfectly beautiful female actresses. If you are unaware of, you cannot imagine that these female actresses were actually male from origin!"* I hasten to add, I resisted the temptation.

However, it's not the sexual proclivities of Pattaya that stuck in my mind, but 'The Catch of the Day' swimming in a tank, waiting to be eaten. The whole place is a vegetarian's nightmare. Then there was this guy with an iguana stuck on his shoulder. I told him what I thought and he was none too pleased. I was feeling rather grumpy and decided to put a few things down on paper.

10 THINGS TO CAST INTO ROOM 101

1. White men with dreadlocks and goatee beards - like Fu Manchu - shave it all off and give them a Grade 0. I can almost feel myself reaching for the hedge trimmers.
2. Men who wear trousers/shorts which are 3 or 4 inches above the ankle - brand name Diesel is an example. They look absolutely ridiculous, especially with socks. Actually isn't this the kind of attire worn in psychiatric units?
3. People with pea-shooters. Or any other form of juvenile entertainment designed to annoy others.
4. Men with iguanas.
5. People who chain monkeys to trees.
6. People who keep birds in cages.
7. Restaurants who keep 'The Catch of the Day' in tanks ready to be eaten and people who frequent such restaurants.
8. McDonald's and KFC restaurants. The unacceptable face of globalisation. By the way it really cheers me up when I see people wearing 'McShit' T-shirts. "Have a McDonald's Crappy Meal. Eat Shit!!!"
9. People who eat snails, frogs' legs, dogs and tiger penises.
10. Men with big beer-bellies.

Somehow I knew that as my travels progressed, this list was going to get longer. And it's a good idea to say I'm from Scotland as it avoids all those David Beckham discussions. Who's he? Though everyone seems to know about Johnnie Walker. The best country to come from is Iceland I think.

Ko Samui is Thailand's third largest island and is part of a larger archipelago of mainly uninhabited islands. It lies just off the east coast in the Gulf of Thailand, and is one of the Kingdom's most popular tourist destinations. I suppose together with Phuket it could be considered the Ibiza of Thailand, but like that island you can still 'get away from it all'. There are over a dozen daily flights from Bangkok to Samui, or you could go by train or bus (approx ten to twelve hours, plus ferry crossing). If you want plenty of shops, bars and night life, then head to Chaweng and Lamai beaches on the eastern coast. If you want peace and quiet the northern coast beaches of Mae Nam, Bo Phut and Bang Rak (Big Buddha) are your best option. The west and south are the least developed, being furthest from the airport. To me it was only a few days' rest to recharge my batteries, but there are some items of interest other than lazing in the sun.

Water sports abound of course and diving in particular. There are some walking trails in the interior - the land rises to over 600 metres with a couple of waterfalls and splendid views. A few Buddhas of course, namely the 12-metre Big Buddha, built in 1972 near the airport. You'll see it as you come in to land. A local speciality is buffalo fighting, where water-buffalo butt one another and lock horns until one backs down. Some say it's pretty tame, certainly when compared to bull or cock-fighting, others that it can still be a bloody experience. Not for me either way. Nor hiring a motor-bike, though I did ride as a passenger a couple of times - you can't avoid it. In one incident I recall a biker was pushed off the road straight into some barbed wire. Samui has the worst traffic accident record in Thailand.

To the north-west of the island lies Ang Thong National Marine Park, containing some forty small islands with sheer limestone cliffs, white sand beaches, hidden lagoons and dense jungle vegetation. It was somewhere here that the location of the book *The Beach* was set, though the film version was located at Maya Bay on Ko Phi-Phi Leh. Day trips to the park are run from Mae Nam and Na Thon.

The neighbouring island of Ko Pha-Ngan is famous for two things: chilling out and Full Moon Parties. It's true to say there's a beach for everyone - from the biggest beach party in the world at Hat Rin to remote palm-fringed bays accessible only by boat. I did the Full Moon Party on a day trip, or rather a night trip from Ko Samui. It's not really my thing, but I had to see what all the fuss was about. There can sometimes be up to 12,000 participants at these raves, so it was going to be quite a numbing experience.

Heavy House Trance Techno blared out from competing sound systems, loads of spaced-out dudes pissing in the sea or collapsing on the beach and loads of police too checking for drugs. In the early hours of the morning the sight that greeted the revellers was a beach full of plastic litter, food containers and bottles, piles and piles of them as far as the eye could see. It should be renamed 'Bottle Beach' (there is a far better beach on the island with the same name) - what a nightmare for the refuse collectors. I stayed until 6am when the boat took me back to Ko Samui. As to the chilling, try anywhere else on the island - lying in a hammock reading *The Beach* and looking at sunsets, eating banana pancakes and drinking coconut shakes. Well, what else do you do when you chill, but it does get boring after a while.

So here's a ripping little yarn about camping and the idyllic life of the beach bum. 'It was 8pm and we were sitting by the camp fire. The flames were flickering in the soft breeze, but in the distance storm-clouds were gathering. It was rapidly getting darker and there was a tension in the air. One or two people started giggling over the most trivial of matters, but it was quite infectious and soon the whole party were laughing uncontrollably. Some people started wandering around quite aimlessly - where were they going and when were they coming back? Three of the group collapsed on the beach, just outside the bar, and started to stare vacantly at some guy chatting to a girl. They suddenly burst out into laughter and could not stop however hard they tried. Then they remembered someone saying earlier "You will never reach the bar."

'The sky was getting blacker and blacker as the moon was obscured by clouds. Back at the campsite everyone wondered what was happening. Were they the only one affected? What was the time? What was the day? What was the year? Slowly the laughter subsided, to be replaced by animated chattering. Everyone was thirsty - but for what? Were they drinking coffee, tea, water or more beer? Was it hot or was it cold? No-one knew. No-one cared.

'The wind was starting to get up. A few spots of rain hit the ground and the fire started to hiss. All around the trees rustled and many decided to head for their tents. Problem - where was the tent, let alone the zip to pull up to get inside. And if you did get inside, how would you get out again? Time stood still. Then went backwards.

'Haven't I been here before? Have I met these people before? Is this the previous evening? There doesn't appear to be any wind or rain. And the fire is much bigger. Nobody wants to talk to me - don't they like me? I think I'll head to the bar.

'The bar was only about fifty or so metres away, but it might as well have been fifty miles. It could have been hours or even days, but I made it - or almost. It seemed unusually busy, or so I thought, and who were all these strange people? I didn't know them and they certainly didn't know me. Was I becoming paranoid? I decided to make another attempt to get back into my tent.

'I lay in the tent for what could have been an eternity and then woke up - but not quite - it was like being in a dream-like trance. I felt terribly alone, as if I was the only person in the world, and struggled for ages with the zip. Sub-consciously I again headed to the bar. I heard screaming. Was someone shouting out "They're trying to kill me" or something like that? Other voices talked of snakes and drowning and everywhere was filled with the terror of persecution. Then everything went quiet - the silence of the grave. I hasten to add I did not reach the bar.

'The next thing I remember was sitting again at the campsite. Was it raining, was the fire out, or was it still glowing in the night air? And was it night anyway? Had the people around me changed or were they the same? Was this déjà vu or was it something different? Was I going insane?

'I made one final attempt to get to the bar, just to prove them all wrong. And this time I succeeded and ordered a Coke. Ha! Ha! But I still wasn't quite sure whether this was illusion or reality. As it was only 8.30pm.'

Is all that we see or seem, but a dream within a dream! Edgar Allan Poe.

The Class of '99. Lay off the pizza; no more camping for me.

CHAPTER 21

PIERCED IN PHUKET

I am going to begin this chapter with a few words on the tragic tsunami which hit the region on Boxing Day 2004. The earthquake that caused it off the Sumatran coast at Meulaboh measured 9.3 on the Richter scale and was the second most violent in recorded history. The worst affected areas in Thailand were on the western Andaman coast, namely Khao Lak, Phuket, Krabi and Phi Phi, and these are now indelibly linked to the tsunami. It was the elephants that felt it first, with their ultra-sensitive feet detecting vibrations in the earth we don't even notice.

Five hundred miles away the tectonic plate that held the Indian sub-continent plunged beneath the S E Asian plate and in a matter of eight minutes, 750 miles of fault had been ripped away. Earthquakes usually only last for seconds; this one lasted nearly ten minutes, displacing a huge body of water. This travelled across the ocean at over 100 mph, though at only a foot high, boats out to sea hardly noticed it.

In Thailand some 5400 lost their lives; two in five of them were foreigners. When the waves first hit the Thai coastline, people were mesmerised, as it was the trough that hit first, not the crest. This had the effect of sucking the water away from the land for up to two kilometres, leaving fish and boats stranded until the crest arrived in all its ferocity. There are some amazing stories of people clinging to palm trees, of a lady rushing towards the incoming wave to save her children, and divers being trapped in a sea cave waiting to be rescued.

So many people commented that it was straight out of a disaster movie, but fact turned out to be far more horrifying than fiction. Some were swept out to sea, along with the beach huts and sun loungers. One person recalled it was like being spun in a giant washer. Roads were instantly turned into rivers of debris, with people being hit by, among other things, fridges and TVs. A shark ended up in a hotel swimming-pool, with cars on hotel roofs and stuck in trees. There was a desperate scramble for higher ground - with their sixth sense the dogs and cats knew where to go.

You may well remember the story of Boon Ya Nee, just 15 months old, naked and vulnerable, separated from her mother during the tsunami, her tiny hands reaching up for help from strangers. Her picture was on the front page of the Daily Mail, Friday December 31, symbolising the plight of all tsunami survivors. Luckily she was soon reunited with her mother, but many thousands of children have now been left as orphans.

In Phuket, pictures of the missing were pinned up outside the town hall, and friends and relatives came searching for loved ones in hospitals and makeshift morgues. In the BBC documentary 'The Killer Wave', Trevor Fisher, a volunteer at Phuket International Hospital, said in an eulogy *"We also owe them a promise this day to make the rest of our lives a beautiful and noble example to all."* A quite profound and moving message. The tsunami relief effort is the biggest humanitarian operation ever mounted. And it is a continuing effort - the recovery will take many years as people rebuild their lives.

However, my story about Phuket really has little to do with the sea or the beaches or the bars and night life of Patong, but a lot to do with piercing and pain. For it is in Phuket Town that one of the most amazing spectacles in S E Asia takes place. But unlike a lot of celebrations and festivals this one is not at all touristy. The tourists all stay on the beaches. I'm talking of the Vegetarian Festival, which takes place during the first nine days of the ninth lunar month of the Chinese calendar. In 2003 this was from 25th September to 5th October.

I arrived on the bus from Bangkok on my birthday, 27th September, a most auspicious day. Not surprisingly, it was extremely busy - those motor-bikes again. Many people were dressed in white for purity, and there were vegetarian food-stalls, Chinese lanterns and banners everywhere. There is a lot of Chinese influence in Phuket - the architecture, old shop-houses, the language and of course the food.

The festival began in 1825 when a theatre troupe from China fell ill for failing to propitiate the nine emperor gods of Taoism. In penance they performed acts of self-piercing, meditation, a strict vegetarian diet and abstinence from sex. Altars are set up by shopkeepers to offer tea, incense, fruit, candles and flowers to the nine emperor gods evoked by the festival.

During the processions, those participating as mediums enter into a trance-like state and their cheeks are pierced with a bewildering array of knives, spears, poles and tree branches. Other activities include climbing knife-blade ladders and running over hot coals. It is believed the event owes much to the influence of the Hindu festival of Thaipusam held in Malaysia. In Phuket the activities are centred around five Chinese temples, the most important being Bang Neow and Jui Tui. There are similar festivals in Trang, Krabi and other southern Thai towns.

I started my 'Don't try this at home' experience with the food offering to the warriors at Bang Neow shrine, consisting of wooden barrels laden with rice, noodles and vegetables. There was lots of drumming, cymbals and fire-crackers, and a Chinese opera going on at the same time. Quite deafening. And the white T-shirts they wore had the Tesco Lotus logo. Well that was a good supermarket advertisement. There are Tescos in Thailand if you didn't know. Then to the Birth-Death Gods Propitiation at Jui Tui Temple. Loads of people lining the streets for this one. Long horns with bulbous middle pieces (more reminiscent of Nepal or Tibet) were being played and a gong and yet more fire-crackers. I didn't really see as much as I would have liked because of the crowds, but it was a great atmosphere. And the meal I had afterwards was as hot and spicy as the procession.

Right, back to Bang Neow Shrine for the Propitiation of the Seven Stars (isn't that the name of a pub?). You'll find yourself running all over Phuket with excitement as the processions progress from street to street, and the temples stage their different spectacles. There were some guys up on a podium - lots of chanting, dancing, drumming and cymbals crashing again. Then some mad axe-men started swinging axes over their heads - actually I think the axe head was made of wood and covered with sheet metal. Otherwise there could have been some nasty accidents. Also metal balls with spikes - like an instrument of torture.

The next morning, there was a street procession from Bang Neow Shrine, with some seriously spiked dudes waving black flags and everyone kneeling down in front of them and praying. Yes, they had steel rods and skewers through their cheeks with fruit attached. Sweets and fruit were thrown to onlookers. And I'm sure the fire-crackers are getting louder and louder - they drive away the evil spirits. It was all followed by a Chinese Lion Dance. And maybe those axes were for real - there were several people covered in blood and not from the piercings.

The fire running took place near the Sui Boon Tong Shrine. Even young girls were braving the hot coals, though they were sprinkled with water first. Maybe it's not as dangerous as it looks, but if you slipped over you'd be for it. Something I wouldn't do.

Another day, another street procession with a cast of thousands - more cheek piercings - a flag pole, a fishing net, a hose-pipe through three men's cheeks and a camera tripod. Bizarre. But most harrowing of all was four large hacksaw blades. Quite a few women had piercings as well. Then there was a guy licking an axe blade with his mouth full of blood. I'm certain now that the axes are for real. Frightening. On top of all this was the bathing in hot oil - towels are soaked in the stuff and then wrung out over their bodies. And it is boiling hot. By the way all this was in the pouring rain. The streets were flooded afterwards. But I still have to see the slide trombone piercing as mentioned in the Lonely Planet. Finally come the sedan chairs carrying the emperor gods and the fire-crackers go off. And that's before breakfast.

In the evening came the bladed ladder climbing at Bang Neow. 36 rungs up and 36 rungs down with a small platform at the top. The devotees wear gags (presumably to stop them biting their tongues from the pain). It was certainly mortifying to watch. My final street procession was from Yokkekeng Shrine. At least the rain eased off for me to take some photos. Piercings today included a one-inch diameter hose-pipe, an axe handle, radio antennae, palm fronds, four daggers, a rifle and best of all - a fluorescent light tube! Ouch!!!

It rained really heavily that night and there was flooding everywhere, though not uncommon this time of year. The fire engines were out in the morning to pump all the excess water into the river. I was wading about up to my knees. When the water finally subsided, the nine emperor gods were given their rapturous send-off amid a huge cacophony of fire-crackers. Really loud - I had to retreat to my hotel to escape the noise. Like a continual barrage of gunfire lighting up the streets, and the air full of acrid smoke. I was a little shell-shocked. So it was all over for another year and time for me to leave. But if you're into fire-crackers and body-piercing, Phuket is the place to come.

The influence of Western media and culture on the world is huge. I watched a quiz show on Thai TV on *Lord of the Rings* and the characters involved. They were likened to the Beatles, with John Lennon being compared to Gollum. Prizes included plastic replicas of the characters and battlefield scenes, some tickets to see the film and bottles of 'Big Chang' from the sponsors. It was worse than 'Blankety Blank' or 'The Generation Game', if you're old enough to remember them. There was also a version of 'Who Wants to Be a Millionaire.' Afterwards the 1998 film *The Avengers* was shown, starring Sean Connery, Ralph Fiennes and Uma Thurman, dubbed into Thai. Really funny.

While I was in Phuket, I did take time out to do a couple of touristy things. One was visiting James Bond Island in Phang-Nga Bay. This was where *The Man with the Golden Gun* with Roger Moore and Christopher Lee as the protagonists, was filmed. The Thais call it Ko Phing Kan - Leaning on Itself Island. The focal point is the cone-shaped rock called 'Nail Island', a limestone sea-stack eroded around its base by the action of the waves. The film was made back in 1974, but now thirty years or so on, the only action is from the coral and shell vendors - definitely bad karma. And boatloads of camera-snapping Japanese.

You can also visit some caves with thousands of roosting bats, or go out in a sea canoe to explore tunnels and lagoons. Many boats stop off in Ko Panyi, the Muslim fishing village on stilts with its green mosque and yellow onion dome. It has a superb backdrop of towering limestone cliffs, and is home to some 2,000 people, complete with shops, a market and health clinic. What I would like to ask is, when fish are caught, do they have to be swimming in the direction of Mecca? About 10 km south of Phang-Nga is Wat Tham Suwankhuha or Heaven Grotto Temple, a cave shrine full of Buddha images. There are two main caverns, the largest containing a 15-metre long reclining Buddha and a Buddha footprint - he must have been a pretty hefty dude. An elderly monk was sitting with his legs crossed, looking very much like the wax figure in the Tiger Cave in Krabi, my next port of call. And macaque monkeys were waiting eagerly for us to emerge and provide them with food. But sadly on this occasion they were out of luck.

CHAPTER 22

CLIFFS AND CAVES IN KRABI

"At first, the unusually large wave out to sea did not seem anything to worry about. But as the wave thundered closer, a few saw how it violently rocked the boats and yachts anchored offshore. Word spread quickly around Rai Leh Beach that this really was a big one. Then came the chilling realisation that this was something much more sinister - and deadly. Swimmers began frantically racing for the beach, tripping over rocks and struggling to run through wet sand. But one mother in a pale blue bikini, thinking only of her children in the surf, ran more than 200 yards straight towards the foaming wall of water. *'I had to try and save my children and nothing was going to stop me.'* Moments later, the raging monster crashed on to the beach, swamping everything in its way."[8]

Daily Mail, Friday December 31, 2004
and Monday January 3, 2005

Miraculously the mother, Karin Svärd from Sweden, and her three sons, survived.

I was on the very same beach just a few months earlier, never thinking once that such a dreadful calamity would befall this beautiful area. Always expect the unexpected I suppose. Ao Nang and its surrounding palm-fringed beaches, cliffs, caves and offshore islands are what everyone imagines a tropical paradise to be. And thankfully there was relatively little damage caused by the tsunami here. Some long-tail boats were lost, the sea-wall breached in places, and a few shops flooded. Physical repairs have been quickly put in place, with signs showing evacuation routes and warning towers with klaxons constructed. But the psychological damage may take a bit longer to heal.

Between Ao Nang and Krabi to the east lie the picture postcard beaches of Ton Sai, Rai Leh and Phra Nang, all easily reached by long-tail boats. This area is a rock-climbing Mecca - some of the best in the world, with steep pocketed walls and overhangs. I watched one young girl attempt a particularly precarious climb with a seemingly impossible overhang, but she made it one piece. I had to satisfy myself with a rather muddy and rocky path, pulling myself up by ropes attached to tree roots. Rather hard work in my Tevas, but at least there was a great view of the double bays of Rai Leh from the top.

At the bottom of the cliffs is the Princess Cave, the home of a sea princess. Offerings of carved wooden phalli are made to her, with bright red and yellow ribbons wrapped around the Phallic Princess, a large penis-shaped stalactite. Nearby is Diamond Cave, consisting of three caverns and a golden stone waterfall of sparkling quartz. This is the grand palace of the sea princess. To the north at Ao Thalen you can go kayaking amidst the mangroves and sea caves. Watch out for the crabs, macaques, mudskippers and kingfishers. And other kayakers. At nearby Than Bokkharani National Park there are some more caves, hot springs, mini waterfalls and a large turquoise pool. It reminded me of the Blue Pool in Wareham, Dorset, but no doubt a lot warmer, and it is a popular weekend playground for the locals. A magical place.

Back over towards Krabi is the legendary Wat Tham Suea or Tiger Cave Temple. The area used to be the natural habitat of tigers, but they're long gone. The abbot is Luang Por Jamnien Seelasetho, and inside the temple are portraits and a lifelike replica of him in a glass case. He is a well known teacher of vipassana (insight meditation) and metta (loving-kindness). The Tiger Cave is situated at the back of the main cave and is reached via some marble stairs. A Buddha footprint is laid out on a gilded platform.

Outside the temple is a statue of Kuan Yin, the Goddess of Mercy. There's a forest trail around the temple with dozens of monastic cells built into the cliffs and caves. Some have light-switches so you can find your way round. Huge dipterocarp trees with massive buttress roots line the way. But the best is yet to come, for there's a truly exhausting climb up 1237 extremely steep steps to the top of the 600-metre limestone peak. I was sweating buckets as it was so humid. There you will be greeted by the meditating Buddha seated on lotus petals, supported by Yaksa guardians and the naga serpent with ten heads, five at each end of its body. There's also a golden stupa and a Ganesh in the small temple there.

If you're a glutton for punishment you won't mind the further twenty-five steps to the Buddha's footprint. I had the place to myself for at least half an hour, before a group of Thais (even they were sweating) and other visitors came. There are some absolutely fabulous views over Krabi and Ao Nang, the sea in the distance and the stunning karst limestone scenery. On the walk back down some macaque monkeys were having a bit of rough and tumble, so I gave them a wide berth.

The Krabi area is also renowned for snorkelling, scuba diving and sea-borne activities of all kinds. There is a bewildering variety of tours and excursions that can be organised from the resort of Ao Nang. Probably the two most popular are the Four and Five Island trips. You'll get to see dazzling white beaches, crystal clear waters for swimming, peaceful turquoise lagoons, undisturbed mangroves, magnificent corals and bright exotic fish in every colour of the rainbow. There was some excellent snorkelling at Chicken Island - the rock formation really does look like a chicken. And Tup Island where you can walk across a sand spit at low tide. Quite a few women were walking about bare-breasted - even Thai girls. It's outrageous. But even more outrageous were men wearing Speedos.

My next destination was Phi Phi, 28 km from Ao Nang by ferry. It's actually two islands - Phi Phi Ley where *The Beach* was filmed, and Phi Phi Don, where all the tourist developments are. The latter was badly hit by the tsunami, but sterling efforts have been made at a recovery. Seventy per cent of the buildings were destroyed here and there has been some debate on how redevelopment is proceeding. Stories abound over individual land rights, government and big business corruption, and money not getting to the right people at the right time. Just like Britain really.

It is interesting to note how much better Nature has fared when compared to man's flimsy structures. Tall coco palms still swaying in the breeze amidst all the flotsam and jetsam of humanity. In the final analysis, Nature predominates and Man is cast asunder. Wasn't it the Marquis de Sade who said something like 'Nature cares not whether Man thrives or perishes.'

The town of Ton Sai, at the centre of all the devastation, is built on a bridge of land forming two beautiful bays and beaches. It is full of bars, restaurants, tour agencies and dive shops, but somehow has quite a homely, rustic feel about the place. It helps that no cars are allowed, so it's great to wander around the sandy pathways. But the stinking fish in the market and all the flies were a real shocker. Post-tsunami, the biggest change seems to be in the expansion of the resorts.

A scenic boat trip will take you first to Viking Cave, where vine and bamboo scaffolding is used to gain access to swiftlet nests high up in crevices in the rock face. The nests, made from the bird's saliva, are turned into birds' nest soup for the Chinese. A profitable, but dangerous occupation. Severe injuries and even fatalities are part of the job, and offerings of incense, tobacco and alcohol are made to appease the cave spirits. There are some prehistoric paintings of human and animal figures in the cave. And much later ones of Chinese Junks, resembling Viking longboats, from which the cave gets its name. Then it's off to the fabulous Maya Bay for some great snorkelling, although bad anchorage has caused damage to the coral reefs. Butterfly, zebra and needle fish, groupers - in a kaleidoscope of colours - a giant clam and an eel about two feet long were amongst the inhabitants. But unfortunately I saw no sharks, even at Shark Point. It must have been a great location to film *The Beach*, the story of a beach Utopia going horribly wrong. A modern version of *Lord of the Flies*.

Between three and four tonnes of rubbish had to be moved from the bay before filming commenced, putting paid to the rumour that the film company trashed the place. Unfortunately Thailand does have a litter problem. But doesn't everywhere! One benefit from the tsunami here - it actually flushed out a lot of the rubbish and built up the beach with more sand.

I was headed south to the border with Malaysia, a different culture and certainly a different religion, a country where Islam predominates. But I decided to overnight in Hat Yai first, Thailand's most southerly city. It's like a mini Bangkok, with large department stores, Chinese gold and jewellery shops, street vendors and pavement food-stalls. There are also the infamous 'Barber Shops', where Malaysian men come over the border to take advantage of the more relaxed attitude to sexual services - and cheaper rates. So if you go in for a short back and sides you might get more than you bargained for.

What most disturbed me was seeing an elephant with its mahout (keeper/trainer) walking down one of the main streets as a tourist attraction. In recent years, demand for these majestic creatures in logging, transport and other industries has dwindled, creating unemployment for their owners. So they bring them to town selling bananas and sugarcane to feed them. Elephants and the urban environment do not mix; in 1998 an elephant died in Bangkok after trapping one of its legs in a sewer culvert. Many other domesticated elephants are neglected, ill-treated or abandoned. Is their only future to be in elephant shows and performing circus tricks? There are perhaps fewer than 2000 wild elephants in Thailand today; their conservation is paramount - the Asian elephant is rightly regarded as an endangered species. But the jungle is their only true home and in the jungle they should stay.

The southern provinces of Songkhla, Pattani, Yala and Narathiwat have a strong Muslim character with an abundance of mosques - the largest in Thailand. The Yawi language (local Muslim dialect) is often spoken more than Thai. Malay restaurants serve roti, a round flat bread and dhal curries - and the music's different too, with Malay and Arabic influences. Most notable are the women in their headscarves and long dresses.

Although Muslims make up only 4% of Thailand's population, most of them are concentrated here. They complain that they feel like second-class citizens. Bombings and shootings are commonplace; with the resurgent Muslim separatist movement being blamed. Schools and police stations have been set on fire and in one gun-battle in April 2004 one hundred militants were killed in a single day. Police fired tear-gas and rocket-propelled grenades into a mosque in Pattani, and 78 men died of suffocation whilst in army trucks. There is also widespread police corruption, protection rackets, drug-running and general lawlessness. Local Buddhists say that support from Bangkok is not forthcoming and so are arming themselves. The area seems to have become Thailand's 'Wild West' or rather 'Wild South', and the fatalities have topped 2700 over the last four years. I suppose every country has its internal tensions. Indeed my next destination Malaysia has a wealth of such issues, and I was already at the border.

STREET VENDOR, KYAIKTIYO, MYANMAR, NOV 2003

COOKING IN KALAW, MYANMAR, NOV 2003

MUSLIM FISHING VILLAGE, PHANG-
NGA, THAILAND, AUG 2003

DHAMMIKARAMA BURMESE BUDDHIST TEMPLE,
GEORGETOWN, PENANG, MALAYSIA, AUG 2003

SNAKE TEMPLE, PENANG, MALAYSIA, AUG 2003

UNCLE TAN'S JUNGLE CAMP, KINABATANGAN,
SABAH, MALAYSIA, APR 2002

SARAWAK LADIES, KUCHING, MALAYSIA, MAY 2002

MINANGKABAU WEDDING, BUKITTINGGI,
SUMATRA, INDONESIA, AUG 2003

CHILDREN, TUK TUK, SAMOSIR, DANAU
TOBA, SUMATRA, INDONESIA, JULY 2003

BOROBUDUR, JAVA, INDONESIA, JULY 2002

CHAPTER 23

PENANG, PEARL OF THE ORIENT

The country of Malaysia is in three parts - peninsula Malaysia bordering Thailand, and the states of Sabah and Sarawak forming the northern part of the island of Borneo. In some ways it's a microcosm of S E Asia, but without the hassle. Travelling is easy and most parts of the country are easily accessible. It has a wealth of natural beauty from the heights of Kinabalu to the jungles of Taman Negara, coral reefs and white sandy beaches and an amazing variety of wildlife - the famed orang-utans, proboscis monkeys, tigers, elephants, monitor lizards, hornbills, green and leatherback turtles. There's an extensive network of national parks to help preserve all this beauty. Of course like every other country in the world there's intense pressure on the environment; forest clearance for the planting of oil palms and dam-building are just two of the damaging human activities.

With a population of just over 22 million, with 85% living on the peninsula, there seems plenty of space for everyone. The legacy of colonialism means there is an interesting cultural and racial mix. Islam, Buddhism, Hinduism and Christianity are all in the melting pot. The

Chinese and Indians are mainly found in the urban areas of Penang, Kuala Lumpur and Melaka, with a sprinkling of Chinese throughout Borneo. Native peoples, known as Orang Asli, are found in the jungle areas of the interior of all three states. The Malays, at about 57% of the total population, are pretty much evenly distributed, though it is on the eastern side of the peninsula that their culture is most distinct.

There is a certain amount of political, economic and religious rivalry within this disparate group, but it is the Malays who hold the reins of power. Malaysia also combines the old and the new - from godowns (river warehouses), mosques and ancient temples to the Petronas Towers of KL, the tallest buildings in the world. It is reckoned that the country will reach 'developed status' by the year 2020 in its mad rush to catch up with the West. The motto of the tourist board is 'Malaysia, Truly Asia' and this more or less sums it up.

I started my journey in Penang where this concept was going to be well and truly tested. Penang is an island off the west coast of peninsula Malaysia, and was the oldest of the British Straits Settlements. Georgetown, its capital, is a sprawling, mainly Chinese city with a wealth of temples, mansions, and shop-houses, but also lots of colonial architecture. There have been some modern developments on the outskirts of town and at the Komtar shopping complex, but by and large it retains an authentic oriental character all but gone elsewhere.

A good place to get an overall perspective is in the excellent museum, highlighting the multi-cultural nature of the island *"They came to Penang from all over the world."* The Indian Festival of Thaipusam is well represented with offerings of coconuts, milk and honey to Lord Subramaniam, his jewel-encrusted image borne on a silver chariot drawn by oxen. Devotees were piercing their tongues and cheeks with spears, barbed hooks and skewers. There was an opium pipe made of bamboo with a jade mouthpiece and an accompanying amber bowl.

The smoker would then lie down on his opium bed, elaborately carved with mother-of-pearl inlay, and 'chase the dragon'. Opium was not banned in Malaysia until the 1940s.

A Baba Nonya (Malay/Chinese intermarriage) Wedding Ceremony was underway with tea-drinking and hair-combing, complete with bridal chamber and wedding bed. Those brides again!!! There was a lot on the spice trade and the Jinrikisha, a two-wheeled man-pulled passenger-carrying vehicle eventually replaced by the trishaw. The Chinese festival of Chingay was shown, where a guy was balancing a forty-foot flagpole in his groin. I bet that hurt. A collection of landscape paintings of old Penang, some costumes and the keris, the asymmetrical Malay dagger, can also be seen. Perhaps this was used in circumcision ceremonies. Even more hurtful.

St George's Church next to the museum is the oldest Anglican church in S E Asia and dates back to 1818. I had a great conversation with a lady here about religion, politics and culture - these subjects were going to crop up quite a lot in Malaysia. She was well-travelled and what I remember most was her saying how quiet England was, in particular Oxfordshire, in comparison to Penang. No peaceful country lanes here, but are there any left in England. And she didn't try to convert me. But I didn't get to find out what was so bad about yoga, from a Christian perspective.

Over the way is Fort Cornwallis, one of the oldest buildings here, built between 1808 and 1810. This was the military and administrative base for the East India Company and its whitewashed battlements are surmounted by an array of cannons. One of them, Seri Rambi, dates back to 1603 and is regarded as a fertility symbol, with childless women placing flowers in its barrel. The fort is adjoined by a *padang* (open playing-field) with a vista of neoclassical colonial buildings, such as the City Hall. Just opposite in the middle of the roundabout is the Victoria

Memorial Clock Tower, a dazzling white tower topped by a Moorish dome. It was built to honour the Queen's Diamond Jubilee in 1897. It is 60 feet high, each foot representing a year of her reign.

In the Little India enclave the elaborately sculptured and painted Sri Mariamman is Penang's oldest Hindu temple, built in 1883. It is the starting point for the festival of Thaipusam. Kapitan Keling Mosque was built in 1801 by Indian Muslim settlers brought over by the East India Company. It has a single minaret and is crowned with yellow domes; unfortunately I couldn't go in as it was closed for renovations at the time of my visit.

At Kuan Yin Teng, the Goddess of Mercy Temple, there were some more fertility rites with the offering of food, flowers and oil and the burning of incense. It must have been her birthday, as in the evening there was a performance of Chinese opera. I'm not sure what the opera was all about, but Chinese dramas have a moral dimension - dark and light, Yin and Yang with a happy ending. Four themes of grief, joy, separation and union. The actors/singers were garbed in colourful and elaborate costumes with gold and silver headdresses. The music was provided by drums and various percussion instruments, a long thin three-string guitar and circular moon guitar.

I went backstage to see the actors and musicians. It was hot, smoky with two huge braziers and incense being burned. But most interesting of all was the chat I had with two Chinese guys afterwards. The usual West versus East stuff and how shitty the Malays are, but also astrology, Buddhism and religion in general, free-thinking, did man only originate in Africa and yes also vegetarianism and animal welfare. One of the guys wanted to set up a company dealing with animal welfare issues.

We got onto the 'Bumiputra' (Sons of the Soil) policies of the Malaysian Government and principally Dr Mahathir Mohamad, the Prime Minister who in 2003 was stepping down after 22 years in office.

In essence 'Bumiputra' means giving jobs, shares, loans, government contracts etc. to the Malays over the Chinese and Indians, purely because the latter groups are more economically successful. A catching-up exercise, so to speak. It smacks of racism whatever way you look at it.

While we are on the subject of racism (what with the Big Brother row in 2007), I too was accused of being a racist - by a rather irate young lady traveller. I made a seemingly innocuous, jocular remark over a couple of dirty Chinese hotels with bed bugs and unfriendly proprietors. I wasn't attacking the whole Chinese race - far from it, these guys were very much exceptions to the rule. The Chinese virtually run S E Asia - without them I think the entire economy and infrastructure of the region would collapse. But it was interesting how racist viewpoints can develop through misunderstandings.

The debate went onto issues like the Tiananmen Square massacre, the killing rooms and general human rights abuses in Communist China, but that was nothing to do with racism. However the lady concerned was adamant I was a racist and the discussion, or rather argument, ended in stalemate. Up your Bumiputra I say. (As a footnote to this, if I were to be considered racist it would be against white people - they cause me the most grief.)

The best Chinese temple in Georgetown is Khoo Kongsi, an extremely ornate temple/clan-house built in 1906, which has been recently restored. The Khoos were wealthy Straits Chinese of the Dragon Mountain Hall clan from Hokkien province. I met Benny Khoo, a trustee, and he explained some of the temple's features. Firstly, the difference between male and female lion guardians - the male has the money, the female the cubs. Well that's appropriate. Then the nine old men 'to observe the two spheres regulating Yin and Yang between

Heaven and Earth, to play a game of chess reflecting on the strategies of the past and the present.' Not quite sure what that meant.

Benny asked me to give a talk to a group of 16-year-old English language students about the UK, differences between East and West, lifestyles and culture. So I rambled on about my travels, environmental concerns…politics, with the condemnation of Bush and Blair and their crusade in Iraq. (Don't get me started, but we're not all Bush's poodles). And what an attentive, well-behaved bunch they were. Would put UK kids to shame. No Grange Hill or Waterloo Road antics here. The going rate for teaching English in Malaysia is a damn sight more than the minimum wage in Britain, and just look at how low the outgoings are. Much better than slaving away in our sweat shop low-wage economy. So what is everyone waiting for - Malaysia needs you - for a few months anyway. Actually I read on the web recently about one woman funding all her world travels by teaching English in exotic lands.

The Cheong Fatt Tze Mansion or La Maison Bleu, from the indigo paint used on the walls, was the creation of the rags-to-riches Hakka entrepreneur of the same name. He came to S E Asia at the age of 16 and during his life had eight wives with numerous concubines. Such was his aura and fame that when he died in 1916; flags were flown at half-mast throughout Dutch and British colonies.

The Mansion was one of five - the others being in Medan (Sumatra) and China (still standing), Singapore and Hong Kong (destroyed). It has 38 rooms, five courtyards, seven staircases and 220 windows. It combines cast-ironwork and tiling from the West – Glasgow and Stoke-On-Trent, with Venetian Shutters, Shanghai woodwork and Chinese ceramics and decorations in an Art Nouveau style. The dilapidated mansion was acquired in 1990 and has slowly been restored to its original glory. It was the winner of a UNESCO conservation award in 2000. And you can stay there for about £50 a room per night.

Just off the road to Batu Ferringhi, Penang's beach resort, are two Buddhist temples opposite each other. The Dhammikarama Burmese Buddhist Temple is Penang's oldest, founded in 1803. There are scenes of the Buddha subduing the fierce, drunken elephant, Nalagiri, released by the wicked Devadatta. And a diorama of the Epic Renunciation with Prince Siddharta riding his stallion Kan Thaka. Statues of the naga, the mythical five-headed dragon and garuda, king of the birds are particularly striking. At the Thai Buddhist Temple, Wat Chayamangkalaram - what a mouthful, there's a 33-metre-long gold-plated reclining Buddha, and within the structure pigeon-holes with urns containing ashes of devotees. Also some International Meditating Buddhas from surrounding countries e.g. Thailand, Myanmar and India. The Burmese temple was much more ornate and interesting though.

Georgetown is as colourful and vibrant by night as it is by day. There's a wide range of bars, some with live entertainment, cafés, coffee houses, Indian, Chinese, Malay, Thai and Western-style restaurants, night markets, numerous street hawkers - you can even catch up on the latest Bollywood movie. And when everything starts closing down the hookers and ladyboys come out, especially in the Love Lane area - the centre for backpackers. And some are really brazen. "Hi Honey" is the usual retort in a rasping husky voice.

One place I really liked was the Hong Kong Bar. It had guest-books going back to 1955 with plaques from the Army and Air Force on the wall. There was hardly anybody in there - just two guys playing cards (one with a handlebar moustache - a throwback to the old colonial days - Chocks Away!) and that was about it. Actually I had a word with the gentleman concerned. He had lived in Malaysia since the 1960s - had to keep renewing his visa and he quite vividly recalled the Chinese/Malay riots of the time, when hundreds of Chinese were killed. There was a map of the world with New Zealand blown out of all proportion, showing all its positive points and other countries as negatives. Best of everything in the world, the most modest people and Australia described as an uncharted desert island off NZ, populated by a backward tribe known as STRINES.

To the west of Georgetown are the Botanical Gardens and Arboreta, a fascinating array of trees, palms, bamboos, ferns, orchids and other herbaceous plants. Apart from the lush tropical growth, the gardens boasted huge colourful butterflies, red dragonflies and ants over an inch long. Also squirrels, a monitor lizard emerging from a lily pond and a grey and red striped lizard. Then hordes of long-tailed macaques made their appearance, grooming themselves one minute and fighting the next. I walked to a nearby waterfall where there was an image of Ganesh (the Hindu elephant god) in what appeared to be a Muslim shrine. Was this a sign of religious tolerance?

I continued my journey up to the top of Penang Hill. It was so bloody hot, and then it poured down, one of those sudden tropical cloudbursts that appear from nowhere. And I was drenched; so much so I decided to replace my dripping wet T-shirt with a new one. That doesn't happen very often. I was tempted to buy one which read 'I have an occupational disease - I'm sick of work.' Can anyone out there relate to that? The hill is 830 metres above Georgetown and you get an amazing view over the city as well as to Penang Bridge, the longest in S E Asia. I took the funicular railway back down. This was built in 1923 by a Swiss company in two sections and is an incredible feat of engineering.

Just to the south on a hilltop at Ayer Itam is Kek Lok Si, the largest Buddhist temple in Malaysia, and Ban Po Thar, the Ten Thousand Buddhas Pagoda. It was constructed in the late 19th and early 20th centuries and is reached via a covered walkway with souvenir-stalls and a turtle pond. As I entered, a yellow-bellied hummingbird came flying past, which is a sign of good luck. Its nest was built just above a Chinese lantern. And they were playing that latest Buddhist hit 'Om Mani Padme Hum'. I bought one of the CDs so that when I play it, memories of my trip come flooding back.

There were lots of fat smiling Chinese Buddhas with lighted pink candles arranged in the shape of the lotus flower. And the original meaning of the swastika was explained. In ancient India it was a symbol of auspiciousness, purity and perfection, and was not tilted. The symbol was also used in Greece and Persia. In the large hall there were three gold meditating Buddhas and hundreds more in cavities around the walls. Ceiling decorations in bas-relief depicted scenes from the life of the Buddha. Both male and female monks were serenely chanting. I climbed to the top of the seven-tier wedding cake pagoda for a great view. It is said to be Burmese in style at the top, Thai in the middle and Chinese at the bottom.

Behind the pagoda, a massive bronze statue of Kuan Yin, Goddess of Mercy, the female form of Buddha had just been erected. It was cast by the China Aerospace System Engineering Corp Shanghai Qunli during 1998-99. Standing on a bed of lotuses the statue is over 30 metres tall and fronted by two elephants, two dragons and two Chinese warriors. The logistics of getting it there must have been enormous; the Chinese certainly have plenty of ingenuity - and money. I went up to it by the incline lift, like a cable-car - must be getting old.

Probably the only thing worth visiting in the south of the island is the Snake Temple, dedicated to the Buddhist priest and healer, Chor Soo Kong. It is named after the pit-vipers and green tree-snakes which appeared in the vicinity after the completion of the temple in 1850. These coil round pillars and beams and are said to be rendered harmless by the burning of incense. There are two stone lions guarding the temple, with doors brightly painted with warrior gods. A black statue of Chor Soo Kong was draped in red and yellow robes. Unfortunately the custodians of the temple were really persistent in asking for money, even after I'd made my donation, which made me feel just a little uncomfortable.

It is generally recognised that if you want a beer in Malaysia, you head to a Chinese bar. Even in the Muslim-dominated states on the east coast, you'll usually track one down somewhere. The Chinese are great traders, stall-holders and shop-owners and they'll generally find what you're looking for. For some reason many Chinese men love Guinness, so that particular product is quite easily available.

And in every Chinese bar you'll see Guinness posters with the semi-naked female form being used to sell beer. They read something like this *'Rank the Guinness Beauties. Round 1 - Enticing Elegance, Round 2 - Alluring Adventure. Win a Mitsubishi Storm.'* If somebody was to say to me what encapsulates Malaysian culture, I would say something like "A Chinese bar with the aforementioned posters; the proprietor with a beer in one hand, a leg of pork in the other and clad only in shorts and sandals. And just opposite this bar a mosque with imams calling the faithful to prayer and the women most definitely not in a state of undress."

CHAPTER 24

A CAMERON HIGHLANDER

The Cameron Highlands are situated in the central part of the peninsula in the state of Pahang. They lie at an elevation that ranges from 1300 metres up to the highest point, Gunung Brinchang, at 2032 metres. This provides for a very temperate climate of between 10 and 21°C, in which vegetables, fruit and flowers are widely grown; but it is the tea plantations for which the area is renowned. The Highlands get their name from a William Cameron, a surveyor who mapped the area in 1885. A hill station was soon established, encouraging wealthy colonists and farmers to set up businesses here and escape the oppressive heat of the lowlands.

The area still has a British colonial feel to it, with mock-Tudor style houses, red telephone boxes, golf courses, tea shops, rose gardens and plant nurseries selling a whole range of garden accessories. Unfortunately there's a major development boom going on, with new apartment blocks and a reservoir being constructed. Forests have been cleared, hills levelled and streams diverted to make way for farmland. Landslips and flooding are frequent in the heavy rains. A new road is being built to link up more easily with the coastal highway and the future is looking pretty bleak. So make the most of it while you can.

The Highlands are famous as being the final resting place of Jim Thompson, the American silk magnate. He went missing in March 1967 while trekking here and has never been seen since. Many theories abound as to his disappearance - was he kidnapped or was it suicide, maybe killed by a tiger or knocked down by a truck driver. But I think he was spirited away by aliens. I certainly never saw him. When you're out on one of the many jungle trails just keep your eyes open. These trails surround the major towns of Tanah Rata and Brinchang and most can be walked in just a few hours.

My base was in Tanah Rata, where most of the backpacker accommodation is, and where you can find great Indian food. Most of the Indian population here are descendants of the first tea-pickers. My first outing was to the Bharat Tea Estate via, I believe, bits of trails 6 and 10 (the trails are all numbered). It didn't compare to Thailand or Laos, but there were certainly some strenuous and tricky sections. I was accompanied by Hans, a German guy aged 65, who really put me to shame as he was so fit. Though for a rumble in the jungle it does help being short and stocky - I kept hitting my head on overhanging branches. We met again on Kinabalu - he was climbing up and I was coming back down.

For most of the day it was pretty cool with low cloud, but when the tropical sun does come out, the temperature jumps by several degrees in minutes. We had a relaxing break for tea and scones - how very English, with a grand view of the tea terraces. But if you were expecting tea-pickers toiling away in saris forget it - that's the past. Tea-picking in Malaysia is now all mechanised.

My second 'rumble in the jungle' was a walk from Tanah Rata to Brinchang via trail 4 to the Parit Falls, then by road and trail 1 up to Gunung Brinchang. I went past Ye Olde Smokehouse Hotel in the traditional mock-Tudor Style (the place serves up traditional Western food and cream teas) and an old red telephone box. Then to an Anglican Church called 'All Souls', where they were half way through a service. And there was an old pillory. I wonder when it was last used. Almost the stereotypical English village. Further on, the golf course reminded me of the one at Crask of Aigas near Inverness. In fact the Cameron Highlands are quite similar to the Scottish Highlands in some ways, though there are more trees. And then there's the rain. It had started drizzling.

Anyway I was now on Trail 1, trekking and scrambling up to the highest point in the Highlands. I met a metre-long green lizard on the way, devouring an insect. That was about the only wildlife I encountered - certainly no tigers, they had all disappeared with Jim Thompson. At the top is a transmitter tower you can climb with a great view if the mist allows. A few people were milling around and one Indian guy I spoke to was complaining at how the 'Malay' government had allowed all the forest clearance. Environmental issues in Malaysia are certainly on the agenda. On the way down I got drenched and almost lost my footing on slippery boulders and tree roots - the path was now more like a raging torrent than a trail. Getting more like Scotland by the minute. (While I was writing up this book at my home near Inverness it always seemed to be raining.) The Scottish Highlands are spectacular in the sunshine, but when the hills are cloaked in mist and the all-pervading gloom descends it can be quite miserable.

Back in Tanah Rata, a lady in one of the cafés gave me a book to look at called *The Blue Day Book* by Bradley Trevor Greive. A lesson in cheering yourself up. *'Everybody has Blue Days. Oh what to do, what to do? Who knows what fantastic things are in store just round the corner? Get out there and go for it! Live every day as if it were your last, because one day it will be!'* Yes, that's my motto. And there were some wonderful pictures of animals in the book with a grinning frog at the end. I thoroughly recommend it.

CHAPTER 25

OM AMRITESWARIYAI NAMAH
(SALUTATIONS TO THE IMMORTAL GODDESS)

Kuala Lumpur is very much a blend of old and new, with the modern and hi-tech on the ascendance. The name in English means 'Muddy Confluence' as the city sits on the meeting points of the Klang and Gombak rivers. It started life in 1857 as a tin-mining town, became a colonial capital and look at it now - all glass, steel and concrete. But it still has an abundance of colonial buildings and lots of museums, galleries, parks, gardens and historical sites. There is an astonishing variety of things to see and do, but unfortunately KL, as it is affectionately called, is horrendously busy. Six-lane roads and flyovers chop up the city, making it a nightmare for pedestrians.

It is difficult to know where to start a tour of the city, but why not at the cricket ground, its colonial heart. It was here in August 1957 that the Union Jack was lowered for the last time and independence declared. On 1st January 1990 Padang Kelab Selangor (the cricket ground) was proclaimed 'Merdeka Square' (Freedom Square) by P M

Dr Mahathir Mohamad. A one-hundred-metre free-standing flagpole was erected, the highest in the world. And at the Royal Selangor Club it was members only, so things haven't changed much. It's just not cricket!

Surrounding Merdeka Square are the splendid colonial structures of the Supreme Court (Sultan Abdul Samad Building), a strange mix of Victorian kitsch and Moorish domes, the Old City Hall, the National History Museum and Memorial Library. To the south is an extravaganza of Moorish spires, minarets, towers, cupolas and arches. It is actually the train station, built in 1911 by British architect A B Hubbock and paying attention to local tastes.

The two main mosques are Masjid Negara and Jamek. The former or 'National Mosque' is one of S E Asia's largest, with a 73-metre high minaret, surrounded by a pool. The main dome consists of an 18-pointed star - 13 for the Malaysian states and then the five pillars of Islam. There are 48 smaller domes covering the courtyard. To me it looked like a launch pad for the next space mission and I think the minaret is about to take off. Or it could be compared to a crumpled umbrella. Which would be useless in all these tropical rainstorms. It was bucketing down when I was there. Tasteless 'sixties architecture. Masjid Jamek was a bit more to my liking; an early 20th century creation in pink and cream on the Indian Moghul model, delightfully located in a grove of palm trees. And I noted that there's been a few Mormons about recently - aren't they risking it a bit?

The National Museum is a modern building on the edge of the Lake Gardens - its predecessor was destroyed in World War II. It's hellish to get to the museum on foot (even from the nearby Central Station), forcing most people to take a taxi. But not me - I managed to brave the traffic. Its main exhibits are to do with culture - shadow plays (Wayang Kulit), traditional dancing, Indian and Malay weddings, another

Chinese bridal chamber, various costumes and a Royal Circumcision Ceremony, last performed in 1933. They must have nipped off to get that keris from Penang.

In 'Faces of Malaysia' there was something on the original inhabitants, the Orang Asli and the longhouses in Sabah and Sarawak. More on the Indian community and Thaipusam - Batu Caves in particular, the Chinese Lion dance, fortune-telling, kites, fishermen and the Malay house. An interesting item was a giant drum 'Rebana Ubi' - 1 metre high, 70cm in diameter, which was used in the Commonwealth Games opening ceremony.

I didn't see any 'Amok Catcher', which I believed was described in the Lonely Planet at one time, so was a little disappointed. Maybe so many people were running amok during the Merdeka celebrations, the authorities were out catching them with it. But I did see what I think was a similar device in 'Tortura' later on in an exhibition in Melaka. A long wooden pole with a circular metal brace (spikes on the inside) at the end, for the person's head with two V-shaped appendages. Nasty.

But enough of the past, it is time to come up to date with Malaysia's more recent architectural achievements. During the boom years of the 'nineties when the Malaysian 'Tiger Economy' was in full flow, tall buildings shot up almost overnight. Foremost among these were the Petronas Towers, at 452 metres high the tallest buildings in the world, when I visited anyway. Generally I am not a lover of modern architecture, but these are a majestic sight, the design based on the eight-sided star found in Islamic art. The five tiers to the building represent the five pillars of Islam and are topped with masts that resemble minarets. They have come to symbolise modern Malaysia.

Unfortunately you can't get higher than 146 metres, at the skybridge that joins them on the 41st floor. So as an excellent alternative I went to the KL Tower, at 421 metres the world's 4th highest, making the BT

Tower at 189 metres look puny by comparison. It has the advantage of being situated on a 90-metre hill, and with the observation deck at 276 metres, gives an amazing view of KL, including the Petronas Towers. Would be great for a bungee jump. The tower was opened in July 1996 and the authorities were at great pains to explain that its position was shifted to accommodate a 100-year-old Jelutong tree. The tower is lit up for the various celebrations - red for the Chinese New Year, purple for the Hindu festival of lights (Deepavali) and green for Ramadan. Other modern buildings include the Tabung Haji shaped like a drum, the Telekom Malaysia Tower like a bamboo shoot, and the Maybank resembling the scabbard of the keris. Out with the old and in with the new seems to be the order of the day.

A vision of the future can be seen at Putrajaya, the nation's sparkling new administrative centre to the south of KL towards the international airport. Contained within landscaped parks, gardens, lakes and a wetland area, the complex purports to be a city of the 21st century, a showpiece of Malaysian engineering and architecture. There is the Perdana Putra (Prime Minister's Office) with its blue domes, the Putra Mosque in pink and the Putra Bridge, copied from Isfahan in Iran. Though if Malaysia is truly multicultural, where are the Chinese and Indian monuments? Critics of the project say that it has sucked up billions of dollars that could have been spent on schools and hospitals.

Just 15 km north of Kuala Lumpur are the famed Batu Caves, a Hindu shrine to the elephant god Ganesh. The main cave (Gua Kecil) is 100 metres high and reached by a steep flight of 272 steps. Monkeys can be found clinging to statues, rocky outcrops and overhanging branches, waiting for temple food offerings or somebody's packed lunch. They also go after such items as cameras, handbags, sunglasses and wallets. The monkey I saw was a wallet-snatcher, which he proceeded to take up into a nearby tree and rip to shreds. But all the money drifted down to the people waiting below as the monkey was distracted by a bag of peanuts - more useful to a monkey than cash. What was that about getting monkeys if you only pay peanuts? Another interesting diversion was watching a cockroach being devoured by ants.

Once inside the cave there are statues of Shiva, Rama, Murugan and Ganesh, and an excellent audio presentation is available. The caves are partly illuminated by spotlights, but sunlight streams through a hole in the roof giving very much a cathedral-like atmosphere. At the base of the steps another cave (Gua Galeri) contains more colourful Hindu sculptures and dioramas - Shiva, Durga, Krishna, Rama and Hanuman, the monkey god. There was even one called Thatchnu - must have been a pretty evil god. And of course the beloved Ganesh.

The caves have been a Hindu shrine since 1892 and are the setting for the legendary 'Thaipusam' festival in January/February. Lord Subramaniam and his chariot make their way from the Sri Mahamariamman Temple in KL's Chinatown amidst a crowd of a million devotees. The festival lasts three days and is particularly noted for the *kavadi* carriers, wire frames piercing the flesh and decorated with flowers, pictures and peacock feathers. Tongues and cheeks are pierced with hooks, spears and tridents.

As in the Vegetarian Festival in Phuket, the preparations include a vegetarian diet and abstinence from sex. However, with so many followers it would be extremely difficult getting anywhere near the action. Arriving at dawn is the best option and I'm not an early riser. I was there at the wrong time of year anyway. But I did celebrate with a banana leaf vegetarian meal. Very nice it was too.

On the 27th of March I received darshan (blessing) from Amma (Mata Amritanandamayi), a holy woman from Kerala in India who was touring Malaysia. She is affectionately known as 'The Queen of Hugs'. Amma has spent most of her life travelling the world offering her message of love and compassion. And bestowing an estimated 30 million hugs and blessings. She has also created a vast network of charities for the poor. You may have seen a Louis Theroux TV programme about her. The experience was very moving and emotional, and I was quite touched. I think I was the only Westerner there, apart from the helpers, amongst thousands. The 27th is quite an auspicious day for me. I was born on the 27th, so was Amma - she is exactly one year older than me. I left the UK on the 27th and now the blessing.

And when I went to the KL Tower the lift girl remembered me - it's amazing how people's faces lit up when I mentioned Amma. You can go to Amma's website for more information - it's very good. A couple of interesting sayings - *"You cannot change the direction of the wind. But you can change the way you set the sails."* And, *"Anger is like a knife that is sharp at both ends - it injures both the victim and the assailant."* And something I saw written in the Reggae Bar in KL. *"Yesterday is History. Tomorrow is Mystery. Today is a Gift. That's why they call it the Present."*

On the way back to my hotel, minus my sandals which got lost in the mêlée, the Hindu taxi-driver was complaining about the state of the nation. He wanted the British to come back. Didn't Gandhi say something like that? But I shall leave the final words to Amma *"Children, I need nothing from you except your burden of sorrows. Mother is here to shoulder it."*

CHAPTER 26

MERDEKA MELAKA

Melaka, more popularly known as Malacca, has had the distinction of trading with or being colonised by just about every nation on earth. That might be a slight exaggeration, but in its long and turbulent history it has had trading agreements with China, India, Siam (Thailand) and Indonesia, been colonised by the Portuguese, Dutch and British, occupied by the Japanese and finally another, albeit brief return by the British.

Melaka's history dates back to the 14th century when a Hindu prince called Parameswara arrived from Sumatra. Its favoured location on the Straits, half way between India and China attracted merchants from all over the east, namely Admiral Cheng Ho, the 'three-jewelled eunuch prince'. He was bearing gifts from the Ming Emperor and the promise of protection from Siamese raiders. But without his own three treasures I hasten to add. More about him in 'Singapore Sling'.

Chinese settlers soon followed in his wake and are now known as Baba Nonya or Straits Chinese. In the 15th century, with the arrival of traders from India, Melaka converted to Islam. The following century saw invasion by the Portuguese, enticed by the wealth of the spice and other eastern trades. They fortified the city against attacks from neighbouring states and also a fresh assault from Sumatra. To the south the power of the Dutch colony of Indonesia was growing, and in 1641 the Dutch took over and constructed many fine public buildings and churches. In 1824 the Dutch swapped Melaka for British held Bencoolen (called Bengkulu today) in Sumatra. It then became part of the Straits Settlements, along with Penang and Singapore, but took very much a back seat to its more prosperous rivals.

During the Second World War, the whole of Malaya and Singapore was in Japanese hands and most of the British were POWs. With Japanese surrender in 1945, the struggle for independence led to a communist insurgency, and in 1948 a State of Emergency was called. This was not lifted until 1960, but sporadic fighting continued until a formal surrender was declared in 1989.

Melaka is a very compact city despite a lot of modern development, and is very easy to explore on foot or trishaw (bicycle rickshaw). These can be seen touting for business in the environs of 'Red' or 'Dutch Square'. They are bedecked with flowers (usually plastic, but sometimes silk) and sound systems blare out such greats as 'Hotel California'. But Hindi music is also popular. The square is dominated by the Stadthuys (Municipal Town Hall). This was built in the 1650s and painted brick-red in the traditional Dutch style.

There's a lot inside about colonial struggles, obviously always showing the Malays as victors. Still they were eventually, after 500 years. And then the political movement for independence with all the main characters gawping down at you. Cheng Ho makes an appearance with a small replica of his statue - the original is in Kunyang in China. And a book: *1421 - the year China discovered the world*. Well, that puts a different perspective on things. It is reported that the Chinese made contact with Australian Aborigines and kept kangaroos in zoos.

Opposite is Christ Church, again in red - built in 1753 and taking 12 years to complete. No expense was spared - a whole tree used for each ceiling beam, with elaborately carved pews and a frieze of the Last Supper. It was originally Dutch Reformed - now Anglican. Independence was proclaimed in Melaka in 1956, although it wasn't actually granted until the following year. There was a historic procession through the town and this is celebrated in the Proclamation of Independence Hall. A Merdeka Car, Merdeka Road, Merdeka Parade, Merdeka Table, Merdeka Flag, Merdeka Movie - what a song and dance. Rather ironic that it was once the home of the Malacca Club, the bastion of colonialism. The Merdeka celebrations were in full swing at the time of my visit in August with lots of shouting, singing and flag-waving. A bit too jingoistic for me and not a Chinese or Indian in sight.

There is a high concentration of Malay Islamic culture in Melaka. In the Islamic Museum there's a replica of the Koran, a chronology of the life of Mohammad, and the history of Melaka from a purely Islamic perspective. A giant drum was on display called the Beduk, which is used for the call to prayer and for the start and cessation of fasting during Ramadan. What I liked were pictures of various Islamic punishments under Hukum Kanun Melaka - the Laws of Melaka. Like stoning to death for adultery, 100 strokes of the whip for alcohol consumption and hands dipped in boiling oil for giving false evidence. The left hand amputated for stealing, then the right hand and finally the legs for subsequent offences. And something about a Mufti issuing Fatwas. I believe the state of Kelantan wants to bring back this code of justice.

The Melaka Sultanate Palace is a replica of an original 15th century palace, and contains a museum with more on the influence of Islam, though there was a little about Indian, Siamese and Chinese traders. Various artefacts were on display including clothing, knives, daggers and the keris, with last but not least, the Sultan's Bedchamber. The Sumatran-style Kampong Kling Mosque was completed in 1746 with a strong Hindu influence. The minaret resembles a Chinese pagoda. There are Corinthian columns and symmetrical arches in the main prayer hall and wooden pulpits with Chinese/Hindu carvings. I wonder whether the preaching is also in such a hybrid manner.

One of the most photographed sites is A' Famosa (The Famous), one of the oldest surviving European architectural remains in Asia. Once part of a mighty fortress constructed by the Portuguese in 1511, this tiny gate, called Porta de Santiago, was originally one of four. The rest of the complex was destroyed by the British during the Napoleonic Wars. Up on the hill is St Paul's Church, 'Our Lady of the Hill' built in 1521 and regularly visited by St Francis Xavier, the itinerant Spanish preacher. Following his death in China, his body was brought here for nine months, before being interred in Goa in India where it remains to this day. A marble statue of St Francis was erected in 1952 to commemorate the 4th centenary of his passing. There is also an interesting connection with South Africa, as the site contains the grave of Frau Van Riebeck, the wife of John, founder of Cape Colony.

A walk around Chinatown on the western side of the Melaka River will reveal an abundance of shop-houses, antique shops, Buddhist temples, ancient mosques, atmospheric restaurants and cafés. Jonker Street (now renamed Jalan Hang Jebat) in particular retains a lot of charm and character, though some of the residents complain it is being turned into a 'ludicrous theme park of fake heritage at bargain prices'. Many traditional trades such as goldsmiths, shoemakers and barbers it seems are being forced out due to traffic restrictions and rent rises. That must happen in every high street in the world. But it is very sad to note that between 2000 and 2002, some forty-two buildings were demolished in Melaka's conservation area. Well that's not going to get them World Heritage Listing is it?

Dating back to 1646, Cheng Hoon Teng is the oldest Chinese temple in Malaysia - again dedicated to the Goddess of Mercy. It is decorated with golden phoenixes and dragons, blossoming flowers and guardian lions. There are some fine carvings and lacquer-work in a riot of black, gold and red. Restoration of the main hall took place between 1997 and 2000. The Baba-Nonya Heritage Museum is situated in a traditional townhouse with a selection of Chinese hardwood furniture, multicoloured ceramics and costumes. It is a not only a good example of conservation in action, but also a fascinating insight into past lives. Who loves ya Baba-Nonya.

Melaka is excellent for museums. One of the best is the People's and Beauty Museum. Slightly quirky and off-beat; the concept of beauty - how and why the human body has been modified, decorated and ornamented. Tattooing, scarification, slimming and anorexia nervosa. Lip-plates, lip-plugs, dental alterations - filing and removal of teeth, nose ornaments, ear embellishments, ankle rings. And of course the 'Long-Neck Karen'. Head-flattening and deformation and the highlight of them all - foot-binding. A local speciality in the Chinese community.

Pretty dainty feet - at four years old, girls of noble birth had their feet bandaged, so that the foot was eventually forced upwards with the toes curling underneath. It was called the golden lotus and considered the height of beauty at the time. Bandages were only unwrapped when feet were washed with 'min fan', a Chinese medicine. The girls were not allowed to perform menial tasks - well they couldn't because they could hardly walk. Some of the shoes I saw were only 3 inches long, but very neatly and exquisitely embroidered. Fortunately the practice has long since been discontinued. Wouldn't have been very good for the bunions. Though I did see something on TV recently about a woman binding her own feet. Unbelievable.

At the Maritime Museum there is a replica of a Portuguese galleon, the 'Flora de la Mar'. Much emphasis was placed on the trading importance of Melaka during the Malay Sultanate and colonial eras. *"Whoever is the lord of Malakka has his hand on the throat of Venice."* The decline of Melaka was blamed on European powers, but what has happened since 1957? By the way, the ship sank in 1512 in the Straits of Melaka on a voyage to Europe.

Inside an adjoining building there was an exhibit called 'Ocean and the Mankind'. *"The museum is built as mark of appreciation to the oceanic realm with their beauty and uniqueness, besides testifying to the greatness of Allah."* The exhibits included a diorama of a fisherman's village, a Kelantan boat, the 'Warrior Crow' - looked like it had been crossed with a rooster. Then some pictures of European explorers in portholes - many were missing, perhaps on purpose. An exhibition on marine life and coastal habitats was sponsored by the World Wide Fund for Nature - a good way of getting the environmental message across. My favourite was 'Too many fins spoil the broth'. The Malaysian Navy Museum was closed, but outside was a collection of rusty guns and armoury.

An interesting connection with Portsmouth - the Sri Terengganu, a patrol craft built by Vospers, launched in 1961. It served in the Indonesian conflict in 1965 and for patrol operations during the Indo-Chinese war of the 1970s, then decommissioned in 1994. You can go inside - it was obviously only designed for midgets; I knocked my head at least three times. And the entire structure is slowly falling apart.

But I am saving the best until last. 'Tortura', an exhibition of torture and punishment with authentic instruments on loan from the Medieval Criminal Museum, San Gimignano, Siena, Italy. As used by the Inquisition in Spain, Portugal and Italy. This was really up my street. I spent hours there. The Malays were making the most of how brutal, intolerant and cruel us Europeans can be. Firstly an import from Holland, the 'Dutch Barrel' which was used locally. The victim was placed in a barrel, nails driven inside and the barrel rolled about until the body was torn to shreds. People were rolled down St John's Hill, about 3 km out of town to their deaths - for unnatural offences. Red-hot pincers and tongs being used to rip and burn off genitals was a popular one. The oral, rectal and vaginal pear was the punishment for sodomy and adultery. The device was inserted into the chosen orifice, and then opened up using a screw mechanism.

A full scale model of the Bull of Falaride was on display. Once the victim was inside the hollow metal structure, a fire was lit underneath with the cries sounding like the bellowing of cattle. Then there was Breaking with the Wheel, the *"Victim transformed into a sort of huge screaming puppet writhing in rivulets of blood, a puppet with four tentacles - a sea monster."* The limbs were then braided into the spokes of the wheel, allowing the crows to take the shreds of flesh and peck out the eyes. Or how about being impaled through the anus, the point coming out between the shoulder blades. After that you will never be able to look at another stick of *satay* in the same way again.

Other exhibits included thumbscrews, chain scourges and flails with stars, collars, belts, leg irons and gags, the guillotine - this was used in France until the abolition of the death penalty in 1981, the rack and the saw. The body was turned upside down; then cut in half through the genitals and abdomen - the victim stayed alive longer that way - used for homosexuals. I don't think the Catholic Church liked gay people. And did you know that a swiftly and neatly severed head, is fully aware of its fate as it rolls along the ground or falls into the basket. Perception is extinguished only after a few seconds. Worth bearing in mind if you're a naughty boy (or girl) in somewhere like Saudi Arabia. And if that wasn't enough you could always be hung on the gallows in the courtyard at A'Famosa. Does this beat the London Dungeon?

To the north-east of town is Bukit China or China Hill. At its base is Poh San Teng Temple, built in 1795 and containing images of the Taoist entity Dabo Gong. Next door is the Sultan's well, built for his princess Hang Li Poh in 1495. The well has been poisoned many times as a means of sabotage. It must be OK now as there are some fish swimming in it. I wouldn't want to drink the water though, but if you do it is said you will return to Melaka. A monument for the Chinese victims of the anti-Japanese occupation was constructed in 1948, and there was mention of people being thrown in the well and of bayoneting babies.

On the path up the hill are models of Stadthuys, A'Famosa and 'Flora de la Mar', but unfortunately these were in a state of disrepair. At the top the Chinese Cemetery, the largest outside China and containing some 12,000 graves, had also seen better days. The Eng Choon Communal Ritual Tomb, erected in 1873 has a plaque which reads 'A record and commemoration of our esteemed forbears.'

Its great fun twisting round those arrows (Kiblat) on the ceiling in hotel rooms (used for praying in the direction of Mecca), to perhaps the South Pole or worst of all New York - modern day Babylon itself. Only joking!!! The chorus of shutters being pulled down or security gates closed is a regular feature of S E Asian life about 9 or 10 pm, when business finishes for the day - this sometimes includes hotels. So the hotel you'd thought you checked into earlier in the day seems to have disappeared, as you wander around in a desultory, semi-comatose state. There is in fact a secret entrance round the back, but you're often not told that on arriving.

I'm going to make a final comment here about religion and culture in Malaysia (and Indonesia). First there was animism, then Hinduism, then Buddhism, then Islam and finally some places adopted Christianity. Religious beliefs have been discarded like worn-out clothes. Under Islamic jurisdiction, the current flavour is very Arabic - and not just religion, law and architecture. The clothes, the Tommy Cooper 'fez' for men and headscarf for women, the names - everybody's Abdul or Mohamad - and Arabic script. This goes to prove that the true coloniser of Malaysia and Indonesia was not European, but Arabic.

Finally, a soft drink for sale called SARSI - I think I'll give that one a miss.

CHAPTER 27

SINGAPORE SLING

There are certain things that are perceived as 'must dos' in certain places e.g. a gondola ride in Venice, a camel ride at the Pyramids, hot-air ballooning over the Serengeti, or eating witchetty grubs in the Australian outback. Well in Singapore it's got to be the Raffles Hotel and splashing out nineteen quid on a Singapore Sling. I've been to all of the above, but done none of the aforementioned, and I wasn't going to buck the trend now. So you can go and sling your hook, Mr Raffles. Still, if somebody else was paying that might be different.

Singapore is an expensive city - it rivals London, New York, Hong Kong, and Tokyo. Over £4 for a pint of beer and that was in an Irish pub, not Raffles. Singaporeans think it's dear too. The girl in the bar who's worked in London and San Diego still has to live with her mum to make ends meet. And Singapore is also full of ex-pats who think the 'eighties haven't finished. There were loads of them in 'The Penny Black', a pseudo-Victorian pub with old prints, old books, Toby Jugs, pictures of Queen Victoria, a map of the London Underground and an old style letterbox.

I managed to get two pints of draught cider for £5, as I was having a meal. That's about UK prices. It went down my throat like golden nectar: it's my favourite drink, and almost impossible to get elsewhere in S E Asia. One must pay for life's little luxuries. And in the cool, dark, air-conditioned environment I could almost imagine myself being in a London pub. But something you wouldn't get in a typical British pub - an Indian woman offering palm readings. This is Asia after all, if rather sanitised.

Singapore is the most popular stopover destination for those heading to Australia and NZ, with over 450,000 Brits making it their pit stop in 2005, though most never leave the airport. And those that do head straight for the shops. I didn't touch the airport, having come over the causeway from Johor Bahru. I didn't go shopping either, well apart from having to replace my rather knackered Tevas. The stereotypical view of Singapore is of orderliness, of fines for smoking, spitting, litter and improper disposal of chewing gum. To a certain extent that is true - and why not - but I did see litter and people smoking in enclosed public spaces. Singapore just acts like a Western city, from an Asian perspective.

The city started life back in 1819 with the arrival of Sir Thomas Stamford Raffles, who set the island up as a bastion of the British Empire, and it has prospered as a trading hub ever since. You can see a statue of him, peering out over the Singapore River in the direction of 'The Penny Black' and all the other trendy bars and restaurants. I bet he was dying for a pint of cider too! The fall of Singapore was Britain's largest defeat in the Second World War. Churchill remarked that 15th February 1942 was the 'blackest day in the history of the British Empire.' Over 130,000 allied troops were marched off into captivity by the Japanese, many having not fired a single shot in anger.

Since the war, the city had a brief flirtation with its neighbour Malaysia, but this came to an unceremonious end in 1965. The government has very much been dominated by a single individual, Lee Kuan Yew, a third-generation Straits-born Chinese. Although now taking a back seat, he has been responsible for much of the city's success as a modern industrialised nation.

Singapore today is the world's second largest port after Rotterdam, and one-fifth of the globe's merchandise comes to its shores. There are huge skyscrapers and shopping malls, boardwalks and highways, a railway transit system second to none, but amidst all this modernity there are still some colonial remnants, the odd Chinese shop-house or Indian temple. Staying in the area of the river, a circular walk round the colonial district will reveal a potted history of the city. From the Raffles landing place, head north past the Old Parliament House, Victoria Theatre and Concert Hall and onto the cricket ground at the Padang. On your left will be the City Hall and Supreme Court, creations of the inter-war years, and then St Andrew's Cathedral.

In the War Memorial Park there is a memorial to the civilian victims of the Japanese Occupation. Four white vertical pillars, known locally as the Chopsticks, soar to over 70 metres symbolising Chinese, Indians, Malays and others who died. In the East, chopsticks standing upright are a symbol of death. Unofficial estimates give the total as 50,000, mainly Chinese in the Sook Ching (meaning purge through cleansing) massacre. Remains of the unknown victims are interred beneath the pillars. The monument was unveiled in 1967, 25 years to the day since Singapore fell to the Japanese. They surrendered at City Hall on 12th September 1945.

One block on is the Raffles Hotel, opened in 1899 by the Sarkies brothers, migrants from Armenia. It soon epitomised the ultimate in oriental luxury and opulence. During the 1970s the hotel became rather dilapidated, but it has since been designated a national monument and an expensive restoration project took place from 1987 to 1991. With room prices from £200 per night they're obviously trying to recoup their money. Noel Coward would be weeping into his G & T.

Now head back south through the Esplanade Park past the Cenotaph and the Indian National Army Monument. Over to the east you will see the twin glass and aluminium domes of the Theatres on the Bay, Singapore's equivalent to London's Gherkin. Perhaps they were designed by the same architect. Locally they have been likened to durians, and there is a passing resemblance. The area is bristling with activity - restaurants and cafés galore and cultural entertainment both in and outside the auditoria. Then on to the Lim Bo Seng Memorial, which is guarded by four Chinese lions. Major General Seng led the anti-Japanese movement in Singapore. He was tortured before being executed in Ipoh in Malaysia.

Cross over the Anderson Bridge to the Merlion statue, which has now been moved to its permanent position at the Fullerton Promenade. The Merlion is the surreal half-fish, half-lion icon of Singapore, which after all means 'Lion City', and the connection with the sea is obvious. *'This lion of the sea. Salt-maned, scaly, wondrous of tail.' Edwin Thumboo February 1977.* Mind you don't get wet from the huge water spout shooting from its open jaws. And there's a much bigger one you can climb up inside in Sentosa. Go past the Fullerton Hotel - there is often live music playing on the promenade and back over the river on the Cavenagh Bridge (built in Glasgow 1869 says the plaque) to the Asian Civilisations Museum. Virtually everything you wanted to know about Asia - history, culture, festivals, religion and music. Need I say more? And you're then back where you - and Singapore - started. Of course to save your tired and weary legs, you could always ride the wacky duck. Give Singapore Duck Tours a ring.

On my second trip (like Bangkok, Singapore is a major transit centre), I arrived on the National Day, the 9th of August. They were celebrating 38 years of independence. I saw most of it on TV - the march-past of the president, and multicultural dancing. And I'm sure you will love this little rhyme - *'One Singapore, one nation strong and free - A thousand different voices sing in harmony.'* Then the strains of Also Sprach Zarathrustra and the 1812 Overture. I saw the firework display from the hotel window. SARS was still very much on people's minds and there was much praise for the healthcare workers. But let's face it - SARS, like BSE and Foot and Mouth before it, was caused by flagrant animal abuse - a lesson for all humans to learn.

It was late - almost 10 pm, so I headed straight to the nearest Indian vegetarian restaurant - in Little India of course. And it was just about to close, so I was lucky. Indian food is very cheap here - about £2-£3 for as much as you can eat. So the day ended quite well. But next day it was hard work getting a decent breakfast - a lot of places were shut - it was a Sunday (it's always Sunday when you arrive somewhere) and everybody seemed to be recovering from the celebrations. I eventually found something at Clarke Quay, usually packed with shoppers, diners and the like, but not today. I decided to go on a Chinatown and Little India tour.

The Thian Hock Keng Chinese Temple (Temple of Heavenly Bliss), recently restored, was built in 1842 and dedicated to Ma Chu Po, the sea goddess. It is noted for its rooftop dragons, carved screens, intricately-decorated beams and towering granite columns. The entire structure was assembled without a single nail. Right in the heart of Chinatown, surprisingly, is the Sri Mariamman Temple. It is Singapore's oldest. The ornate gopuram or tower is literally crammed with Hindu deities and floral decorations. If you come in October, watch out for the Thimithi fire-walking festival.

For the real low-down on city life, the Chinatown Heritage Centre on the appropriately named Pagoda Street is a must, where you can... *"Journey to a time of coolies and immigrants who risked their lives in search of a better life in Singapore. Discover the trials and tribulations of our early settlers and relive the love, life and passion of early Chinatown."* There are some great displays on 'Facing the Four Evils' - opium smoking, prostitution, gambling and secret societies, and also cubicle-living, street-stalls and night markets.

Probably the most colourful (gaudy reds, mauves and gold come to mind) and elaborate temple in Little India (and most difficult to pronounce) is Sri Veeramakaliamman. It is dedicated to Kali, the bloodthirsty consort of Shiva, a popular deity with the Bengalis, who constructed the temple. She is shown garlanded with skulls whilst disembowelling her victims. The Sri Srinivasa Perumal Temple is dedicated to Vishnu, with the garuda making yet another appearance. The gopuram is quite recent, dating back to the 1960s. It is the starting point for Thaipusam. Finally, the Sakaya Muni Buddha Gaya Temple, founded in the 1920s by a Thai monk, where the 15-metre-high seated Buddha shares the place with his Hindu buddies Ganesh and Brahma. With Kuan Yin, the Chinese Goddess of Mercy, as an added extra. It is known as the Temple of 1000 Lights - are there really that many light bulbs on the premises?

I love gardens as you will probably realise by now, so a visit to the Botanical Gardens was a must. The gardens were established in the 1860s and cover some 52 hectares, a green lung for the city. But they were so manicured. Admittedly there is a remnant of the original rainforest that once covered the island - a shame it wasn't more extensive. There are numerous bamboos, palms, figs, sweet-scented frangipani and large kapok trees with huge buttress and surface roots. The gardens contain the world's largest collection of orchids. One was called Princess Di and one called Thatcher. Oh no!

Water features abound - I almost expected to see Charlie Dimmock performing an installation. And they're building an air-conditioned cool house, completely the opposite to Kew. Actually I crave air-con, I love air-con, I am addicted to air-con. Air-con is my god. I'll even walk into a shop to get that freezing cold blast of air and stand there luxuriating in its icy embrace. I'm not sure if many in the UK will be feeling the same way.

Apart from attracting tourists, joggers, plant lovers and tai chi enthusiasts, the gardens are also a great backdrop for wedding photos. The brides were everywhere; in fact they were also by the Raffles monument, by the war memorial and by the Cavenagh Bridge. Is marriage coming back into fashion? And the number of times I've been asked to take photos of couples is unbelievable. Perhaps I should set up in business as a wedding photographer. Or maybe as a porn director. In particular directing Annabel Chong in the 'World's Biggest Gang-Bang', where she was serviced by 251 men. She is from Singapore.

The Light Railway System, or MRT (Mass Rapid Transit), of Singapore is excellent - clean, efficient, comfortable - but has really boring names like East/West and North/South lines. Some station names are copied from England e.g. Somerset, Redhill and Dover. A message in one of the compartments *"Worry gives a small thing a big shadow."* Swedish proverb. It's no use worrying when you're travelling. The 'in-flight' movie, if it could be called that, was base jumping from Petronas Towers - wicked.

I was off to Sentosa Island to amuse myself for a few hours. Sentosa means 'Tranquillity' in Malay, although it was anything but tranquil. In some ways it reminded me of Sun City in South Africa, or Singapore's version of Disneyland. There's a lot of new development at the harbour front, a new train line is being built and new lagoons and artificial beaches created. I went over by cable-car, which gives a fantastic view of the city, just showing how massive the docks and shipping areas are. At the Guardian Dragon of Lung Ya Men (Dragon Teeth Gate) there is a plaque which reads *"After a long hibernation, this custodian of Lung Ya Men has arisen to greet a new and prosperous Singapore on its doorsteps - in itself an economic dragon of the East."*

I went up into the Merlion, 37 metres tall on Sentosa's highest point, and looked down at the 120m-long mosaic of colourful phosphorescent animals. Legend has it that they laid down their bodies to enable the Merlion to make his way up to Merlion's Rock. One even looked like Nessie (Loch Ness Monster).

There are many items of interest on the island about the culture and history of Singapore. Stories of the Sea went back to the first aboriginal settlers - everybody after that was a coloniser. The Admiral Cheng Ho Puppet Theatre was fun. He was the early 15th century Chinese Muslim mariner and adventurer. Some say he became a eunuch voluntarily as the traditional way of courting favour with the Chinese Emperor. Others claim he was captured by the Chinese army and castrated as a boy of thirteen - hardly a consenting adult. Either way he had obviously paid a visit to Tortura. Shame they didn't show a re-enactment of the operation.

Some 300 vessels and 27,000 men were under his control, and his flagship, at 400 feet long was more than four times the length of Columbus' Santa Maria. He was the world's greatest voyager to that date - seven trips to S E Asia (including Singapore), India, Persia, Arabia and Africa. And all this sixty years before Columbus even set sail for the New World. It is interesting to note that after his death, China banned all further expeditions.

'Pioneers of Singapore' shows a tableau of merchants, administrators, property-owners, businessmen and artisans and the historic signing of the trading agreement in 1819. With the coolies' living quarters in Chinatown, opium-smoking, harbour, dockside and street scenes of the 1930s. Also a recollection of the Japanese in Singapore with tableaux of the British and Japanese surrenders in the Surrender Rooms. 'Festivals of Singapore' displays Chinese Lion Dancing, the Lunar New Year, Indian Fire Walking and Thaipusam.

Fort Siloso was built in the 1880s to protect the western entrance to Singapore Harbour, and is the last remaining British coastal fortification. It was turned into a concentration camp under Japanese occupation during 1942-1945. British troops finally departed in 1967. There are interactive displays here with battle and firing drills. Other exhibits include the Dolphin Lagoon, Underwater World, Butterfly Park and Insect Kingdom if you are so inclined. Finally, the musical fountains were very impressive with the water shooting skywards in time to the music. A sound, light and laser extravaganza. Blue Danube and Morning Mood to Walking On Sunshine. At night the dancing fountains are lit up, so Dancing in the Dark would be an appropriate number now.

I think the Merlion was very angry - his eyes had turned yellow and his mouth was a scarlet red. Must have been chewing too many betelnuts. Then came the lightning and the thunder and the rain, which had been threatening all day. And I got drenched again and decided to leave. So this was the end of my Singapore Story and I never did enter the hallowed enclaves of the Raffles Hotel.

CHAPTER 28

THE OLD MAN OF BORNEO

Up a Mountain...Down a Beer. Altitude and Attitude. Seen it, done it, got the T-shirt and the certificate. (Even though later they were to go missing in the post - in the Royal Mail Sorting Office in London of all places, along with many of my photos. Should have bought myself a digital camera). Well, what can I say...the climb up Kinabalu was incredible, with impressive views all the way to the Philippines. The mountain is a huge granite outcrop and at 4095 metres, the highest point between the Himalayas and New Guinea. It reminded me somewhat of the granite wonderland that is Yosemite, with the famed El Capitan and Half Dome.

The last few hundred metres are climbed (it's really just a scramble) using fixed ropes. Nearing the summit, I looked down into Low's Gully where those marines went missing a few years back and the guide pointed out where 17-year-old Ellie James died of hypothermia. She was climbing the neighbouring St John's peak in thick mist. Luckily for me and my climbing companions it was a very clear day, at sunrise anyway, with almost perfect visibility. But when it's not - and the rain-polished stone is very slippery, it can be a pretty dangerous place.

Mount Kinabalu is the biggest tourist attraction in Sabah (Malaysian part of Borneo) and is climbed by some 30,000 people a year. It is a relatively easy climb - no mountaineering skills required - just a little determination with lots of stamina and the ability to cope with the altitude. At the summit the air pressure is 50% that of sea level, and consequently half the oxygen. On the walk up you progress through the various vegetation levels of rainforest, then oaks and chestnuts, rhododendrons and finally stunted shrubs before reaching bare rock devoid of plant life. Unfortunately however I missed out on spotting the *Nepenthes rajah*, that species of pitcher plant lucidly described by David Attenborough as *"so monstrous that occasionally it succeeds in drowning one of the mountain's rats."* [9] Another wonderful evocation in 'Life On Air' about Kinabalu, is that of the *"tropical crescent moon hammocked between the Donkey's Ears, two extraordinary black pinnacles."* [10] He goes on to say, *"If I had ever had any doubts about abandoning a career that would keep me sitting behind a desk in London, I lost them there."* [11] Probably the wisest and most prophetic words ever spoken.

The first recorded ascent was by Sir Hugh Low in 1851, and the main peak and gully is named after him. The mile-deep gully was created surprisingly recently in geological time, when one million years ago it was gouged out by a huge glacier. It is appropriately called 'The Place of the Dead.' And it was here that the ten-man British Army expedition got lost in 1994. They took only ten days' rations, no radios or flares and not enough rope - the expedition finally took four weeks.

Things did not start well - the Chinese in the team had no experience in abseiling and one team member was suffering from the climb up. So they split into two groups before starting their descent. The fickle weather quickly deteriorated, with the rain gushing down the sides of the rock and filling the gully with water. So the escape options were either impenetrable forest or impassable waterfalls. Reaching the point of no return, they were like spiders in a bath, they could only go down. The weaker group lagged behind and when they could go no further left an SOS made of stones. The stronger group forged on down a mile-long staircase of water - some full-on canyoning here. They were clambering up and down sheer cliff-faces, fighting through jungle with loose vegetation on rock and living off berries, with subsequent food poisoning. This group split up again, with two of them finding a road after seventeen days, and then back to civilisation. Their three companions soon followed.

The Malaysian Army then sent out a helicopter to find the remaining five, but without success. The RAF Mountain Rescue team took up the search and their sixteen best climbers descended into the gully - twice the height of Ben Nevis. But they too had to give up due to the appalling weather conditions. On the 31st day, the Malaysians saw the SOS and airlifted out the last five members of the team. They were emaciated and skeletal, having lost a fifth of their body-weight. The ten men had underestimated the scale and ferocity of Kinabalu's unique terrain and unpredictable weather. It was not until 1998 that a joint British-Malaysian expedition properly explored the bottom of the gully, finding several new species of plants and insects.

Well if that isn't enough for you adventure buffs, why not try the four-day 200-mile Borneo Challenge. Running up and down Kinabalu, roller-skating and mountain-biking in the rainforest; then canoeing and white-water rafting. In 35 degree heat and 90 per cent humidity. The competitors needed six weeks of intensive training for six hours a day using up 1000 calories per hour.

After the climb, we retired exhausted to Poring Hot Springs for some R&R in the sulphur heated pools. This complex of pools and hot-tubs was developed by the Japanese during World War II and is a popular weekend retreat for the locals. It was quite weird being in a swimming-pool in the middle of the jungle, surrounded by huge bamboos forty feet high and three-horned rhinoceros-beetles whizzing about our heads like something out of Star Wars. And then the deafening chorus of the giant cicadas. I saw one being eating alive by ants, and it seemed as if it was screaming in agony. There were butterflies, moths and bats everywhere. And if you're a twitcher you'll be in bird heaven.

The evening meal of Massaman curry on the veranda was delicious, if you didn't mind the odd bug or two falling in your food. I think a lot of these insects are quite poor flyers and being attracted by the light, hit the ceiling fans. And hey presto, the dining table becomes alive. They're all pretty harmless though, and the waitresses had great fun picking them up as they lay helpless on their backs, legs flailing in the air, then releasing them back into the trees. On another occasion, two geckos fighting on the ceiling fell into my beer, but both managed to make a quick exit from the slippery glass to continue their merry pranks elsewhere. It really added some flavour. As I collapsed back into my room amidst all this mayhem, I was confronted by a spider four inches across - don't go there.

The next day I was headed to the orang-utan Rehabilitation Centre in Sepilok, but before I left had the great privilege seeing a mother and baby orang-utan in trees by the side of the road. This was like Africa. The wildlife comes to you. The name 'orang-utan' means 'person of the forest'; these majestic animals in their highly-organised social groups are just that. And the adult males are the old men of the forest, indeed of Borneo itself, just in case you thought the reference might have been to me. The orang-utan is the 2nd biggest great ape after the gorilla, and the largest tree-dwelling and fruit-eating mammal. In the wild they can live up to forty years old. Sadly there are probably less than twenty thousand orang-utans left in their forest homes in Sumatra and Borneo, mainly due to forest clearance. They are a critically endangered species and reproductive rates are low. A female rarely has more than three young in her lifetime. It was said at one time an orang-utan could swing through the forest canopy from one side of Borneo to the other without touching the ground. Those days are long gone.

The centre at Sepilok is one of only four in the world; it was established back in 1964 and has so far handled about a hundred and seventy orphaned and injured animals. They are fed fruit, mainly bananas, twice daily from a platform in the forest only a few metres from the viewing area. If you are patient and wait until the package tourists have gone, you might be lucky enough to have one come right up to you. Of course he/she ran off at the moment I was taking a photo. But I saw a couple more on one of the forest walks. The male orang-utans are most imposing, great ginger-haired hulks five feet tall, weighing in at close on 200 pounds with an arm span of eight feet. But it is the babies with their innocent trusting eyes that are the most appealing, and people are tempted to pick them up.

Sepilok is not just famous for its orang-utans - superlatives include 450 species of tree, 200 species of bird and 90 species of mammal. I saw the pig-tailed macaques (stealing the orang-utan's food), monitor lizards two metres long (not that far short of the Komodo dragon), hornbills and egrets. At night-time, flying foxes (a large fruit bat) and flying squirrels (true squirrels with wings, or rather flaps for gliding) eerily screech through the trees. And then I watched 'Jessica' making her nest in the tree canopy above as all wild orang-utans do every night. Apart from the care and rehabilitation of orang-utans, the centre also organises educational programmes and there are various practical projects and donation schemes that volunteers can be involved in.

Staying on an environmental and nature theme, Uncle Tan's Wildlife Camp on the Sungai Kinabatangan is an opportunity to see even more amazing wildlife - probably the best place in Borneo. The Sungai Kinabatangan, at 560 km long, is Sabah's longest river, and although the upper reaches have been cleared to make way for palm-oil plantations, the riverine forest near the coast has been left more or less intact. You can go on jungle trails day and night, or go out in Uncle Tan's boat, and in a couple of days you would expect to see the following: proboscis monkey (only found in Borneo), long and pig-tailed macaques, gibbons, orang-utans, bearded pigs, civet cats (like a racoon), otters, tarsier (like a small squirrel), crocodiles, eagles, kingfishers, hornbills, snake-birds, owls, bee-eaters - well I did anyway - the list is exhausting.

Accommodation is pretty rustic with bamboo shacks open to the elements and a bucket of cold water for a shower, but hey, you're in the jungle and there's not much left of it to enjoy. Uncle Tan is a very genial agreeable guy with a wry smile and a jocular expression. He told me he served in the British Army back in the 'fifties, which must make him seventy-something. He has been a great champion of conservation in the local area, railing against government, loggers and oil companies alike.

The high spot for me was the proboscis monkeys, the male with its huge pendulous nose, pot belly and waistcoat attire, sitting upright in trees overhanging the river, arms nonchalantly splayed out. Back in camp, while enjoying our evening meal, we were greeted by Gum Gum, the resident bearded pig (wheee...wheee) eagerly awaiting some leftovers. To be followed by the civet cat on the prowl.

Ending on a very sad note, even this wildlife haven is under threat. Vast areas of Sabah's rainforest have been cleared to make way for palm-oil plantations - some say 80%, others say as much as 92%. And with them an amazing diversity of plant and animal species. Larger animals such as elephants and rhinos are almost extinct, with orang-utans and proboscis following in their wake. The river is now slowly choking on silt caused by soil erosion upstream, the result of extensive logging. Hunting parties from the logging camps have been responsible for shooting many animals. Extensive areas have been put to the torch and the remaining animals burnt alive. It is reckoned one third of orang-utans have died in this way. In 1999 part of the lower Kinabatangan was declared a protected area, but it seems loggers and plantation owners (backed by the banks) have the most clout.

The rainforests of Sabah and Sarawak have become Malaysia's 'Killing Fields', with the unique ecosystem the battered and bloodied victim. It is not as though Malaysia is a poor country - it is the richest in South-East Asia, apart from the City States of Singapore and Brunei. The number of people I saw driving around in 4x4's was astounding. Most of the money of course does not go to local communities but to the government and big business interests - and overseas. The local people - Dayaks, are as much the victims as the wildlife as they are evicted from their forest homes.

All I can say is avoid any wood or palm-oil product (used in many food products, cooking oils and soap), sourced from Malaysia. According to the Environmental Investigation Agency, Britain is the largest importer of illegal tropical timber in the EU. And imports a million tonnes of palm-oil each year. Protest and make your voice heard to all concerned.

On the return journey between Ranau and Kota Kinabalu, where I had begun my trip to Sabah, I gained a most spectacular view of Mount Kinabalu. It was about six pm, most of the cloud had cleared and a mist was slowly rising from the forest. And before my eyes the most vivid and gorgeous sunset I have ever seen. As I was on the bus, a decent picture was out of the question - the best ones always get away. But it was rather propitious as the pictures were destined to go missing in any event. Still I have my memories and that's what counts.

CHAPTER 29

A SARAWAKY DUDE

Flying out of Kota Kinabalu is when the true extent of rainforest clearance hits you. Great swathes of oil-palms reaching as far as the eye can see. An environmental crime if ever there was one. My destination was Gunung Mulu National Park, the largest in Sarawak, where hopefully there was still some pristine rainforest left. It is truly an adventurer's playground, with amazing wildlife, jungle trekking, rock and mountain-climbing, caving and river-rafting in an incredible wilderness of rugged forested mountains. Some of the superlatives include eight types of forest, 170 species of orchid, 10 types of pitcher plant, 8000 types of fungi, 262 species of bird, 75 mammals, 74 frogs, 281 butterflies and an unbelievable 458 ant species. Better go and see them before they're all gone.

Mulu is really just a clearing in the jungle with a resort, the Park HQ, and huts for sleeping in while you await your big endeavour. However they are extending the airstrip to take larger planes. The weather was OK until about 2pm, and I was about to go to some caves when the heavens opened. It rained until well past midnight, even though this was the dry season. Living up to its reputation as a rainforest. I stayed in the dormitory, a large barrack-style hut with 18 beds, and had the place all to myself. Well not quite - I had to share it with a foot-long lizard and a frog, and perhaps a few more things besides. All other flights that day were cancelled. It was a really eerie feeling - I'd been with quite a lot of people in Sabah and now was alone again with the rain pelting down and the barking frogs outside - they sound just like dogs. And all these empty beds reminded me of *The Shining*. "All work and no play makes Jack a dull boy. *Here's Johnny.*" Fortunately the night was uneventful.

The next day I set off for the Deer and Lang Caves, the Deer Cave so-named because at one time deer used it for shelter. But sadly no more. The caves are reached via a 3 km boardwalk from Park HQ through peat swamp and alluvial flats, and past limestone outcrops. They contain the world's largest cave passage and natural chamber. Deer Cave is 2160m long; never less than 90m high and the main chamber at 122m is quite overwhelming. It is said the cave could contain St Paul's Cathedral five times over. The aptly named Garden of Eden has been created where a hole in the roof allows dappled sunlight to bathe the luxuriant undergrowth. Another interesting feature is the Abraham Lincoln profile.

As soon as you are inside, you will notice the stink of ammonia from the two million free-tailed bat droppings. Don't look too closely - the floor is alive with a great abundance of creepy crawlies feeding on dead bats and various detritus. Within a few minutes you will probably be retching and gasping for air. At dusk the bats emerge in a huge black cloud, spiralling and circling through the evening sky to catch insects on the wing. They are estimated to consume up to three tons of insects every night - that'll keep the mozzies at bay. This aerial performance can last up to an hour before they disappear into the forest. An unforgettable experience - one of nature's great marvels.

Clearwater and Wind Caves are along another 3 km boardwalk and forest path, which was very slippery and undulating - up and down over rocks and streams and crevices, and along the Melinau River via Moon Milk Cave. This cave is at the top of some steep stone steps and is difficult to negotiate with rocky overhangs and myriad tree roots. A torch is essential. Clearwater Cave is 107 km long with the longest cave passage in S E Asia, and a subterranean river that small boats can navigate. Or you can go swimming if you like. Though I thought it was uncannily like the River Styx of Greek legend. Just outside the cave I was surrounded by a cloud of Rajah Brooke (a Victorian adventurer who we will be meeting later) butterflies with vivid green wings. They are attracted by the mineral salts in human sweat and urine, so your arms will be covered - and you can have them on your privates as well. But they don't bite, unlike the sand flies in New Zealand, who would give you an instant circumcision. And guess what, I met Hans again, the German guy I first saw in the Cameron Highlands, then Kinabalu and now Mulu.

If exploring these show caves is a little too tame for you, then there is always adventure caving, with climbing, abseiling - and wading through underground rivers. The routes are graded 1 to 5, with 5 being described as 'A very difficult cave with many hazards. Requires a high technical ability. Very difficult route finding.' Just up my street then. I think not. It is reckoned to date that only 40% of the cave system has been surveyed, let alone opened to the public, so there are plenty of opportunities for that 'virgin' conquest.

It was most definitely time for me to go above ground - to the Pinnacles to be precise, for yet another 'bit of rough and tumble in the jungle'. The second night in the hostel could not have been a greater contrast. A large group of Malays had arrived, mainly women as it happens - I was surrounded by them. And surprisingly there was no segregation in the dorm, despite Malaysia being a predominantly Muslim country. Another myth shattered, as some hostels in Western countries like, dare I say Australia and New Zealand, are living in the Dark Ages on this score. There were also a couple of guys who had just completed the Pinnacles trek and they looked absolutely shattered. Sweating profusely, covered in mud with tales of wading through rapids, torrential rain, falling and slipping over rocks, their legs bloody from innumerable leeches. It sounded like a great trip, but took a couple of days to get enough people interested and brave enough to go. But if you come to a place like this, wouldn't it be a shame not to experience at least some of the things on offer.

There were seven of us that made this great trip. Two Swedes, one Swiss, one Malay (a partner of one of the Swedes), a Japanese couple and yours truly. What an assortment. The adventure started with a two-hour boat ride from Park HQ along the Melinau River to Kuala Berar. Had to get out of the boat a couple of times as the water was too shallow. A bit tough on the boatman, but I suppose he was used to it. Then a 9 km jungle trail crossing the river with all our gear - that was pretty scary as it was very fast flowing. I didn't want to lose anything or get swept away. Finally arrive knackered at camp and go for a swim in the river, which was quite calm at this point in the proceedings.

On day two the real hiking begins - a 2.4 km trail up through the forest rising 1200 metres to the viewpoint on Gunung Api. The humidity was stifling and I was just covered in sweat, so I stripped down to my swimming-trunks. Nothing is dry in the rainforest. Finally nearing the summit, it becomes an assault course that could be used in army training. Fifteen aluminium ladders, assorted ropes and iron rings all contained within sharp limestone pinnacles, caves, crevices and dense, moss-covered forest. One slip and you would fall onto the rocks and receive some serious damage. The rocks, ladders and latticework of tree roots were so slippery.

So at last I reached the top after four exhausting skin-drenched hours for a view of the stone forest. A wonderland of 45-metre razor-sharp silver-grey limestone spikes towering above the surrounding vegetation, and with the mist swirling about them. A brilliant aerial view of the Pinnacles was shown on *Planet Earth* - on a clear sunny day with great visibility. Something straight out of *Lord of the Rings*. Maybe it's Dwimorberg, the Haunted Mountain. Adventure trekking can't get much better than this. Patagonia, Kamchatka perhaps. Frodo look out.

Not everybody made it to the top - the Japanese guy didn't; he was overweight and he smoked. The trip back down was even harder. Another four hours it took and I was running out of water. At least this wasn't Kilimanjaro - some people there had run out of water on the summit, or it had frozen rock hard. You had to be so damn careful of tripping over. Just to add insult to injury, various tales were told by my guide of having to airlift injured people out of an almost impossible terrain. The Malay girl was one of the first back and there was barely a drop of perspiration on her forehead. Still, she was half my age and probably did this kind of thing all the time.

I ended the day in a rather spectacular fashion. I had been swimming in the river and was now sitting on the boat jetty, enjoying a refreshing tropical shower. I think we were in for a bit of a storm, the wind was picking up and the water was getting rather choppy. Deciding to go for one last dip before supper I prepared to jump in, but slipped awkwardly. The current dragged me under and I hit my head on the side of the jetty. Momentarily I was knocked out, and coming to was swept a few metres downstream. Fortunately, I managed to clamber up the riverbank none the worse for my exploits. My companion Magnus from Sweden was decidedly white-faced when he saw me - thinking I was a goner.

Later on he was to impart many tales of trekking in Nepal with people getting lost, falling down crevasses and breaking bones, spending the night out in freezing temperatures (reminded me of *Touching the Void*), guides with - would you believe - altitude sickness, and being accosted by armed Maoists. One guy I was speaking to not so long ago even had an army rescue team looking for his party, with an incredible catalogue of mishaps and disasters. A three-day detour due to heavy snow, incessant rain, flooding and mudslides with bridges and roads being washed away. Trek ponies dying outside their tent, and a man suffering a heart attack who also died. Fortunately none of that happened on my trip to the Annapurnas. But it would have made a great story if it had.

The rest of my Pinnacles adventure was pretty tame by comparison. On the way back to Park HQ, I managed to traverse a slippery log bridge by sitting on it and pulling myself forward with my hands. It looked very funny to onlookers, but was effective nonetheless. I certainly wasn't prepared to risk falling off, which was a real possibility with my dodgy feet. If you are surefooted enough, try going over in your socks - they give more grip than either boots or bare feet. The worst thing to affect us were the leeches, encouraged out by the recent downpours. They hide in the streams, under rocks and in the undergrowth, and they hang down from the trees. Stop for a moment to tie up your boot laces and they'll be crawling into your socks. One poor guy even got one on his scrotum - they head for any available orifice, so keep well buttoned up.

There are many more forest and mountain trails. Within the National Park, the Gunung Mulu trail is a four-day trek to the summit of the mountain, staying in wooden huts overnight - and the Headhunters Trail, named after Kayan war parties, boating downriver and visits to tribal longhouses. Outside the park the Bario and Kelabit Highlands offer superb rainforest walks, alpine plateaus and wildlife-spotting. There are overnight stays in jungle camps and longhouses, and trips across the Indonesian border. You couldn't possibly do them all - you'd have to be superhuman. And as regards the headhunters, there was a report a few years ago about one tribe of Dayaks, in Kalimantan (Indonesian part of Borneo) headhunting newcomers, beheading them and then eating their body parts. Well that puts paid to Indonesia's transmigration policy.

I flew from Mulu to Miri, which is on the coast; with more monotonous views of oil-palms I'm afraid. It was time to take a rest from being an extra in either a David Attenborough nature documentary or a Harrison Ford adventure movie. Also I was beginning to crave Western food - all this rice and noodles was just too much, and the number of days I had to survive on biscuits, buns and crisps! Imagine dreaming about a cheese sandwich or even bread and jam. I definitely wasn't going 'native', though I knew some that had. Eating noodles for breakfast and spitting in the street.

So this experience enticed me to pen 'The S E Asian Diet.' Sticky overcooked rice with boiled cabbage and onion with a bowl of dishwater. For Laos - add a pig's trotter. For Vietnam - add turtle and frog's legs. For Singapore - add a fish-head. For the Philippines - add a duck embryo - beak, feathers and all. For Cambodia - add human body parts; there have been some more cases of cannibalism recently. For Malaysia - add lumps of fried meat on a stick - it's called satay. What was that about a dog not being just for Christmas? Though it's probably the Chinese who come out on top, or is it bottom. Put the whole lot in a cooking pot with some instant noodles, tiger-penis and monkey-brains for a gargantuan feast. That's why S E Asian restaurants don't have menus - there's only one dish on offer. I may be saying this in jest, but there is definitely a germ of truth in it.

Miri is a pretty nondescript place, originally a fishing village; then it prospered from the oil industry and rubber plantations. It serves many river-towns in northern Sarawak, and like its neighbours to the south-west, Bintulu and Sibu, the main activity today is the logging industry. The main attraction is the caves at Niah on the way to Bintulu.

Back in the 'fifties, archaeologists discovered rock paintings, canoe-like coffins, various tools and ornaments and a human skull here. It is reckoned that people lived in the cave some 40,000 years ago. A reconstruction of the cave, together with various artefacts, can be seen in the Sarawak Museum in Kuching, the state capital. The bus drops you off in Batu Niah and it's a 3 km walk to the Great Cave, 250m across at the mouth and 60 m at its greatest height. I think it looked more impressive than the Deer Cave.

At one time half a million bats and four million swiftlets inhabited the cave. There are far fewer now, especially the swiftlets, whose nests have been harvested for the Chinese market. Like the Viking Cave in Phi Phi in Thailand, bamboo and vine scaffolding is used to extract the nests. Traditionally this has been the preserve of the Penan people with the Iban concentrating on the collection of bat-guano. Beyond the Great Cave, a short forest pathway leads to the Painted Cave, with pictures of warriors and hunters and some of the animals of the forest.

I found both Bintulu and Sibu extremely depressing places. The rivers on which they stand, the Batang Kemena and Rejang are merely muddy, silted-up sewers for the logging industries. Sawmills line the riverbanks, with boats loaded down with timber, and lots of forest debris floating downstream. The receiving end of global market economics. The Bakun Dam project at Belaga on the Rejang, the brainchild of former PM Mahathir Mohamad, has cleared a huge area of rainforest and uprooted 11,000 people from their small river communities. And all the animals killed. A massive reservoir the size of Singapore is being constructed, flooding even more land. And industries such as aluminium-smelting are moving in to further degrade the land and cause health problems.

The Malaysian Government is guilty of the worst kind of colonialism, treating Sabah and Sarawak as vassal states to be plundered mercilessly. All for a scheme that is both economically unnecessary - Sarawak has all the electricity it needs - and environmentally damaging. And a huge black mark against Britain for helping to finance this project. An Orang Ulu native community leader, Jok Jau Evong, opposing the exploitation in lecture tours overseas, had his passport taken away by the authorities. How's that for Malaysian democracy, though he did eventually have it returned. Malaysia is certainly heading down the wrong path in its quest for 'developed' status. But what's happening in countries like China and India, I'm sure is much worse, and certainly on a larger scale. O Brave New World.

CHAPTER 30

KITSCH IN KUCHING

Kuching means 'Cat' in Malay and the city is well endowed with feline images. There are statues of cats everywhere. Sibu and Kuching are known as the Yin and Yang of urban Borneo, the rough river-city of Sibu sharply contrasting with genteel, sophisticated Kuching. Indeed the city is probably the most attractive and pleasant of all S E Asian cities, very laid-back and peaceful with a beautiful riverside setting. It boasts many international hotels, and compared to the rest of Sarawak is positively brimming with tourists. For a great view over the city, head to the top of the Civic Centre Tower - the mountains of Kalimantan can be seen on a clear day. The night-time cityscape is a pretty spectacular sight too. With a population of slightly under half a million, this capital of Sarawak enjoys a very cosmopolitan status. It has Chinese, Malay and a liberal scattering of Sarawak's various ethnic groups as residents.

The city was given its name by Charles Brooke of the famed White Rajahs in 1872. Before that it was simply known as Sarawak. There's a lot to see and do here, especially of a cultural nature - many of Kuching's historic buildings escaped damage during World War II. Most of the attractions are on the south bank of the Sungai Sarawak - the green and white mosque, the Sarawak Museum, the Islamic Museum, the Chinese History Museum, the Courthouse and Brooke Memorial. A pleasant paved walkway meanders around landscaped gardens, and is lined with cafés and food-stalls. Many godowns (river warehouses) and Chinese shop-houses have been tastefully restored - quite often as book, craft or antique shops. There's also a Chinese Pavilion, an open-air theatre and some musical fountains. River-ferries (tambang), with lanterns lit up in the evenings, glide peacefully back and forth to the opposite bank.

Over the river is the white Fort Margherita, complete with battlements, and now housing the Police Museum. There are also some traditional Malay houses in four kampung (villages) which are well worth a visit. The Great White Cat of Kuching, with its bright blue eyes (which everyone comes to see), is situated at the eastern end of town on Jalan Padungan. Other kitsch cat statues are to be found along the waterfront and opposite the Holiday Inn. There is the Cat Museum as well, the world's first, and a must for cat-lovers.

The history and development of Kuching and Sarawak is very much tied up with the arrival of the British and then Chinese migrants. But it was no ordinary colonial backwater. From 1839 with the arrival of James Brooke in his well-armed sloop 'The Royalist', until capitulation to the Japanese in World War II, the state was run as the Brookes' personal kingdom. James Brooke had come to the aid of the Sultan of Brunei, and was rewarded by being installed as the first 'White Rajah' of Sarawak.

He was succeeded by his nephew Charles Brooke in 1868, who kept the reins of power by a policy of divide-and-rule over the local tribes. He was succeeded in turn by his second son Charles Vyner Brooke, who continued the dynasty in the inter-war years. After World War II his nephew Anthony, the heir apparent, made a last-ditch attempt to regain the family estate - but to no avail. The governor was murdered in 1949, and after much deliberation, Sabah and Sarawak joined the Federation of Malaysia in 1963.

The Brookes, in particular Charles, left a wealth of colonial architecture behind them. The Astana, the imposing palace on the north bank of the river, was built as a bridal gift to his wife in 1870. It is now the official residence of the Head of the State of Sarawak. Fort Margherita was built in 1879 to guard against incursions from pirates. Again Charles had his wife Margaret in mind, as the fort was named after her. The fort contains many fascinating exhibits of Brooke militaria, and weapons captured during the communist insurgency. It also houses the famous 'laughing skulls' which many visitors claim have the ability to emit an eerie laughing noise. I couldn't possibly comment as the fort was closed at the time of my visit in 2002 for renovations.

The Square Tower, built in the same year, was another fortification, but no shots were ever fired in anger from its battlements. The Courthouse was completed in 1871 as the seat of Sarawak's Government, and was in use by the state magistrate until 1973. A clock tower was added in 1883, and the small granite Charles Brooke Memorial in 1924. This whole area is being redeveloped as a visitor and cultural centre.

The Sarawak Museum, which straddles both sides of Jalan Tun Haji Openg, is considered to be one of the best in S E Asia. The old wing is designed in the style of a Normandy townhouse, and contains many stuffed and mounted animals. It also has informative ethnographic and archaeological exhibits, including a reconstruction of early human settlements in Niah Caves. There are displays on longhouse life and some fine collections of ceramics, wood-carvings, furniture and musical instruments.

And probably for the first time in Borneo, I was not only spoilt for choice on accommodation and food, but entertainment as well. Eating out was a real pleasure from coffee-shops with their marble tables, food centres, curry-houses, Chinese bars, pizza parlours, hotel buffets and even an English pub, the Royalist, decorated with Brooke-era memorabilia. *'Follow in the footsteps of Sir James Brooke. Let your adventures in Sarawak begin with the Royalist.'* Other themed pubs have such evocative names as 'De Tavern', 'Amigos', 'Eagle's Nest', 'Latino', 'Soho' and 'The Victoria Arms', all catering no doubt for the rich vein of ex-pats and wealthy Malaysian Chinese. Karaoke lounges abound, mainly in hotels, and the odd disco and live Filipino bands are pretty popular too. Cat City had a lively mother/daughter duo (with family backing band) and it was difficult to tell them apart. They may have been tiny, but boy could they sing. There was one really excellent restaurant which deserves a mention - The Life Café, which served delicious Chinese vegetable dumplings and curries, and a wide range of teas and coffees. All in an extremely clean and welcoming environment - just what I needed after all those days and weeks surviving on buns and bananas.

I suppose I should make a brief mention of the shopping opportunities too. Some good buys include hand-woven rugs, wooden hornbill-carvings, silver jewellery, Orang Ulu beadwork, Bidayuh basket-weaving and Penan blowpipes. And the odd mask. Most of the antique and curio shops are to be found in the Main Bazaar along the waterfront, with some in the Padungan area by the Great Cat. With wacky names like Artrageously Ramsay Ong, specialising in bark paintings and ethnic textiles, Gallery Nepenthes and the Artelier Gallery selling hand-made furniture. Apart from arts and crafts, there are plenty of Western-style shopping centres, malls and plazas to satisfy the most avid of shopaholics. So fat and bloated from eating too much and arms dragging along the ground from all those heavy bags, it's time for some proper exercise out of town. However a slight diversion first, and staying on the 'kitsch' theme - a visit to the Sarawak Cultural Village, the *ultimate* tourist destination.

Here goes - *'Experience Sarawak with all of your senses. Savour the sounds, colours and sensations of Sarawak at Sarawak Cultural Village.'* See Sarawak in half a day. Selamat datang 'Welcome' in Malay and you're issued with a passport to a most pleasant and unforgettable experience. The village consists of seven ethnic houses - Bidayuh (or Land Dayaks), Iban (Sea Dayaks), Penan, Orang Ulu, Melanau, Malay and Chinese situated around a man-made lake. The 17-acre site is located at the foot of Mount Santubong, about a forty-minute drive from Kuching. The passport in question is stamped as you enter each ethnic abode - a longhouse, a jungle settlement, a Malay townhouse or a Chinese pagoda.

The traditional longhouse is built of axe-hewn timber, tied with creeper-fibre and roofed with a leaf thatch. It is usually situated close to water with access to a river-jetty. You then climb up a notched log to an open veranda, scene of community and domestic activity. Doorways lead to the rooms of individual families. You can see handicraft-making, traditional games, household chores (I love work, I could watch it all day), rituals and ceremonies. And you can watch welcome and warrior dances, sago dances (sago is a staple food for some tribes), dances to celebrate the harvest, a Malay Joget and a Chinese Lion dance. You can have your picture taken with one of the storytellers (guides), dressed in traditional costumes. You can even get married in the village - perhaps to one of the dusky storytellers.

I never did venture upriver to a 'traditional' longhouse. Perhaps I was a little tired of trekking and I'd already seen the hill-tribes of Thailand and Laos. Horrific tales of logging and environmental destruction and the fact that some of these longhouses had satellite TV and fridges put me off somewhat. Also I felt the experience was going to be far too touristy and commercialised. One hand with a welcoming glass of rice wine, the other held out for twenty ringgit (Malay currency). And buying a pig at a local market as a gift to be slaughtered was certainly not on. At least with the Cultural Village I knew what I was letting myself in for and it was all in good humour - no worse than the cowboys and girls in Dalat. But if I'm in Sarawak again, I might just make a visit to one of the more remote longhouses and be pleasantly surprised. And as for getting drunk on the rice wine and making an idiot of myself (to get in with the locals), I do that anyway.

> Here we are living as one
> Beneath our crescent, stripes and star.
> People everywhere throughout the land
> Love Sarawak and together, together
> Let's make our land of beauty
> The Best...
> *Gerard Law*

Yes, Malaysia, truly Asia!

Bako National Park, Sarawak's oldest, is situated on the coast just north of Kuching. There is a wide range of habitat - mangroves, peat swamp, rainforest, grassland and *kerangas* - sandstone heath forest. This is complemented with an amazing array of plants from the giant dipterocarps down to sundews and pitchers. As for animals, there is the usual gamut of bearded pig, long-tailed macaques, silver langurs, palm-squirrels and monitor lizards. Plus some 150 species of bird, many snakes, pangolins, tarsiers, bats and flying lemurs. The macaques will quite brazenly come into your room or lodge and steal food, clothing and bags, so keep windows securely closed. But best of all I saw a pair of mating proboscis and pretty close too. That was exciting. They certainly made a lot of noise. There were lots of excellent trails and I saw loads of fiddler crabs and mudskippers on the beach. Had the place to myself. But unfortunately could only stay one night as all accommodation was fully booked for the weekend. The Malays love their weekends off.

I wish every day was a Monday. Who was it didn't like Mondays - they're great if you're not working. Actually I was in the queue next to Bob Geldof at Gatwick Airport quite recently and was tempted to remind him of his greatest hit. But he looked pretty pissed off and I stayed silent. Another lost opportunity.

Unfortunately I missed out on Gunung Gading, home to the world's largest flower, the Rafflesia (Stamford Raffles again). The scarlet red Rafflesia can grow up to one metre in diameter, and emits the smell of rotting flesh to attract flies and other insects for pollination. It has no specific season for flowering and only stays in flower for four or five days before dying. You have to rely very much on local knowledge and often it's a mad rush on a motor-bike down some remote jungle track to locate a flowering specimen. Sight of one continued to elude me throughout my travels in Malaysia and Indonesia.

Before leaving Sarawak, a few interesting observations. The Condom Shop - displaying its wares quite openly - and semi-naked women used in advertising - must all be Chinese. Then an advert for shampoo - Sunsilk. You don't even see the girl's hair. Well one might just catch a tantalising glimpse of it, because she's got a scarf over her head. And the condemnation of the West by Dr Mahathir, when the country has imported some of the worst American 'culture' e.g. McDonald's and KFC. Why?

Finally some interesting body-piercing, as advertised in the tourist office of all places. Female genitals - outer labia and clitoral hood. Male genitals - Prince Albert and Reverse Prince Albert, foreskin, Guiche, Frenum, Didoes, Apadravya, Hafada and Palang. This latter piercing originated amongst the various tribes of Borneo and involves the insertion of a metal barbell some five centimetres long horizontally along the shaft of the penis. The Palang (translates as crossbar) is the name for the timber roof supports of longhouses. The device is supposed to give both sexes pleasure, though it sounds to me like something out of a horror movie. No doubt Chris Tarrant could do a programme about it. If anyone wants to take up these offers they can apply direct to the Head-hunters' Tattoo Studio, Kuching. Enjoy.

CHAPTER 31

THE OLDEST RAINFOREST

I was now back on the mainland and heading up the east coast of the Malay Peninsula. This part of the country is more conservative and Islamic in nature, so it was going to be quite an interesting contrast. Could I last several days (or even weeks) without a beer for example? From the airport at Johor Bahru I made my way to the bus station at Larkin and onward to the coastal town of Mersing. Not a lot goes on here apart from fishing - it's merely a stopover to Pulau Tioman and other east coast islands. The island is 20 km long and 11 km wide and, some say, shaped like a turtle. This stretch of coast is certainly famed for its green and leatherback turtles. It is extremely hilly or even mountainous in parts, reaching an altitude of over 1000 metres. There are beautiful white-sand beaches, coral-studded bays in which to snorkel and dive, and some rugged forest trails in the interior.

It was the setting for the 'fifties Hollywood musical *South Pacific* - the mythical Bali Hai, nothing to do with the real Bali, I hasten to add. So get out your sailor outfits, put on a song and dance routine and you can pretend you're here. *"I'm gonna wash that man right outa my hair,"* or so sings Nellie. But how could she if she had a scarf on? Later on, in the 1970s Tioman was proclaimed by Time magazine one of the world's most beautiful islands.

I was led to believe that the island was totally geared to tourism, with all the burgeoning infrastructure of a new airport, express boat services, roads and even a casino. With hordes of visitors far outnumbering villagers, it sounded like the resort island from hell. I went in May, not exactly the off-season and it was as quiet as the grave. Perhaps 9/11 had put everyone off, or was it that the island was teetotal. I think tobacco should have been banned as well and make it entirely drugs-free! I spent most of my time swimming and relaxing on the beach, but did some trekking as well.

An excellent forest trail crosses the middle of the island from Tekek to Juara along a boulder path, across streams, the vast canopy of the jungle arching overhead. You can stop for a refreshing dip in a small waterfall at the top of the hill. On the other side the path drops steeply down to Juara, with another lovely beach for swimming and a stop for lunch before walking back. I heard that a road is going to replace this trail - the horrendous onslaught of so-called progress. There are lots of other great walks on the island, especially along the west coast - through mangroves, over rocks and headlands and across near-deserted beaches. As I think I've said before, get out there before it's all gone.

Cherating, about half-way up the east coast was my next stop. It's known as a traveller's kampong (village), a restful oasis with a few bars (selling beer at rather inflated prices) and restaurants on the beach. It's about the nearest the east coast of Malaysia gets to Southern Thailand, but nowhere near as commercialised.

The highlight of my stay was watching a green turtle laying her eggs. These wonderful creatures have been hunted, captured in drift nets, had their eggs harvested and been subjected to marine pollution and environmental degradation. It is reckoned that only one turtle hatchling in a thousand survives to maturity, and populations have been reduced by 60% over the last fifty years. About 11pm we went to the beach, a short motor-bike ride from town, and saw the metre-long turtle laying around 100 eggs.

We were told very few people would be there, but at least fifty turned up. Poor turtle, all that struggling up the beach to be met by so many people with torches. The eggs had to be taken away by the rangers to be incubated, or else they'd be stolen. Green turtle eggs are still on sale in the markets. Though beach patrols guarding the nests is a better option, with a higher hatching success rate. Then we watched her go back into the sea - what a relief. An amazing sight. I was charged 15 ringitt - just under £3 - for the experience, but would have willingly paid far more. It's the only way to ensure the animals are conserved - to make eco-tourism more profitable to the local people than poaching.

Taman Negara is purported to be the world's oldest rainforest, though there are other places that have also put in a claim. It is reckoned to have existed for the past 130 million years virtually unchanged, having had no major geological activity in that time or strayed far from its current equatorial position. Much of it is still pristine, but you will be lucky to see larger mammals such as elephants, tigers, rhinos or even tapirs. They keep well away from the forest trails. But you will see birds and insects in abundance - I saw swarms of butterflies in forest glades - and of course the leeches will always want to make your acquaintance.

The park sprawls across the states of Pahang, Kelantan and Terengganu in the centre of the Malay Peninsula and covers over 4000 square km. Formed back in 1937, the park now welcomes over 40,000 visitors a year, which puts a lot of pressure on the ecology of the area. But at least the money from tourism helps keep the poachers at bay. Settlements on the park boundaries also contribute to environmental damage and I did notice a lot of litter around. At the gateway to the park is the small town of Jerantut, a stop on the so-called 'Jungle Railway'. I was later to continue my journey from here to Kota Bharu on the east coast. A bus journey to Kuala Tembeling takes just under an hour; then it's another three hours for the 60 km boat-trip to Park HQ at Kuala Tahan. This is interesting enough in itself with sightings of macaques, kingfishers, hornbills, and the odd water-buffalo.

I spent my first night in the hostel at Nusa Camp, which surprisingly was quite empty. In the early hours of the morning I found out why. It was overrun with mice. I awoke to the sound of gnawing and chewing just inches away from my ear. When I flashed my torch, the mouse scarpered, and on further examination I found, to my horror, holes in the walls, floors and just about everything else. Some were covered by flimsy sticky tape as if that would do much good. A lot of the woodwork was rotten and some of the beds covered with mouse droppings. I managed to find a bed as far from a wall as possible, but didn't get much sleep that night. And I had visions of mice crawling into my ears and eating my brain. Wooden structures don't last long in the jungle, a fact that was going to be firmly imprinted on my mind a couple of days later.

I opted for some easy jungle trekking on the Bukit (hill in Malay) Indah trail via the Canopy Walkway, suspended 25 metres above the ground by ropes, chains and netting. At 500 metres in length it is the world's longest, a scary experience for anyone suffering from vertigo. I loved it, despite having to wait at the various viewing platforms in a queuing system. A great way to see the forest from that height - literally a bird's eye view. The trail takes you on to Bukits Teresik and Indah with wide expansive panoramas of the forest and the rapids at Sungai Tembeling. Another trail takes you to Gua Telinga, a cave with a stream running through it. You have to cross the Sungai Tahan by sampan (small boat) first. On my arrival, I was almost hit by a bat making a hasty exit. Once inside, you cling anxiously to the rope as it guides you through the darkness.

Now for the interesting bit. Nearby is the Bumbun Belau hide and it certainly lived up to its name. I was resting underneath the hide, when some rotten wooden supports came crashing down with part of the corrugated iron roof. Just managed to get away in time, but fell over and got very muddy. Must have missed being killed or at least seriously injured by inches. It was like a Buster Keaton movie, when the wall falls down and he's standing at precisely the right spot (where the doorway is) to avoid being crushed. Throwing caution to the wind, I did a brief examination of the building and discovered that the whole structure was indeed rotten and about to be reclaimed by the jungle. Yet another narrow escape. I'm thinking that, like a cat, I must have nine lives. There are numerous other trails in the forest and the spectacular 55 km trek to the top of Gunung Tahan (2187m), the highest point on the peninsula, a bit more taxing than the Cameron Highlands I feel. Maybe tomorrow!

In fact the next day I was leaving the park on the 'Jungle Railway'; eleven hours of stop/start, clackety-clack and shaking from side to side in what seemed an eternity. At several points the train 'jumped', and I thought it was going to leave the tracks. Frightening. Reminded me of all those pleasant journeys by Network South East in the UK. That's showing my age. But the scenery was a lot better - the line is regarded as an engineering marvel and I finally arrived at Wakaf Bharu, the stop for Kota Bharu, in the late evening.

It was the school holidays - isn't it always - and the Chinese were in town and heading to the Perhentian Islands. Never went there - was going to be much too crowded. Anyway, the only place I could find (cheap or expensive) was a dorm some way out of town. It wasn't that bad – clean, and the beds were comfortable, but it's what happened the next night that was the shocker. It was about 2am and I was fast asleep. A Malay couple in their thirties came in and opened the door to a private room opposite me. The light went on and they left the door ajar, a bright beam of light directed across my bed. Then they started undressing; the woman lay on the bed, the man mounted her and they had sex, complete with grunts and groans. After the act the man cleared off somewhere, the woman knelt down to pray and started chanting - maybe it was some verses from the Koran. This must have gone on for thirty minutes or so. Well I was flabbergasted. Shagging in dorms in Oz or NZ, I suppose is pretty commonplace. But in the Muslim-dominated part of Malaysia, and in full view of others, as Victor Meldrew would say, "I don't believe it."

Kota Bharu is a not a place you would probably want to stay in for more than a couple of days. Its main purpose from a Western perspective is as a transit town for the Perhentians or a gateway to Thailand, but it does boast some royal palaces, colourful markets and museums if you're looking for something to do. Wayang Kulit (shadow puppetry), Gasing (top spinning), Wau (kite flying) and Rebana (giant drum) playing appear to be the main cultural activities here, though sadly I didn't see any of them. If you start getting thirsty there is always the odd Chinese bar that sells beer. And I can recommend a couple of excellent vegetarian restaurants - Natural Vegetarian Food with an all-you-can-eat buffet, and the Muhibah Vegetarian Restaurant serving Chinese and Malay dishes.

When the time did come for me to leave, it seemed that Malaysia was at a complete standstill, which I'm sure couldn't have been blamed entirely on the Chinese and the school holidays. All planes fully booked and the bus to Penang full for 10 days solid. Absolutely ridiculous. So I came up with the brilliant idea of going back into Thailand to Hat

Yai and then down to Penang that way. Mad isn't it. But then everyone knows I can't keep away from the 'brides'. And Thailand is always a safe bolthole in times of trouble. I did go to a barber shop by the way, for a Number '0'; keeps the head lice at bay.

When I was in Africa, Cher's 'Believe' was the song of the moment; now it's Kylie's 'Can't Get You out Of My Head' — it's being played everywhere. Or as the bishop said to the actress "I can't get my head out of you." Still, enough of such frivolities, I was now on my way over the Straits of Melaka to Sumatra and my final country in S E Asia, Indonesia.

CHAPTER 32

SEARCHING IN SUMATERA

"We found them sifting resolutely through the putrid carpet of mud and debris covering the remains of their front room; a handsome young couple with three infant children, determined to resurrect their lives when all they could see, smell and taste for miles around was death. The sights were as surreal as they were macabre. Here a headless cow lying in the road, there a heavy lorry somehow standing on end. Beside a rice field, the body of a woman lay beside an upturned armchair as though she had just fallen out of it; other mud-covered corpses were almost indistinguishable from the fallen foliage." [12]

Daily Mail, Monday January 3, 2005

A huge stretch of western Sumatra was turned into little more than rubble and dust, with trees uprooted and buildings destroyed. On the remote Simeulue Islands west of Sumatra, coral reefs and rocks that had been submerged for thousands of years were now high and dry. A huge 60-foot wave tore into the coastline and travelled some four miles inland, destroying all, or almost all, before it. Satellite pictures show the full extent of the damage, as whole communities were wiped out. There are the classic images of the solitary mosque left standing at Lampuuk, or the tanker stranded a mile inland. And the before and after aerial pictures of Banda Aceh, looking like it had been flattened by a nuclear bomb. It is reckoned that over 170,000 people were killed in Sumatra alone.

Seven thousand people once lived in Lampuuk; fewer than a thousand survived - a once thriving community reduced to rubble by the force of the waves. Piles of debris were scattered for mile after mile. It was clear that several months on, the reconstruction work had hardly begun, with people still living in tents or in shacks made from wood salvaged from the wreckage. It will take between five and ten years for lives to reach anything like normality, but for the people of Aceh the iconic vision of that mosque stands as a beacon of hope and optimism for the future. *"The Tsunami is a warning from Allah because we have neglected our faith. Allah decides. If he wants to take us no-one can stop it. It is a punishment. But God willing we are strong."* Good luck to them.

But there is far more to Sumatra than the horrors of the tsunami and the devastated coastline. I was there about eighteen months before these tragic events took place, and almost my entire trip was spent inland, for that is where the treasures of Sumatra lie. Sumatra is the second largest island in the Indonesian chain of over 18,000 islands, the largest archipelago in the world. It is cut in half by the equator, so the climate is about as tropical as it gets. Apart from the Bukit Barisan Mountains, which are decidedly cooler, especially at night. Fortunately this is where most of the tourist attractions are. The range includes many peaks over 3000 metres, and nestled among them a line of nearly 100 volcanoes. There are more active volcanoes in Indonesia than anywhere else on earth.

Culture and religion are extremely diverse - staunchly Islamic Acehnese juxtaposed with the coastal Malays, and the unique and unusual Bataks and Minangkabau with their buffalo-horned houses. Then there are the Mentawaians of Siberut who still live a tribal existence in the forest and have largely kept their animist beliefs. And just like the Malay Peninsula, much of Sumatra has been exposed to the influences of trading and colonisation. The Europeans, Chinese and Indians have all had a go at shaping the history of the island. With a population of about 40 million, out of a total Indonesian population of 250 million, it is relatively sparsely populated, certainly when compared to its neighbour Java.

When you are departing from the port of Penang, across the Straits of Melaka, you will find there are two queues. One is mainly Westerners, the other mainly Indonesian and Malay. Well, the first is for the tourist hotspots of Langkawi, the second for the port of Medan, the major city in Sumatra, where I was going. The ferry journey of some four or five hours is the bumpiest I have ever experienced - if you're prone to sea-sickness, definitely take the pills. Then another bumpy bus journey into the centre of the city. And finally a bumpy becak (bicycle rickshaw) ride to the hotel of your choice (and be taken for a ride in more ways than one). *"No I don't want the most expensive place on the block so you can get your commission."*

There is really nothing positive I can say about Medan. It is choked with traffic, noisy, polluted, but above all there is nothing to do here. It didn't help matters when I was awakened from my slumbers at 4am by the wailings from two competing mosques. It was worse than the Eurovision Song Contest. Get me out of here.

Just under 100 km to the north-west of this ugly sprawling metropolis is the town of Bukit Lawang, home to the Bohorok orang-utan viewing centre. It used to be a rehabilitation centre, run on similar lines to the one at Sepilok in Sabah, and was set up in 1973, nine years after its illustrious predecessor. But due to a lack of funding and the volume of tourists disturbing the rehabilitation process, that has now been relocated to a quarantine centre near Medan.

The orang-utans are reached across the Sungai (river) Bohorok by dugout canoe, and like Sepilok, there are regular feedings from a platform in the jungle. A mother and baby swung down over my head on an overhanging branch - even closer than at Sepilok. However, you should try not to get too close, as some human illnesses like flu can easily be transmitted to orang-utans. Some irresponsible guides feed the apes illegally to get close access for tour groups, and this also disturbs natural behaviour. I decided not to go trekking around Bukit Lawang and the Gunung Leuser National Park. There was a bit too much pestering and hassling by potential 'guides' for my liking.

Bukit Lawang exists solely for tourism and the income it generates, but the emphasis seems to be more on bars, restaurants and discos than environmental issues. It is very popular with day-trippers from Medan at weekends - probably a good time to avoid. Current predictions estimate that the Sumatran orang-utan may become extinct within ten years; don't they deserve a little better? It seems a great shame that such great assets are not more appreciated and better managed; then the locals, tourists, and the wildlife of the rainforest can benefit. But I suppose it's very much the same the world over.

A very sad conclusion to this story was the devastating floods in November 2003, when over 200 people died and much of the town was wiped out. The Environment Minister Nabiel Makarim has said the disaster was exacerbated by extensive illegal logging in the area, which has stripped hillsides. Describing loggers as "terrorists", he also blamed officials and business-people for letting it happen. President Megawati Sukarnoputri exclaimed *"Nature will become angry if we are arrogant. It will show its devastating rage… when we treat nature with violence."* The tragedy has focused attention once again on the rapid destruction of Indonesia's forests. Locals said that the government had ordered the felling of hundreds of trees in the mountains above the village, for the construction of a major highway from neighbouring Central Aceh district. So who is to blame? We all are.

Back in Medan I was organising the next leg of my journey - south to Danau (Lake) Toba. Well from my experiences so far, I would venture the following comments. A good example of Indonesian organisation:- a menu without a meal, a coffee-shop without any coffee, a tour company without any tours, an airline company without any flights - 'It's Merpati and I'll Fly If I Want To.' Something out of *Monty Python* really. But one thing Indonesia is never short of is cigarettes - it's called Indonesian 'style'. *"And no, I haven't got anything smaller"* - the bus journey to Toba was 45,000 from a 50,000 rupiah note (just under £4).

I think I've been 'Horassed' - too many 'Hey Misters' maybe, as I was now on my way to see the Bataks. 'Horas' is the traditional Batak greeting. 'Hey Mister' is the general Indonesian greeting. If there is one thing that unites the country other than the language - Bahasa Indonesia - it is the 'Hey Mister' cult. It starts like the hum of a single mosquito buzzing around your head, but builds up rapidly to a deafening crescendo to frighten even the most steadfast of souls. There is no escape. Night and day it drones on until one becomes utterly exhausted and psychologically drained.

The route from Medan seemed to be uphill all the way and as we gained altitude, the pines replaced the palms (too many palm plantations - I've already said enough on that), the churches replaced the mosques and the women discarded their headscarves. The Bataks are Protestant Christians (from Dutch colonial times), surrounded by a sea of Islam, though animist rituals are still practised. Lots of Christian graves lined the road and then the distinctive buffalo-horn-shaped roofs came into view. And statues of soldiers pointing their rifles in the air - a freedom thing I suppose - the Bataks have always been a fiercely independent people. Until the 19th century they ate the flesh of their enemies, so subduing them was quite a task. There are now some six million of them in the area around Danau Toba, a natural stronghold against attack from outsiders. However, despite all this sense of foreboding, I found the Bataks to be the friendliest of peoples.

Danau Toba is the biggest and deepest crater lake in the world, the size of Belgium, with the island of Samosir, almost the size of Singapore, sitting like a wedge of cheese in the middle. The lake is up to 450 metres deep in places and was caused by a massive volcanic eruption 75,000 years ago, the loudest noise ever heard by man. Covering a massive 1707 sq km, it is the largest lake in S E Asia. The bus dropped us all at Parapat, from where it is a short ferry ride to Tuk Tuk, the main tourist resort on the island.

Tanjung (peninsula) Tuk Tuk is shaped like an human ear (no doubt listening to the strumming of a Batak guitar - the Bataks are very musical) and all the accommodation and restaurants are situated on a road that runs round its perimeter. I stayed at Tabo Cottages run by Anto and Annette Silalahi, an Indonesian/German couple, with excellent vegetarian food and homemade bread. The rooms were spotless, the beds comfortable and the service impeccable. And a beautiful position set in lush tropical gardens overlooking the lake. And like Indonesians, I just love avocados - they're always on the menu.

I struck up some good conversations with a young lady called Melpa, who worked in Tabo. She was 26, and one of eight children. Her hours of work were from 7am to 10pm, very rarely getting a day off work. She spoke very good English and shared a room with two other girls. So welcoming and unassuming, but also with an ambition to better herself, she reminded me very much of the girl in Hanoi. She told me she had worked as a tour guide on a Christian pilgrimage to the Holy Land, but eventually would like to run a guest-house of her own. Melpa was very knowledgeable about the political situation in Indonesia and world affairs in general. Which just goes to show that it is only circumstances that prevent many people in poorer countries from developing their full potential.

The rest of Tuk Tuk is packed with bars, restaurants and craft shops, but strangely there is a lack of commercialism here - it has very much a quaint village atmosphere about it. For an evening's entertainment you could try the Brandos Blues Bar with the latest Indonesian disco craze - girls with hula hoops - full on. Or experience a live band performing such greats as 'A Sing Sing So' and 'Rositta'. One of the songs sounded like 'Saddam's in Toba' and I thought at the time maybe he was in hiding here. Come to think of it, one of the singers looked a bit like him. I was coerced into buying a cassette - I think playing it would be guaranteed to keep the cats away, but would give you a terrible headache. For the record, the instruments used were flutes, guitars, drums and a primitive glockenspiel - with wooden slats.

I wanted to go on a Toba cruise, but unfortunately it wasn't running - not enough tourists, which was quite in evidence despite being the 'high season'. Indonesia does seem to have everything against it - the fallout from 9/11 and SARS, the unrest in East Timor, the Bali and Jakarta bombings, the civil war in Aceh, riots, forest fires and finally the seemingly knockout blow of the tsunami.

I went walkabout in this very peaceful place, far from any of the above. Indonesia is a huge country after all. From top to toe it would be like travelling from London to Afghanistan and what a hotbed of discontent lurks there. Don't believe everything you read in the press. Firstly I met a group of schoolgirls from Siantar, a nearby town, wishing to improve their English. By my reckoning it was pretty good already. And they brought with them a camera of course for lots of photos. I reached Tomok, a quiet idyllic rural setting with rice paddies and water-buffalo, the majestic lake and mountains as a backdrop. More churches with corrugated tin roofs - much cheaper to produce and maintain than the traditional thatch. And then King Sidabutar's Grave - a sarcophagus with sculptured heads and a statue behind. If he really looked like that, no wonder he's six foot under.

At Ambarita there was gospel singing with the congregation dressed up in their Sunday best - flashy suits and colourful dresses. But what I had come to see were the stone chairs and execution block in an adjoining courtyard. There was no guide available, so I didn't get the luridly graphic description of past executions (and ritual cannibalism) as mentioned in the local literature.

Next day it was a 90 km bike ride to Pangururan (there and back) on the other side of the island, to give my ankle a little exercise. Would you believe I was still recovering from a broken ankle? First stop was Simanindo, where there is a fine museum with musical instruments, masks, spears and swords displayed in an old Batak house. I missed most of the traditional dances - a tour group turned up (probably the first one in months) and they changed the timetable to accommodate them. But as one of the dances depicted the slaughter of a water buffalo at the Borotan (slaughter pole) it was probably just as well. Continuing my journey I passed such delights as the Beehive, the Lighthouse and the Horse and Rider statues. There's not much at Pangururan - very much a backwater as far as tourism is concerned. It's okay as a lunch stop though, and then it's time for the return journey.

I was almost back in Tuk Tuk when the heavens opened and I got drenched. There were at least forty lightning flashes and any one could have hit the bike as I was quite exposed. It was also getting very dark

- with no bike or street lights. Somebody suggested later I should have gone by motor-bike. Have they seen the pot-holes, or the state of the bridges with piles of sand and oil drums in the middle of the road? And the general standard of driving. Scary. Though I'm glad I didn't try the trekking option over the hill, which two German girls were considering. Would have been like mud-wrestling. On second thoughts!

Well, all good things come to an end and I waved goodbye to Melpa as I left on the ferry to Parapat. I was bracing myself for the night-bus journey south to Bukittinggi on the less-than-aptly named 'Trans-Sumatra Highway', the greatest misnomer in the world of transport. I think it could all be summed up by a sign I saw in Parapat - Dr Natalia Turnip; if you went to see her, you'd end up in a vegetative state. Which is exactly what I felt like after a horrendous sixteen-hour smoke-filled journey on the so-called Super Exec coach.

Up and down it went on what for much of the time was little more than a dirt-track and so expensive - 190,000 rupiah, or a pound for each hour endured - a similar journey in Thailand would cost half that. I dread to think what it would be like in the wet season. And the smoking on the coach was unbelievable - they were trying to compete with the volcanoes. Talk about passive smoking - one fag lit up after another. Did you know that one in eleven smokers in the world is Indonesian, and they're all on the bus with me. Do you think I'll be able to sue if I get lung cancer?

The next morning we went through Bonjol on the equator, so the rest of my trip was going to be in the Southern Hemisphere. So I finally arrived in Bukittinggi with a sore throat and headache and quite the worse for wear. But I suppose I have to be grateful. A German guy I met (who incidentally spoke fluent Mandarin and had been teaching English in China) had nine hours added to his ordeal due to a massive breakdown. We travellers do torture ourselves.

The hill town of Bukittinggi, home to the Minangkabau people, is a great place to chill out after the labours of such a journey. And at 930m above sea-level it does get a little cold at nights. It is surrounded by volcanoes, lakes and canyons, and there are many interesting sights within an easy walking distance. The focal point of the town is the five-tiered Clock Tower, built in 1926. When Indonesia gained independence, the tower was topped with a Minangkabau buffalo-horned roof. These are constructed at an even steeper gradient than those of their Batak neighbours. Looking towards the tower is a statue of a Sumatran tiger - there's not many of those left.

There are a couple of good museums, by Indonesian standards. The Military Museum has an American Harvard B419 plane mounted on the front lawn. Inside, there's a collection of faded photos, weapons and memorabilia from the War of Independence from the Dutch. Like Malaysia, much is made of the 'Merdeka' story. A footbridge over Jalan (street) Ahmad Yani provides a panoramic view of Bukittinggi's rusting rooftops to Mount Merapi. It leads to another museum, an excellent example of Minangkabau architecture, and housing costumes, photos, kitchenware, models of houses, but also two-headed and eight-legged buffalo calves. They lived for about two hours. I can hardly mention the zoo next door - a very sad and depressing place and not recommended.

On the southern edge of town is the Panorama Park, with views of the 120m-deep Sianok Canyon and the Mount Singgalang volcano. Contained within are the very extensive Japanese Caves, constructed by Indonesian slave labour during WWII. I did a short stroll through the Sianok Canyon past a couple of mosques and a school, with squeals of "Hello Mister" ringing in my ears. It was quite picturesque with banana plantations, the road lined with hibiscus hedges, papaya and bougainvillea. But lots of angry barking dogs - one of my pet hates.

Back in town there were loads of guys sitting around selling durians that had just come into season. Actually not that bad if you can endure the smell. I can think of many worse food items. Further afield, tours can be arranged of local villages, buffalo-horn houses, rice-thrashing and craft workshops. A coffee-mill driven by a water-wheel reminded me of Bateman's in Sussex, home of Rudyard Kipling. Ginger coffee - it might catch on, and the dried banana and papaya was pretty tasty.

The Minangkabau, meaning 'the buffalo wins', is a matriarchal society and everything is inherited through the female line - women hold considerable power. It is also Muslim and to me as an outsider certainly seemed one of the more enlightened models. The culture is extremely colourful and vibrant, and this can be seen in clothing, textiles, jewellery, architecture and probably best of all in dance and music. The dancing was some of the finest I have seen in my travels - a very polished and professional performance. Accompanied by the Indonesian gamelan - tuned gongs, and the saluang - a wind instrument like the flute. There was a strong Arab influence and at one point they played 'Rivers Of Babylon', which I suppose was quite appropriate.

The dances included Silek, or self-defence with very dramatic movements and using a dagger. One false move could have caused real damage. Then the Umbrella dance for young people dating, Tari Indang, the dance of fishermen - sitting as though in a boat and using the arms to imitate waves. The performance concluded with the Tari Piriang - dancing on broken plates. Excruciating. But not as excruciating as me dancing. I was sitting in the front row (a big mistake) and was pulled up on stage by a young lady dancer as a grand finale - it was not a pretty sight.

I decided to go on a trek to Lake Maninjau and en route my guide invited me to a wedding-feast - I think it was one of his relations who had just been married at the local mosque. The Golden Couple

- everything they wear is golden, the bride with a spectacular headdress - sit all day surrounded by gold and red brocades, drapes and parasols, receiving guests. We were invited to partake of the sumptuous feast laid out before them. I think it is considered good fortune for a foreigner to be present at the proceedings.

The trekking was a pretty tame affair, but fun nonetheless, across rice-terraces to local villages. Saw a few people in the paddy fields and some guys pig-hunting with dogs. Not so good. Then just over the crest of a hill we came to a small village and there's a football match in progress. So that's where everybody is. A very rough and uneven pitch - I bet there have been a few broken bones playing there. Wherever you go in the world there's always someone playing football.

At Lawang Top I spent the night at Anas Homestay - just a few wooden shacks with tin roofs, surrounded by the forest, but with a great view of the lake. Maninjau is another crater-lake, as deep but not as big as Toba - 17 km long by 8 km wide. But unfortunately the owners don't run the homestay anymore - they're retired! There were some very good write-ups in the comments book about the food and hospitality shown by Mr and Mrs Anas. Also on sightings of orange monkeys and hornbills and brilliant sunrises and sunsets, which sadly didn't come true for me. But the clouds, rain, spiders and leeches were still there, so it couldn't all be bad. At least I didn't get the smoke from the forest fires which so smothered the area in 1997.

Next day we trekked, or rather ambled, past teak, mahogany and cinnamon groves - also plantations of durian, aubergine, coffee and peanuts. Some trees are actually being replanted as a result of government subsidies - hopefully to replace the two million hectares of rainforest that is lost in Indonesia every year. I went for a swim in the lake. It was actually quite warm. And almost got ridden off into the woods to see a Rafflesia that had just come into flower, but it was a false alarm.

Most of the ones that are in flower only reach about 30cm in diameter - not the 100cm giants seen in David Attenborough programmes. I felt better for that as I boarded the bus back to Bukittinggi up 44 hair-pin bends. Would have been scarier going down them.

My next destination was to be Singapore, a journey by road, air and sea which amazingly I achieved all in one day. Bukittinggi to Padang by minibus, Padang to Batam by plane and Batam to Singapore by boat. Finally a taxi from the ferry terminal to my hotel just in time for my Indian meal. One of those days that just worked like clockwork. I was in two minds whether to head to Jakarta - another bomb had just gone off. Bombs are always going off in Jakarta, an experience now being repeated in many other capital cities. And I really couldn't face an even bigger version of Medan, and none of the people I spoke to recommended the place. Perhaps it would be kinder to remember it by its more romantic name Batavia, city of sails and spices. And all the images of swashbuckling adventure that conjures up. Dream on.

So my journey in Java began with the far more genteel and cultural city of Yogyakarta. Just before I left Sumatra I saw a sign near Padang Airport which boldly proclaimed 'SEMEN PADANG.' If that's what they put in the cooking, I think I'll stick to the pizza after all.

CHAPTER 33

JALAN, JALAN, JAVA MAN

Yogyakarta is the cultural and artistic capital of Java. Here you will find the Kraton, the palace of the sultans, and within a stone's throw, the magnificent Hindu and Buddhist temples of Prambanan and Borobudur. During Dutch colonial times, the city was a symbol of independence for the Javanese and today it is largely self-governing, with a certain amount of autonomy from Jakarta. It is quite small for an Indonesian city, with a population of about 500,000, and it is relatively easy to negotiate the roads in the main tourist areas.

I started by wandering around the Kraton, a maze of alleyways (I didn't get lost) with craft workshops, batik-stalls, mosques, schools and the notorious bird market - unmentionable. You get a good view of the old city from the ruins of the outer walls. And of another Muslim wedding ceremony, though this one seemed a little less inviting. I didn't think they would appreciate me being in the wedding photos clad in my T-shirt and shorts. But didn't the bride look nice. A pity I could hardly see her face under the scarf. The palace itself, where the current sultan still resides, was built in the mid-18th century, but much has been added over the years. The main building, the reception hall, is supported by great teak columns with an elaborately-decorated roof. The whole structure has a very airy and spacious feel to it, with a series of courtyards and pavilions. A museum contains gifts from European royalty, various heirlooms and portraits, and a collection of gamelan instruments. Music and dance performances take place frequently.

There were very few Westerners on my visit, especially considering this is a major tourist attraction. Just after the Bali bombing of 2002, visitors were down by 90%, which in my eyes makes the experience that much more appealing. But Yogya, as it is affectionately known, has to be the noisiest place I've been to so far - at least where I was staying just off Sosrowijayan. It wasn't just the usual coughing and spluttering, the loud blaring TV, the crowing cocks, the calls to prayer at all hours, but also the constant movement of furniture and high-heels on tiled floors - that is agony to hear. And doors banging, locks being played with, a washing-machine that rumbled on all night, the thud of cockroaches being squashed; and finally screaming children who wake you at 6am - if you're not already awake - as they're off to play football.

Borobudur is the greatest Buddhist monument in Indonesia. It was first constructed in the 9th century and re-discovered by Raffles under layers of volcanic ash in the early 19th century. It was restored twice in the 20th century - the supporting hill it was built on had become waterlogged. Surviving ash-flows, subsidence, weather-erosion, terrorist bombs and the impact of millions of tourists, Borobudur stands firm, a monument to man's ingenuity and perseverance.

The temple is constructed from two million blocks of stone in the form of a symmetrical stupa wrapped around a small hill. Six square terraces are surmounted by three circular ones, with four stairways dissecting them through carved arches. Huge bulbous bell-shaped stupas top the massive edifice. The monument is covered in bas-reliefs with serene-faced Buddha images and scenes of Javanese life depicting elephants, warriors, kings and dancing girls. There are many similarities to Angkor Wat in Cambodia, a common ancestry. Many of the Buddhas have lost their heads, some perhaps as a result of the bombs planted by opponents to the Soeharto regime in 1985. They reminded me of the decapitated Thatcher statue in the Guildhall Art Gallery back in 2002, with the appropriate headline from *The Mirror*: 'THATCHER BEHEADED (Sadly, it's only her statue)'.

Prambanan, which is the greatest Hindu complex in Java, was erected some 50 years after Borobudur, a period of amazing architectural creativity. It too lay in ruins for many years and it was not until the 1930s that reconstruction was properly attempted. Pride of place goes to the lavishly-carved Shiva temple with statues of Shiva, Durga, Ganesh and Agastya standing erect and proud. This pyramidal-shaped monolith rises to 47m, and is literally brimming with a menagerie of animals, plants and deities in the true Hindu tradition. Smaller temples to Vishnu and Brahma flank the Shiva temple and again like Angkor Wat, numerous other shrines and monuments lie scattered several kilometres away. Scenes from the Ramayana abound with the story of how Lord Rama's wife Sita is abducted by the evil King Ravana, then found and released by the monkey-god Hanuman.

In the evening I went to a performance of the Ramayana Ballet at the outdoor theatre in Prambanan. With the magnificent floodlit Shiva temple as a backdrop, we were entertained with a spectacle of dancing, acrobatics and battle-scenes with monkey armies. The plot goes a bit like this. Boy wins girl, boy loses girl and then has to fight to win her back. But then is not really sure whether he wants her after all. However love, whatever that is, prevails in the end. Quite a sexist drama I'm afraid, but the dancing and costumes were excellent and VIP seats for only 100,000 rupiah (£7.50).

Also not far from Yogyakarta is the 2900-metre Mount Merapi, one of the most active volcanoes in the world. An eruption killed 69 people in 1994, and in 1998 thousands had to evacuate their homes. Its eruptions continue along with pyroclastic flows and earthquakes. Not least the one in May 2006, which killed 5700 and injured 40,000, devastating parts of Yogya, including the temple at Prambanan. The statistics of death and suffering in Indonesia just seem to get worse. A tourist trail takes you up to see the lava flows. The walk started around 2am, but there wasn't too much activity on the night I went, and the flows were at least a couple of kilometres away. I wanted to get within 10 metres or so. But that would have been too dangerous, and breathing in the noxious gases was not a good idea. I have to say I was rather disappointed, but a brilliant view of the mountain at sunrise was received as compensation.

Back in Yogya I was preparing for the next leg of my journey to the awesome and majestic Gunung Bromo. But first, a minor deviation. A couple I had been travelling with in Indonesia had caught Dengue Fever in Ko Pha-Ngan the same time I was there. It is a most unpleasant illness transmitted by day-flying mosquitoes, and can cause headaches, nausea, vomiting, bleeding and muscle-pains. Hence its old name of 'breakbone fever'. The girl could hardly move for days; her joints were very painful and she started losing her hair - another symptom which can occur some weeks after contracting the illness. I must have been extremely lucky - a lot of people went down with it!

So I was on my way on another long road journey, but this time only a total of 12 hours. The route went via Solo (Surakarta), the riot capital of Java - and Ngawi, home of the famed 'Java Man', as unearthed by Dutchman Eugene Dubois in 1891. Officially called *Pithecanthropus erectus*, but more commonly known as *Homo erectus*, the skull and other remains are reckoned to date back nearly two million years. Quite recently further remains of *Homo erectus* (The Hobbit), have (allegedly) been found on the island of Flores further along the Indonesian chain of islands. This supports the view that humans migrated down this route.

On the last leg, from the town of Probolinggo to Cemoro Lawang, the minibus driver drove up the hair-pin bends like a madman. We were taken to the Cemara Indah Hotel where no doubt the driver obtained a commission. What a shit-hole - the worst rooms I'd seen so far, certainly the thinnest mattresses and most of the bed slats were broken. So I booked into the Hotel Bromo Permai instead with hot showers and breakfast included. But at £10 a night it wasn't cheap, the water was lukewarm and the shower-head was broken. But it was worth every penny for what awaited me, so I wasn't complaining. It was a cold night - you needed your thermal underwear - even in the Tropics it's cold at 2000 metres. Difficult to get used to when you've spent a year in the heat and humidity.

Gunung Bromo lies at the centre of the Tengger Massif (as Ali G would say), and must rank as one of the most spectacular wonders of the natural world. I walked along the outer crater-rim the next day - 10 km across - and looked over to Bromo (2392m), Batok (2440m) and Kursi (2581m), and this strange other-world landscape. Nearby rises Gunung Semeru (3676m), Java's highest peak and one of its most active volcanoes. This supernatural landscape has inspired many myths and legends - one says that the Tengger crater was dug out by an ogre infatuated by a princess, using a coconut shell. A very large one. The area is very much associated with Hindus escaping from the spread of Islam, and a small Hindu temple is situated within the crater at the foot of Mt Batok. That evening out came the noodle knockers and later on the Muslim chanting - karaoke without the music. No wonder the Hindus were trying to escape.

Why rise for the sun at 3am, when you can get a much better view a couple of hours later? Okay, about midday the clouds build up to obscure the view, but there's plenty of time before that, and most important of all, you avoid the crowds. I rose at the reasonable hour of 6am, had breakfast - rubber eggs and burnt toast - had they been microwaved? And set off at 7am. It took only an hour to walk across the lava sand, past the Hindu Temple and up the 253 steps to the top of Bromo. Of course passing all those dudes who came in Land Rovers and on horses hours before, creating clouds of dust after them.

And the sight before me - INCREDIBLE!!! No superlatives can give it justice. Smoke rising from the centre of the crater, a crater within a crater. The first time I had been on the rim of an active volcano. I walked round the rim to a higher viewpoint - nobody followed me. I was truly alone for the first time in months. No Westerners, no Indonesians. I stood admiring the fantastic view when suddenly from nowhere I heard a faint "Hello Mister". Was I dreaming, or more likely a recurring nightmare. And out of the bushes came two Indonesian men, almost planted there to give me this insidious greeting. This reminded me of standing on the top of Bidean nam Bian in Glencoe, Scotland and having a piss. When I started there was literally not a soul in sight, but before the last dribble had left my body, two guys poked their faces round a boulder for a good look. Whether they were into water-sports, or just attracted by my sweaty body odour I don't know, but this kind of thing happens so often.

Which conveniently brings me to the subject of Munro-bagging, and I digress somewhat from the essence of the narrative here. For those who are not aware, a Munro is a mountain in Scotland over 3000 feet in height (or 914.4 metres). I've been up a few, mainly the interesting pointy ones on the west coast. But there is this band of people who get great delight in ticking these peaks off, all 284 of them. Another classic case of OCD. So when I'm out walking, one moment I think there's no-one for miles around, when suddenly a great multitude of Munro-baggers come over the crest of a hill, notebooks and laptops in hand, entering in their latest conquest. Adventure has been turned into a corporate enterprise. I feel like I'm Richard Hannay from *The Thirty-Nine Steps*, and so desperate to escape their clutches. One guy I was talking to in a guest-house on the Isle of Skye, even said he preferred Munro-bagging to say, going up Kilimanjaro or trekking in the Himalayas. Well I suppose it takes all sorts. 'I'm Not a Munro-bagger, Get Me out of Here.' Preferably on the next flight to Bangkok for some real adventure.

Meanwhile, I went on a very interesting walk from Cemoro Lawang to Gunung Penanjakan (2770m), a little bit higher than the Munros, through fields of potatoes, cabbages and onions with the odd drift of oilseed rape. Silver wattles, buddleias, fuchsias, daturas or Angel's Trumpets with their long white, yellow and orange flowers and leycesteria (white flowers and purplish-red bracts) lined the roadside. Also many daisies, sunflowers and marigolds. Quite a garden. Further up the hill it was mainly pine forest with brambles, ferns (and tree ferns) and grasses. There were even more spectacular vistas of Bromo, Batok and Kursi - this is the classic picture-postcard view of the volcanoes at dawn with the rays of the rising sun shining through the mist. It was worth visiting Indonesia just for this. Natural wonders never fail to impress. And it is a sight that has remained with me to this day.

CHAPTER 34

BALI HAI

I left Bromo and Java by way of the Baluran National Park and Banyuwangi. This park is called 'Little Africa' on account of its savannah grasslands and invading acacia-thorn scrub. It still has a fair amount of wildlife, mainly deer, monkeys, pigs and even some leopards. All good African animals. A small fire was raging when I passed through - whether this was to control the scrub or more slash and burn I wasn't too sure. Then it was a short ferry journey to Gilimanuk in Bali.

At Gilimanuk there was the minibus fiasco. It was quite late in the evening and everyone was tired and anxious to get to Lovina Beach for a few chill-out days. But life isn't as simple as that. It must have been at least two hours while we waited for the requisite number of passengers to be squeezed in. We offered to pay more to enable the bus to leave pronto. But no, the driver wanted maximum capacity. So we all huffed and puffed, got out and stretched our legs and even touted for more passengers.

Right, we're ready to go. Then one of the guys decided he wasn't going after all and it was back to square one. Finally at 10pm, the bus still hadn't moved and I'd had enough. So I stayed the night in Gilimanuk, not really a good introduction to Bali. The mozzies in the guest-house were horrendous, so no chilling out tonight. But next day I had a minibus all to myself and at no extra charge. Flexibility is what travelling is all about - sometimes go with the flow, on other occasions stand your ground and say no.

To many people, Bali is the archetypal tropical paradise, with its picturesque palm-fringed beaches, verdant forests and rice-terraces, a rich and colourful culture with festivals and rituals galore. And not forgetting some of the best surfing in the world. Those huge waves come all the way from Antarctica. It became the bastion of Hinduism in Indonesia, as Islam slowly spread is tentacles through Sumatra and Java. Despite the myth of a gentle and peace-loving people, the island has had a pretty bloody history. From the feuding Majapahits (Hindu dynastic rulers) and the Dutch conquest, to the battles for independence and the anti-communist riots in the mid-sixties when eighty thousand people were killed, Bali has seen much death and destruction. More than two thousand perished when Gunung Agung, Bali's greatest volcano, erupted in 1963, devastating vast areas of the island. Most recently of course, the Bali bombings of 2002 and 2005 when 225 people lost their lives, emphasising the very volatile politics of Indonesia.

Bali lies just south of the equator, situated between Java in the west and Lombok in the east. It is a small island, only 140 km by 80 km, and like most of the Indonesian chain, very mountainous and containing many active volcanoes. A combination of high rainfall and volcanic soils creates the ideal conditions for growing rice, coffee and vegetables, many of which are exported to other parts of Indonesia. With a population of over three million it is quite densely populated and urban sprawl is beginning to despoil the landscape, especially in the south around the capital Denpasar and Kuta.

Tourism is by far the largest industry, and this too is threatening the fragile environment. Over 95% of the population are nominally Hindu, but Balinese Hinduism often bears little relation to the Hindus of India or indeed Malaysia. They worship the same trinity of gods - Brahma, Shiva and Vishnu, but there is no caste system and no untouchables. A major difference as far as I was concerned, was that none of them were vegetarian or subscribed to any karma doctrines. Suckling pig seemed to be a substantial part of their diet, an item on nearly every menu. A fact that was very sharply defined when I visited Ubud, the cultural capital of the island.

Hinduism, as it spread through Indonesia, was simply superimposed on the existing religious structures, which already contained gods and spirits aplenty. Bali is Indonesian first and Hindu second. In common with much of S E Asia, animism still prevails, with good spirits dwelling in the mountains like Gunung Agung, the 'Mother Mountain', while demons inhabit the oceans, the people living in between.

The Lovina beaches overlook the Bali Sea on the northern side of the island - no surf here and no surfing dudes. The sand around Lovina is of the black volcanic variety, and sunsets over the mirror-calm waters are spectacular. It is a very laid-back place with just a few hotels, bars and restaurants, but you must remember this is Bali and touts can be persistent. The guy in my hotel kept trying to persuade me to go to the hot springs or see the dolphins. Boat trips to see them are the major tourist attraction here. And the sign outside the tour office said 'Get away from all the hassle for the day'. But it was all pretty good-natured. For an evening's entertainment there's Balinese dancing, some live bands and a couple of nightclubs but it's all very low-key.

Just before I left Lovina I noted down an interesting insight into Balinese culture. Boys and girls walking to school together, the boys were carrying books and satchels, but the girls were only carrying brooms. They're obviously being trained for adult life. Which reminded me of an article I read in a magazine entitled 'The Art of Silence'. This was written by a Western woman married to a Balinese man and underlined the subservience of women in Balinese society. Like in many S E Asian countries, women seem to do most of the work, not only domestic chores but working on the roads and on building-sites. While the men sit idly by on motor-bikes, puffing endlessly on cigarettes and hassling passing tourists, male and female. I just seemed to notice this more on Bali, that's all.

On the way down to Ubud and Kuta I made a slight diversion to climb to the top of Gunung Batur. This volcanic cone was formed in 1917 by a huge eruption, and there are also a cluster of smaller cones. Thousands died in the eruption and it destroyed some 60,000 homes and 2000 temples. During the blood-letting purges of the mid-sixties, many people threw themselves into the volcano. Others were drowned in Lake Batur, accompanied by a huge sacrifice of animals.

I stayed overnight in the village of Toya Bungkah, which overlooks the lake. The drive down to the lake affords some spectacular views. It's a scruffy little place, so not worth staying for more than one night. Even then you're up at 4am for the climb to see the sunrise over Gunung Agung, at 3142m the highest point on Bali. It's not exactly an arduous journey, and if you follow the rest of the climbers up the forested slopes you don't even need a guide. You'll soon be on the main ridge. Stray dogs seemed to be the main problem. Make sure you take a torch, an essential requisite for any traveller. At the top you will be surrounded by guides cooking eggs and bananas for their clients in the steam vents which pockmark the volcano's surface. There is another fantastic view over towards Gunung Rinjani on Lombok, which rises up majestically through the clouds. It is worth having a look at the other craters across the lava fields, before heading back down to Toya Bungkah.

Ubud to Bali is what Yogya is to Java - an arty, crafty place with lots of temples and ancient sites. It is situated in the southern part of the island towards Denpasar, and is full of museums, galleries, book and coffee-shops. Almost everyone seems to be selling paintings, wood-carvings or general curios. But prices are high, certainly by Indonesian standards. Just out of town you can walk through the rice fields to several local villages, where you can purchase even more paintings and souvenirs. At Petulu you can watch thousands of herons nesting in the trees and in Ubud itself is the Monkey Forest Sanctuary which contains ... well, monkeys. The usual warnings apply, so be on your guard. Ubud also abounds in meditation, painting, batik and cookery courses and there's the obligatory evening's entertainment of the Ramayana.

All this aside, what I remember Ubud for is THE KILLING OF THREE PIGS. I was staying in a really nice Balinese bungalow with a huge double bed, wood-panelling, marble floors, an immaculate bathroom and outside a tropical garden full of luxuriant growth. A fine view to the distant mountains completed the idyllic scene. After having breakfast on my final day I went back to my room, when I heard the squealing of pigs. Nothing unusual in that, because they do make quite a racket sometimes for the most trivial of reasons.

But then came a deathly agonised screech. I rushed outside and they were killing the pigs one after the other by slitting their throats - the animals were quite clearly in pain. I told the men they would be slaughtered as pigs in their next life, that they were not truly Hindus, just hypocrites. Exactly as the Crazy Monk in Vietnam said. My perceptions of Hinduism were radically altered after that little incident. Cock-fighting was another issue I found very incongruous, and why

Hindus could quite willingly slaughter and eat a buffalo but not the sacred cow, seemed incomprehensible. Bali to me had become a land of hassle, greed and barbarity. Of course the same could be said about factory-farming and meat-eating in the UK, where indeed the suffering inflicted on animals is much worse.

To most people who come to Bali however, it is the night life and surfing that matters and nothing else. And they can do all that in the Kuta region where the majority of the package tour hotels are concentrated. If you want a busy beach-scene, shopping till you drop, bars, restaurants and night-clubs galore plus traffic-clogged roads and persistent hawkers then this is the place to be. But at least you can get a decent meal. Kuta really got off the ground in the late 'sixties as a hippy hang-out - it is conveniently situated just minutes away from the international airport, with the capital Denpasar over to the north-east. Accommodation, drink and food are generally of a good standard and cheap. However do not drink Balinese coffee. This muddy and treacly concoction has all the attraction of a stagnant pond. When you spoon into its murky depths, you raise up a primeval slime, which gyrates around the cup like the Milky Way. And the taste is as bitter and disgusting as it looks. Guaranteed to open up the sluices at both ends, as *Monty Python* fans would say.

The Kuta region consists of a maze of alleyways called *gangs* lined with guest-houses, bars and souvenir-stalls. As you're walking down them you'll inevitably be met by a motor-cyclist coming the other way. At least the alleyways are too narrow for (most) cars. You'll also be met by loads of guys with surfboards coming up from the beach. Surfboards are everywhere. Under people's arms, on motor-bikes, hanging up in shops, being repaired, lying on the beach, but not very many actually being used for their intended purpose. Are they just another fashion accessory?

The first time I was in Kuta, the waves didn't look that impressive, but the second time! Waves big enough for even the most seasoned surfer. Something to do with low pressure over the Antarctic. Great white horses and all in quick succession, together with a strong undertow. Now that reminded me of St Lucia in South Africa when I nearly drowned in a riptide. I saw a couple of bungee jumps - from the tower in the Legian area into a swimming-pool. The guy from Bali Bungee said it was 140 metres, but it didn't look that high to me. And it could never match the awesome majesty and excitement of Victoria Falls and Bloukrans in South Africa. Standing on the edge of the precipice and it's 5-4-3-2-1 Bungee as you plunge headlong into oblivion. What a shot of adrenaline. Ah, happy memories.

The hotel I stayed at in Kuta actually had a swimming-pool; well, you have to treat yourself sometimes - it's called 'Flashpacking', roughing it most of the time, but then splashing out (forgive the pun) every so often. It was full of Aussie surfing dudes on their two-week package from Sydney or Melbourne. Two Irish girls (from Cork) thought I was French (or some other Mediterranean extract) as I was so brown. They were as white as the driven snow. Then through the speakers by the bar came on the classic 'Chill Out' CD and Samuel Barber's *Adagio For Strings*. One of the most poignant and heart-rending pieces of music ever written. Then I realised that music is something I have really missed. Real music. There's a limit on how much MTV can satisfy.

But I enjoyed Chicane's *Saltwater*, which to be appreciated has to be played at full volume. Then a guy dived into the pool in his Speedos, which rather ruined the occasion. Shortly after that the sound system broke down - quite a common occurrence in Indonesia. And a message to all ice-cream vendors on push bikes "Will you please stop playing that stupid little ditty - it's doing my head in. Arghhh..." I've never seen so many guys with long fingernails. It's meant to be a status symbol, but I reckon it's for picking their noses. That night the shagging in the hotel reached fever-pitch and with all that groaning and screaming I couldn't get any sleep.

Every so often I like to go on an outing with the package tourists for the day. A quick and easy way to get your grounding in a new location. But it is sometimes as much to gain an insight on them, as it is to see the local sights. And to boast that you're not going home - just yet. You can cover a lot of Bali in a day if you are pushed; certainly two or three days would close the deal. In my one day I started off with the Botanical Gardens at Danau Bratan - good for orchids, then the Hindu/Buddhist temple with more gardens, and views across the lake to cloud-covered Gunung Catur. Then for some white-water rafting down the Sungai Ayung, but at grade two it was hardly full on. Was I getting a little jaded?

We dropped down to Ubud for lunch, shopping and the Monkey Sanctuary - already done that. The final stop was Tanah Lot at sunset, the best-known and most-photographed temple in Bali. It is situated on a rocky islet along the coast a few kilometres north of Kuta. If you really want to put the boat out so to speak, why not have a romantic meal there. And watch the JCBs cart around loads of sand for an erosion-control project. Did the earth move for you dear?

Before we leave Kuta for all points east, a brief mention has to be made of the bombing at the Sari Club and Paddy's Bar along Jalan Legian. I must have walked past these establishments at least a dozen times, day and night. Knowing the area quite well, the devastation caused must have been horrendous, both physically and psychologically. Apart from the fatalities, a further 300 people were injured from 23 different countries - like 9/11 before it and the Madrid and London bombings after, it was an attack on *all* faiths, *all* races and *all* cultures. Insanity and madness is indiscriminate.

At the time of the bombing I was in Australia and remember quite clearly the minute's silence held in Hervey Bay, Queensland, famous for spotting the migrating Humpback Whales. 88 Aussies and 28 Brits were killed in the explosions - if it had been a few weeks earlier it could have been me.

As much as 90% of the Balinese depend on tourism, directly or indirectly, and it supports families as far away as Java, Sumatra and Sulawesi. Bali's tragedy is Indonesia's tragedy. And now it seems the world's tragedy. In October 2005 another two bombs went off in Kuta and Jimbaran to the south, killing twenty-three and injuring over one hundred. Whether the bombings (like the tsunami) will have a lasting impact on the culture and economy of the country, only time will tell. I will have to go back and let you know.

CHAPTER 35

ENTER (AND EXIT) THE DRAGONS

The Gili Islands off the north-west coast of the island of Lombok are a world away from the brash commercialism of Bali. OK so they are touristy – well, they cater for tourists, but they are very laid-back, quaint almost, and one can enjoy a brief respite from hawkers and motor-bikes. And in Indonesia that is a major bonus. To get there requires a ferry-crossing from Bali, two bus journeys and then a boat over to the islands. It is doubtful whether you can make it in one day - especially if coming all the way from Kuta. So you will probably find yourself in the resort town of Senggigi at nightfall, not a bad place for a traveller's stop. Senggigi is situated along a series of sweeping bays with some nice beaches. There are amazing views back towards Bali and Gunung Agung, especially at sunset. It has plenty of hotels and restaurants and is very good value for a beach resort, so you may decide to stay on for a few days.

Getting to the Gilis is no mean feat. Having arrived at Pemenang on the main road, you then have two options. The option I chose was to walk to the boat terminal at Bangsal, about one kilometre. Don't under any circumstances let anyone carry your bags - it pays to travel light. The second option is to hire a cidomo (horse drawn cart); though I don't think it's much fun for the horses concerned, in the heat and glare of the midday sun. Whatever you do, avoid eye-contact with the touts - everything they sell is at ridiculously inflated prices and they're pretty persistent. I always wear shades in these circumstances and say nothing. Get a one-way ticket, jump onto the public boat, wait for it to fill up and you're off.

There are three Gili islands - Gili Trawangan, Gili Meno, and Gili Air. The first is the party island with plenty of visitor facilities, the other two much quieter and until quite recently without electricity. You can always stay on Trawangan and make day-trips to Meno and Air. Accommodation is mainly in beach-huts and bungalows. There are the usual water-based activities, and I went snorkelling with turtles and a giant clam, narrowly escaping its deathly embrace. Just pretending. But unfortunately missing out on the rays, sharks and barracuda. The corals were most impressive, though I have to say I still preferred the snorkelling at Phi Phi.

The evening's entertainment on Trawangan often commenced with a movie - everywhere seemed to be offering the latest blockbuster. Which made me think about the consequences of long-term travelling. I would liken it to sitting in a cinema watching (and sometimes appearing in) about forty or fifty movies, one after the other without a break. Eventually the conflicting images become blurred, and one is overwhelmed with all kinds of emotions and feelings. And there comes a point where you have to slow right down, take stock of the situation and try and make sense of all you have experienced. Do fellow-travellers agree?

I was about to commence the final, and perhaps most epic, leg of my South-East Asian journey. From Gili to Mataram, the capital of

Lombok, past the majestic Gunung Rinjani, then to Labuhan Lombok for the ferry to Poto Tano on Sumbawa. I was feeling very vulnerable again as the only Westerner amongst all the Indonesians staring at me glassy-eyed. 'I've come to look for dragons, not for dragons to look at me.'

The overnight bus went via Sumbawa Besar to Bima, where in the gloom of early morning at 3.30am it came to an abrupt halt. The road ahead was just too narrow and winding for the larger buses. And the hordes of humanity just piled off the bus into the murky depths of the town and disappeared from view. In the darkness we had passed the volcano of Tambora, the eruption of 1815 being the greatest ever recorded. Nearly four thousand feet was blown off the mountain - the volume of material ejected was estimated at 100 cubic kilometres, or ten times that of Krakatau.

It left a crater five miles wide and ¾ of a mile deep, the biggest volcanic crater in the world. The resultant gas and ash was sent 30 miles into the atmosphere, and caused cooling on a global scale, the temperature dropping on average by 1°C and in some places by as much as 5°C. The death toll in Sumbawa was at least 120,000, or 90% of the population. There was a massive crop-failure throughout Europe, and a further 200,000 died from famine. What was that about the Gaia theory of interconnection - the butterfly fluttering its wings. An epitaph to the event might be "*It reminds us of how small we are next to the violent forces of nature. We are here in an instant. The volcano is here for millions of years and will erupt again, again and again.*"

The bus terminal at Bima was virtually deserted within minutes, and I was meant to be in Sape awaiting the ferry to Labuanbajo on Flores. There were obviously going to be no more buses of any description at this time of the morning, but luckily I managed to hop on a bemo. For the princely sum of £8, I hitched a ride down this long, winding and very bumpy road in almost complete darkness. Two hours sharing with half a dozen strangers who spoke little or no English, and could quite easily have mugged me and got off with my belongings. Scary. But nothing happened and I was delivered to my destination safely and securely. Another myth exploded. It isn't necessarily more dangerous in the developing world.

Once in Sape I waited for the sunrise on the upper deck of the ferry. How romantic. I spotted a couple of Westerners, actually the only Westerners, just before the ferry left - more Germans would you believe. They had managed to get an earlier bus to Bima and had spent the night in Sape. Trust them to get it right. And with a decent breakfast inside them. On the trip over, again I felt a bit like an ambassador for the West (as in the Philippines) with girls wanting me to be photographed with them. Is this what it's like being a celebrity? But one false move and I could really let the side down.

Flores (Portuguese for Flowers) is a long, narrow and rugged island, dominated by mountain ridges and a string of volcanoes. Fourteen of these are active and the caldera of Kelimutu with its spectacular coloured lakes is a 'must see' if you make it this far into Nusa Tenggara. The optimistically named 'Trans-Flores Highway' traverses the whole island from Labuanbajo to Larantuka, as it twists and turns over the unforgiving terrain. The mountain and sea-views are stupendous, and this is rightly regarded as one of the finest bus journeys in the world.

Quite recently Flores has become famous for the discovery near Ruteng of the Hobbit, a metre-high hominoid. Proof that early man did have the ability to make the sea-crossings from Java and Bali. But this was not the reason I had come to this part of the world. For there be dragons…

In the Flores Sea between Sumbawa and Flores lie the islands of Komodo and Rinca. They are dry, parched and desolate with savannah and scrubland - surprising for the tropics. Though I think large areas have been burnt by poachers hunting buffalo. The seas are very choppy here, so make sure you don't get swept overboard on the short crossing from Labuanbajo. I chose to go to Rinca rather than Komodo - fewer tourists and the dragons are not stage-managed. No dragon-viewing platforms here.

As soon as we arrived at the jetty we saw them, and even more lying in shade under the trees. Quite cute with their grinning faces, long forked tongues, rippling muscles and sharp claws. I managed to get really close to one - maybe 3 metres away - for some good pictures. It certainly wasn't as dangerous as all the literature makes out. I was used to seeing the smaller monitor lizards and most of the time these dudes are pretty sluggish. However if provoked they can sprint for short distances up to 20 mph, so be prepared to make a quick dash.

For the record, the Komodo Dragon is the largest lizard on the planet and can grow up to three metres long. Not quite the four-metre fighting giants filmed by David Attenborough. Were they really that big? They can weigh in at 135 kilos and are capable of killing pigs, deer, buffalo and even horses. A goat could be wolfed down in a matter of minutes. There are reports of humans being eaten too, and the island of Komodo used to be a place of exile for miscreants. Sometimes they eat their own young. And if the prey animal isn't killed after the first couple of bites, it will die from infection caused by bacteria in the dragon's saliva. The dragons can live to be fifty years old and for some reason males outnumber females 4:1.

There are only about three thousand dragons left in their native habitat - Komodo, Rinca, Padar and Flores, and there are more in captivity than in the wild. Definitely an endangered species, and they are now protected. The dragons, along with hippos, gorillas and the cassowary are amongst my favourite animals. They really know how to kick arse. But isn't it ironic that so many 'dangerous' animals are threatened by something far more dangerous?

If you hire a driver and guide for the journey through Flores it will cost you over £30 a day, plus your own expenses of course. That may be OK for a small group, but for the lone traveller, a bit too much. So it was going to have to be the public bus – well, that was going to be a travel experience. The first part of the journey was to Ruteng, a hill town just four hours away on the legendary Trans-Flores Highway. This road is nearly 700 kilometres long, nearly twice the length of the island itself. Like a snake it writhes and twists in tandem with the contorted geology of the island. It reminded me somewhat of 'The Mad Little Road of Sutherland' as coined by Alfred Wainwright, which he describes as *"a tortuous journey of ups and downs and ins and outs through a tangled landscape of low hillocks, gneiss outcrops, peat bogs and small lochans…an undisciplined maze."*[13] The road runs from Lochinver to Badnagyle, in the Highlands of Scotland. Only this road was on a much, much grander scale. There are dramatic vistas of rice-terraces, native rainforest, black-sand beaches, and always with the backdrop of volcanoes. The travelling is hard, bumpy and very crowded, and you share your journey with the usual bags of rice and baskets containing chickens.

Ruteng has now been put on the map by the discovery of *Homo floresiensis*, the one-metre-high Hobbit, which apparently lived there as recently as 13,000 years ago. The skeletal remains were found in a cave at Liang Bua, about fourteen kilometres away. No species of human was believed to have reached this far along the Indonesian chain and it most resembles that of *Homo erectus*. It quickly adapted to its new environment, along with miniature stegadon elephants, three-foot rats and the giant Megalania, twice the length of the Komodo Dragon.

Homo erectus left Africa two million years ago and its estimated arrival in Flores via bamboo rafts was about 800,000 years ago. Interestingly, the brain of the creature was also scaled down in size to smaller than a chimpanzee, but retaining human intelligence. According to the locals the Hobbits existed as recently as 300 years ago. They were known as *Abu Gogo* - the grandma who ate everything, including babies, or stole them anyway. Still there are many tales of human and animal sacrifices in Flores, so take care. And before anyone mentions it, another school of thought reckons the creature is a microcephalic, a pathological condition that reduces the size of the head and brain. Making the above a glorified hoax.

Actually I know someone who would fit the description of the Hobbit - the missing link - though her demeanour has most definitely transmogrified into that of an Orc. Her appearance most closely resembles that of the Venus of Willendorf, with its fat bloated ample protuberances; and the blanked-out face that would otherwise turn onlookers into pillars of stone. Even the hairstyle is the same. The other common denominator is the name given to this illustrious creature. I suspect everyone has a similar claim to having met a Neanderthal. We can't all be beautiful in mind and body.

Bajawa, at 1200 metres above sea level and surrounded by even higher volcanoes, is very cold at night. I needed my thermal underwear, fleece and two blankets and I was still shivering in bed. I had to get up early to catch the 6.30am bus to Moni, which proceeded to do the rounds for a couple of hours. Then I was told by the driver that because there weren't enough passengers, I had to take a bemo to the bus terminal 3 kilometres away. Doesn't this kind of thing piss you off? And the guy sitting next to me had a machete. Come to think of it loads of people had machetes - just like Bwindi in Uganda, but that's a different story. Luckily it wasn't the same outcome. There was another motor-cycle crash, but I saw no dead bodies - they must have dragged them away just in time.

I was nearly at my last spectacular sight in Indonesia - the coloured lakes of Kelimutu. In Moni, which is the usual base for visiting the lakes, I enjoyed watching some traditional dancing and ikat-weaving. I was even persuaded (retail therapy?) to buy a shawl. The traditional colours are indigo, black and maroon and guess what the design was… yes, there be dragons. I still have the piece to this day. Moni is a pretty little village with a colourful market and all the guest-houses and shops are strung along the main road. And you don't have to go for miles to catch the bus. It stops right in the village.

For the trip up to the lakes it's another early start to catch the full brilliance of the colours as the sun rises. The lakes are located in three deep craters near the summit of the volcano at 1600 metres. The colours I saw were lime-green, brown - cappuccino one person called it - and black. Though they have changed over the years, sometimes with shades of blue and red. It is thought the colours are caused by mineral deposits. A concrete stairway leads up to the highest point, where you can see all three lakes, and then you can go down to the crater rims. It is best to stay until at least 8 or 9am when the green lake becomes most luminous. Local belief has it that the souls of the dead are contained within the lakes. The young in the green lake, the old in the brown and thieves and murderers in the black one.

The most hectic part of any journey is usually the last and this was certainly true on the Moni to Maumere run. Hell on Four Wheels, in more ways than one. Nearly five harrowing and tremulous hours in the hot sun, crammed between bags of rice, spare tyres, motor-cycle parts, chickens, buckets of stinking fish, children puking and toothless old women chewing betel-nuts looking as if they've got TB. Plus three live goats and a turtle on the roof. And the bus went everywhere - markets, farms and outlying houses. God, have I got a sore bum.

THE CRUCIFIXION OF A TURTLE. The live turtle was tied to a bamboo cross (something like it anyway) and put on top of the bus in the baking sun for four hot and tiring hours. It was then dragged unceremoniously across the road to be prepared for the pot. Would Christians say "Forgive Them Father for They Know Not What They Do?" Bearing in mind Flores is 85% Catholic. Some young girls reading their Bibles by the roadside merely added to the irony of the scene. But like the Hinduism of Bali, Christianity here is an add-on to more deeply held animist beliefs. And these include some horrendous rituals. Like a water-buffalo having its rear legs amputated and body slashed before it was put out of its misery. And a local in one of the restaurants in Maumere recalling how fishermen chopped off shark fins, throwing the dying fish back into the water. Whaling still takes place off the island of Lembata to the east of Flores, Moby Dick style with small boats and hand-held harpoons. In 1994 two such boats sank after being dragged almost to Timor by a wounded whale. Perhaps an example of instant karma.

Also in the early 1990s the port of Maumere was flattened by an earthquake with a twenty metre high tsunami, killing three thousand people. The town is the largest on Flores, so the effect on the economy and social life on the island was devastating. Although Flores is a very beautiful island, life is hard, the climate and geography of the place reflected in a harsh day-to-day struggle for survival. There certainly seems little understanding on the issues of animal or even human welfare. It wasn't that long ago that blood sacrifices of children took place to propitiate the gods. A world away indeed from Western civilisation, where we have the luxury of informed choices. Cruelty can *never* be justified, but shouldn't it be a case of condemning the sin, and educating the sinner. I know this conversation could go on *ad infinitum.*

We must end on a happy note. I spent a couple of days relaxing on Waiterang Beach, just outside the village of Wodong, some 28 kilometres east of Maumere. I stayed at Ankermi, run by an Indonesian/Swiss couple in a bamboo hut complete with veranda and hammock. It's a wonderful little place with a great atmosphere, and you can go snorkelling or diving or even climb the nearby Gunung Egon, an active smoking volcano. But I just chilled and waited for the boat that was to take me back to Bali and beyond. So now I was leaving behind not only the Komodo Dragons, but the Cultural Dragon that is S E Asia, so emblematic of that civilisation. It was the end of my journey.

CHAPTER 36

IN CONCLUSION

Were I so tall to reach the pole,
Or grasp the ocean with my span,
I must be measured by my soul:
The mind's the standard of the man.

Isaac Watts 1674-1748

No more cockroaches, bedbugs, rats, mice, crowing cocks, noisy fuming motor-bikes, chain-smoking in competition with the volcanoes, spitting and coughing and puking and having to take your shoes off every time you go through the door and people staring as if you're a trained circus animal ready to perform some clever tricks. But best of all no more karaoke - that horrible high-pitched whining some regard as singing. Not another rendition of 'Unchained Melody'.

Travelling in S E Asia is a rewarding but demanding psychological challenge, and my perceptions and attitudes towards the developing world have been changed forever. There are huge cultural and social (but refreshing) differences between not only West and East, but also between individual S E Asian countries. The forward-looking friendliness of the Thais, the unsophisticated warmth and generosity of the Lao, the genocidal trauma of Cambodia, the dollar-hungry hassle of Vietnam and the American-hugging Filipinos. To Burma, or Myanmar as it is now called, the Golden Wonder, stuck in a time warp under a brutal military dictatorship. Malaysia, with its mix of Malay, Indian, Chinese and native populations, presents a very diverse picture - from almost backward introspection to extrovert, brash modernity. The City State of Singapore with its skyscrapers, shopping malls, parks, river frontages and colonial buildings - a reminder of the West in Asia. And then to Indonesia, the world's greatest archipelago and cultures to match, land of smoking volcanoes, dragons and the "Hey Mister" cult. Travelling changes the traveller, hopefully for the better, and you learn as much about yourself as the country visited. I would do it all again at the drop of a hat.

Finally a message to fellow travellers. "So here I am heading back home from Bangkok where I started my travels two and a half years ago. It's all gone so quickly - the twinkling of an eye, and I hardly think I've stepped out of the front door. I've come to the end of another stage in my travels - now for a few months to write it all up. Then it'll be back on the road again for another instalment. Best wishes and lots of love to everyone, whatever road you choose, and I may be catching up with you sometime."

Quotations

1. Page 8 - Mail On Sunday - Associated Newspapers Ltd.
2. Page 9 - Natasha Courtenay-Smith, Daily Mail, Wednesday March 12, 2003. Used by permission.
3. Page 61 - By kind permission of Rose Waldron - 2001.
4. Page 69 - © J.R.R. Tolkien - The Lord of the Rings - The Two Towers - Reprinted by permission of Harper Collins Publishers Ltd 1954/55.
5. Page 84 - Country Joe and the Fish - I Feel Like I'm Fixin' to Die Rag. Words and Music by Joe McDonald © 1965 renewed 1993 by Alkatraz Corner Music Co. Used by permission.
6. Page 129 - By kind permission of Rose Waldron - 2001.
7. Page 176 - Ma Thanegi - The Burmese Fairy Tale - Far Eastern Economic Review - 1998.
8. Page 193 - Sam Greenhill, Daily Mail, Monday January 3, 2005 from Karin Svärd; Olinka Koster, Daily Mail, Friday December 31, 2004. Used by permission.
9-11. Page 246 - David Attenborough - Life on Air - David Attenborough Productions Ltd - BBC Books 2002. By kind permission.
12. Page 277 - David Jones, Daily Mail, Monday January 3, 2005. Used by permission.
13. Page 311 - Wainwright in Scotland by A. Wainwright, is reproduced by kind permission of the Estate of A. Wainwright - © The Estate of A. Wainwright 1988.

About The Author

I live to travel. It is in my blood. It is when I am at my happiest and most exuberant, confident and full of the joys of life. In my twenties it was Europe by InterRail, in my thirties it was the odd package tour, but in my forties I finally broke free from my humdrum bourgeois existence and headed to Africa. Five months in trucks, buses, coaches, pick-ups and God knows what else, overlanding across ten countries from Nairobi to Cape Town.

But I also have a passion for the natural world. My idea of heaven would be somewhere in the rainforest, home to over half the earth's plant and animal species. I've worked in an animal sanctuary, a garden centre and plant nursery, and been involved in Green politics and campaigning. And I'm vegetarian. So I suppose you could say travel, trees and the environment are my bag.

South-East Asia was next on the list and this is what the book's all about. With a slight diversion to Australia and New Zealand. Nine countries this time over two years, unfortunately interrupted by falling off a mountain in Australia and breaking my ankle. Backpacking With A Broken Ankle. As soon as I was fit and well, off I went again. Never once was I homesick; if I grew tired of one place, one city or one country I could always move on - and move on I did, following the sun.

But all good things come to an end, and back home I came to write up the book - and this is where I am now. And eager to get that backpack on and go travelling.